The Gardener's Guide to Growing

ASTERS

The Gardener's Guide to Growing

ASTERS

Paul Picton

DAVID & CHARLES
Newton Abbot

TIMBER PRESS
Portland, Oregon

NOTE Throughout the book the time of year is given as a season to make the reference applicable to readers all over the world. In the northern hemisphere the seasons may be translated into months as follows:

Early winter	December	*Early spring*	March	*Early summer*	June	*Early autumn*	September
Midwinter	January	*Mid-spring*	April	*Midsummer*	July	*Mid-autumn*	October
Late winter	February	*Late spring*	May	*Late summer*	August	*Late autumn*	November

First published in the UK in 1999 by David & Charles Publishers
Brunel House, Newton Abbot, Devon
A catalogue record for this book is available from the British Library.
ISBN 0 7153 0804 1

First published in North America in 1999 by Timber Press, Inc.
133 SW Second Avenue, Suite 450, Portland, Oregon 97204, USA
ISBN 0-88192-473-3
Cataloging-in-Publication data is on file with the Library of Congress

Book design by Ian Muggeridge
and printed in Italy by Lego SpA

page 1 *A. novi-belgii* 'Coombe Radiance' (p.54) is one of the most brightly coloured of the late-flowering cultivars.
page 2 *A. amellus* 'Gründer' (p.114), an exceptionally strong-growing cultivar.
page 3 Cultivars of *A. novi-belgii*, *A. ericoides* and *A. cordifolius* in a container.

CONTENTS

FOREWORD

by Roy Lancaster

Aster alpinus was the very first aster I grew. It was one of a beginner's collection of six rock plants I planted on the heap of soil, bricks and concrete chunks I called a rock garden. I was 15 years old and had yet to acquire the skills needed to construct a natural-style rock garden. Still, my alpine aster thrived and the next spring I enjoyed its violet-blue daisy heads that continued into early summer, their golden-yellow 'eyes' attracting a steady cavalcade of insect visitors.

It was at about this time that I came across *A. tripolium*, the sea aster, a fleshy-stemmed biennial. It was growing in the salt marshes of the Ribble estuary. The sea aster is one of only two British native species, though there are many more that have arrived here in more recent times, most of them via gardens.

My very first recollections of asters go back to the 1940s and 1950s. Like many other schoolboys of my era, I was a steam engine enthusiast, and at weekends, I travelled the railways, visiting main line stations and engine depots. I didn't go all that far afield but I did see an awful lot of asters. Each autumn they covered the embankments and sidings with a rich tapestry of royal shades, blue, violet and purple, often gilded by the yellow plumes of golden rod. These plants were throwouts or escapees from railside gardens and allotments and their displays played a considerable role in brightening the untidy and often depressing railway landscapes of post-war Britain.

I was reminded of them years later when I saw Michaelmas daisies in their natural state near Toronto in Ontario, Canada. There must have been several acres of them, as far as the eye could see, down to a lake and continuing on the far side, their massed heads presenting a haze of violet-purple in the bright sun. They were all *A. novae-angliae*, the New England aster. There are many other asters in North America, some of which, with their equally abundant hybrids, have provided gardens with a wealth of ornamental perennials for late summer and autumn display.

It was waist-deep in a colourful display of Michaelmas daisies that I found Paul Picton one bright September afternoon in 1997. I had arrived in Colwall to give an evening lecture and called in at the Picton Garden to see the asters in flower. It was a privilege to be on the site of the old Colwall Nursery where the legendary Ernest Ballard had raised and grown so many award-winning hybrids. Paul's father Percy continued Ballard's work, and now it is Paul's turn with his National Collection. I have never seen so many Michaelmas daisies in one place. Their variety and exuberance are a tribute to Paul's patience and determination as a collector, and to his skills as a gardener.

This book also draws our attention to a host of other aster species. It includes the equally popular *A. amellus* and its many cultivars and hybrids, and *A. sedifolius*. I am pleased to see *A. albescens*, a shrubby aster I once collected in a good blue form in Nepal almost 30 years ago. Another Himalayan species that is described is *A. diplostephioides*, a striking alpine with large violet-blue flowerheads above low leaf clumps.

All in all, the genus *Aster* offers a rich palette of ornamental attributes to the gardener, and in describing and illustrating so many of the best in his book, Paul Picton deserves our gratitude and admiration. Asters can have no better champion.

Among the small-flowered asters, *A. ericoides* 'Yvette Richardson' (p.99) is unusually short in stature.

PREFACE

Gardens and nurseries have been virtually my only home throughout my life. I was born in a head-gardener's cottage, and at an early age took my first shaky steps into the seemingly vast and exotic world of a large country-house garden, a world that was about to change radically with the end of the Second World War in 1945.

My first conscious memory connected with a plant is of peering inside the apparently giant bloom of a 'black' tulip. Its stem slightly exceeded my eye-level and I had to stand on tip-toe to explore the wonders of the interior of the flower. The distinctive fragrance was powerful and I can still recall my sense of frustration at my lack of vocabulary to describe this new experience.

New experiences with plants are daily occurrences but they have never become routine. My first encounter with asters came in 1948, soon after my father moved to Colwall to manage Ernest Ballard's well-known nursery. Several fields around the village glowed with the mid-autumn colour of Michaelmas daisies. Walking through the plants released clouds of butterflies that drifted from group to group of flowers so that the sea of colour occasionally seemed to spray into the air. In neighbouring orchards yellow, red and russet apples were ripening, and many hedgerow and garden trees were assuming their vivid autumnal tints. On local farms the hops had been picked and the corn was gathered. At the age of six, it was not the individual qualities of asters that impressed me, so much as an overall picture of rural, harvest-time richness.

My interest in Michaelmas daisies deepened when I was privileged to walk through the fields of flowering seedling asters with Ernest Ballard and my father as they selected the most promising new plants. During the 1950s the nursery presented an incredible scene through the autumn months when thousands of people came to see the displays. At weekends all the nearby roads were lined with parked cars, many of which would soon be filled by enormous bunches of cut flowers. As Britain emerged from the grey austerity of the immediate post-war years, people were desperate for colour and cheerfulness, and Colwall had acres of both on offer for free.

With the exception of roses, few plant genera could have been in receipt of such mass adoration, but public and media popularity are fickle companions and history has shown time and again that they cannot be relied upon for long-term security. The sudden decline in commercial demand for asters meant that the nursery had to adapt to produce other plants and launch into new horticultural areas when my father acquired the business after Ernest Ballard's death. It was difficult to justify maintaining the stocks of many aster cultivars and at one time only about 40 sorts were preserved. By the 1980s most of the old nursery had been given over to The Picton Garden, to house the stock of plants gathered together by my father Percy Picton and promoted by him over many years of growing, lecturing and broadcasting.

My father died in 1984, at about the time when my wife Meriel and I had realized that our gardening enterprise needed a new lease of life. We decided that nothing could be more appropriate than rekindling an interest in asters by presenting colourful displays reminiscent of Edwardian borders and offering healthy stock, produced by modern methods, for sale. We were well aware that it was a risky gamble and proceeded steadily over a number of years, investing the proceeds into further garden and production improvements. A great boost to our efforts came about with the formation of the National Council for the Conservation of Plants and Gardens (NCCPG), a charitable organization that aims to care for endangered garden plants and gardens. With the help of Isabel Allen, Ron Watts and many other generous plantspeople our collection of asters was growing steadily, and it was recognized as a National Reference Collection by the NCCPG. The success of the National Collections scheme is such that there are now about 600 collections throughout the British Isles. All are cared for at the expense of the Collection Holders and most are very work-intensive. Many of the plants, including a number of aster species

Asters with other perennials in The Picton Garden in early September.

and cultivars, have little or no commercial viability. Their 'value' lies in historical interest and the availability of plant material for new breeding programmes. The growth and (hopefully) improvement of our aster collection would not have been possible without the awakening of the public, via the media, to the work of the NCCPG. Every autumn, Colwall once again throngs with people coming to see asters flowering where they have done so for nearly a century. And many of the visitors are happy to load their cars with pots of these colourful plants.

I am a lover and grower of plants, not a botanist or a skilled writer. What I have written about asters is based on my 'hands on' experience of growing the plants in my gardens in Colwall for more than 40 years. During that time I must have done most of what can be done with asters, although I have yet to cook and consume any shoots!

INTRODUCTION

The name *Aster* has been in use since the time of Ancient Greece and can be translated from Greek as 'a star' or 'star-like'. The generic name *Aster* is wonderfully appropriate since the plants bearing this heavenly epithet have, without exception, starry flowerheads, and asters are truly the 'stars' of autumn gardens throughout temperate regions of the world. Some asters have flowerheads that are individually large and carried in solitary glory on fairly short stems; at the other extreme, there are those with graceful, many-branched sprays bearing hundreds of tiny, star-shaped heads, in a cloud-like effect.

It is easy to see why ancient Greeks and Romans considered asters to be sacred and created some wonderful myths to explain their origins. One story told of the departure of the gods from an increasingly evil earth in the Iron Age of Greek mythology. Astraea, the goddess of Justice, was the last to leave and was set among the stars as the constellation Virgo. It was believed that glittering stardust from Virgo had fallen over the Earth and that the first asters had grown in the places where it had settled. An alternative theory concerned Asteria, a daughter of the alliance between the formidable Titan, Coeus and Phoebe (the wife of Perseus and the mother of Hecate). It was said that Asteria looked down on the Earth from her heavenly abode and was sorrowful to observe how barren it looked without any stars. She wept with sadness and wherever her tears fell to earth asters sprang up and bloomed.

I wonder what the people who believed in these lovely legends would have said had they been aware of the great number of asters growing in Northern America, compared to the miserly share of the genus to be found around the shores of the Mediterranean.

MICHAELMAS DAISIES

In Britain 'Michaelmas daisy' is the popular name applied to the many sorts of autumn-flowering *Aster* species and cultivars. Some gardeners make a distinction by using the term only when referring to the cultivars of *A. novi-belgii*. The use of Michaelmas daisy evolved through the latter half of the eighteenth century, before which, if asters were accorded a general popular name, it was 'starwort'. This name was first applied to a British native species, *A. tripolium*, the sea starwort, and, later, to the late sixteenth-century introduction *A. amellus*, Italian starwort. Now yet another name has come into popular usage: 'September flower' seems to be a recognized term for the many small-flowered asters sold by florists, whatever the month. In a hundred years' time, it would be interesting to know if this new name had spread over the whole galaxy of autumn-flowering asters and, perhaps, replaced Michaelmas daisy as the most commonly used.

The name Michaelmas daisy came into use very gradually, and as a result of a coincidental alignment of two unrelated events. After the discovery that the Julian Calendar had been miscalculated, Pope Gregory XIII decreed a revision of the calendar in 1582. However, the response in England was tardy and it was not until 1752 that the government took any action. At that point it was decided that the third day of September in that year would be counted as the fourteenth day of September, and thus eleven days never dawned. Subsequent dates remained the same but in relation to the natural seasons everything was eleven days earlier. In eighteenth-century Britain the religious and secular festival of Saint Michael, or Michaelmas day, was always celebrated on the 29th of September. Because of the 'advanced' date many more flowers were still in bloom than previously. Among these were the asters. Asters from other areas of Europe were already being cultivated in Britain and, in the latter half of the eighteenth century, a great many asters were being introduced from Northern America. They soon dominated the hardy flowering plant scene of mid-autumn. Naturally, churches and houses throughout the British Isles were decorated with asters or starworts for Michaelmas day and it was not too long before 'Michaelmas daisy' was rolling off people's tongues much more lightly than 'starwort' had ever done.

However popular the new familiar term was among the general public, it certainly did not find much favour with some of the great botanists. In 1785, Thomas Martyn, Professor of Botany at Cambridge University, wrote about 'many *Asters* as confounded under the vulgar title of Michaelmas daisies'. William Curtis published the first volume of his sumptuously illustrated *Botanical Magazine* in 1790 and featured *A. tenellus*. He voiced his opinion by writing: 'most of the numerous species of *Aster* flower about Michaelmas, hence their vulgar name of Michaelmas daisy, a name exceptional not only on account of its length but from its being a compound word.' To be fair and accurate, it should be pointed out that the use of 'vulgar' in the eighteenth century would probably be replaced by 'common' in modern writing, and it is unlikely then to have been meant to indicate something crude or coarse. Botanists then, as now, would have been mistrustful of the general application of plant names that had no direct connection to their carefully construed scientific epithets.

OTHER COMMON NAMES

In the USA many other popular names have been attached to asters when referring to the genus as a whole. These include daisy and fall rose (Ohio), frost flower (Maine, New Hampshire), frost weed (Maine), goodbye summer (North Carolina), it-brings-the-fall (New York Indian).

To illustrate the diversity of local names for particular species, here are some examples for *A. cordifolius*: heart-leaved aster; beeweed, blue devil, stickweed and fall aster (West Virginia); common blue wood aster;

and tongue (Maine). *A. lateriflorus*, the calico aster, has been blessed with the following, all from West Virginia: devil-weed, farewell summer, hairy-stemmed aster, Michaelmas daisy, nail rod, old-field-sweet, old-Virginia-stickweed, starved aster, Tradescant's aster, white devil and wireweed. I need go no further in emphasizing the importance of using botanical names when it comes to identifying plants.

SPRING-FLOWERING SPECIES

Asters are the 'stars' of autumn gardens and this flamboyance has tended to overshadow the rather more subtle attractions of the many spring- and summer-flowering members of the genus, many of which are inhabitants of mountainous regions and are only happy in cultivation where a rock garden or raised bed partially recreates conditions of life at high altitudes. However, there are many that are worth attempting to grow and they do not deserve to be ignored by the gardening enthusiast.

AVAILABILITY

A number of the species and cultivars described in this book are not widely available, but most can be found with a little diligence. See Where to Buy Asters p.156 for information on the best sources.

CALLISTEPHUS

It is unfortunate that the name 'aster' was usurped by the genus of showy plants called *Callistephus*, which are known colloquially as 'China aster'. The genus belongs to the Asteraceae and the name is derived from *kallistos* (most beautiful) and *stephos* (crown). It consists of just one species, *Callistephus chinensis*, a native of China, which, over the years subsequent to its introduction to Europe, has had countless seed races developed from it. The species is up to 80cm (32in) high with ovate or triangular-ovate, coarsely toothed, alternate leaves up to 8cm (3in) long. It produces solitary flowerheads, up to 12cm (5in) in diameter, with an involucre of many fringed bracts. The receptacle is naked and pitted; the pappus are double.

I love the beautiful China asters and greatly admire the skill of gardeners who grow them, but it is the true aster that is the subject of this book.

1

A HISTORY OF ASTERS IN CULTIVATION

In Britain, the native *Aster tripolium* was the first Aster to be cultivated and it was used as a herbal remedy for eye ailments. *A. amellus*, from the more southerly countries of Europe, is known to have been grown in Britain by 1596 as a medicinal plant. The first of a veritable tidal wave of asters across the Atlantic came from Virginia to English shores in 1637, when the younger John Tradescant brought back the aster that bears his surname, *A. tradescantii*. The year 1687 saw the introduction to Europe of *A. novi-belgii*, which arrived in Britain in 1710 along with *A. novae-angliae*. *A. laevis* came in 1758 and is largely forgotten today, other than receiving recognition for its part in the breeding of the *A. novi-belgii* cultivars. Most of the 'important' aster species from North America reached Europe in the eighteenth century, with those from India, China and Japan arriving in the nineteenth century and the early years of the twentieth century.

ALDENHAM

For most of this period, asters were not generally highly regarded except for their being useful at a season in the year when few other hardy garden plants were still in good bloom. *A. grandiflorus*, introduced in 1720, is so late flowering as to be called 'Christmas daisy' and, because of this, was one of a small number of species to be valued. However, the fate of the genus changed when fortune threw together a family called Gibbs and a farsighted head gardener. This fortuitous alignment lifted asters out of obscurity and placed them in the exalted realm of garden-worthy plants.

Henry Hucks Gibbs, father of the more horticulturally renowned Vicary Gibbs, began the transformation of the Aldenham estate in Hertfordshire during 1871 and his younger son continued the work. By the turn of the century, the gardens housed one of the finest collections of plants in Europe, cared for by 58 gardeners under the command of head gardener Edwin Beckett. The cultivation of plants and the standards maintained in the garden were of the highest order: the *Kew Bulletin* obituary for the Hon. Vicary Gibbs in 1932 commented 'Aldenham has many rare plants but after a tour of the garden one always felt that a weed was the rarest'. A collection of nearly all the available species of aster had been established largely due to Beckett's interest in the genus and the inevitable hybrids came along. The aster border was some 150m (yd) long by, in places, 15m (yd) wide. The best of the species and hybrids grown at Aldenham found their way into other private gardens, and eventually into the commercial world. In fact, during the early years of the twentieth century, William Wood Ltd. of Beechwood Nurseries in Buckinghamshire had an arrangement to propagate and sell many of Beckett's cultivars and raised several new cultivars directly from Beckett's original plants.

FIRST COMMERCIAL GROWERS

The great Edwardian gardening writer, William Robinson (1838-1935), expounded ideas that revolutionized the way in which many plants were put to use in gardens, and his opinions are still highly respected by gardeners worldwide. He did much to set asters on the horticultural map and stimulate public demand for them (see p.89). This, in turn, led to a number of plantsmen looking at them afresh and setting about the task of breeding new varieties.

A contemporary and friend of Robinson, Ernest Ballard of Colwall in Herefordshire, was a knowledgeable amateur gardener. He took the brave step of becoming the first commercial grower to specialize in breeding and selling asters. Amos Perry of Enfield in Middlesex had a distinguished horticultural career concurrent with Ballard; he was responsible for introducing many fine asters, including the popular cultivar A. amellus 'King George'. Perry grew a wide range of asters in his nursery including many species other than the A. novi-belgii group. Unlike Ballard, he was not an aster specialist, having a comprehensive list of herbaceous perennials and water and bog garden plants.

With the commercial emphasis so firmly placed on breeding A. novi-belgii cultivars with larger and brighter flowerheads, many other growers entered the scene; some of the most prominent are mentioned in chapter 3.

GARDEN CENTRES
In the early 1960s, the hand of fate once again touched asters by combining the advent of the garden centre with the arrival of tarsonemid mite among borders of A. novi-belgii cultivars. Initally, garden centres lured the public towards the 'look good in container' types of plant such as shrubs, heathers and conifers; herbaceous perennials did not feature greatly in the first flush of garden centres and were left to the domain of those traditional nurseries that managed to survive. Added to the problems of keeping their stock free of mildew, a long-standing curse of the A. novi-belgii cultivars, the arrival of the tarsonemid mite proved too much under the economic strictures facing hardy plant nurseries. Asters vanished from catalogues almost as quickly as deleting a file on a modern computer. By virtue of association, even those not of the A. novi-belgii group suffered a similar period of both professional and amateur disdain lasting for some twenty years.

Although this was the lowest period for asters, a great many cultivars (especially of the previously over-produced A. novi-belgii group) had already vanished from nursery catalogues, under the heading of 'superseded by a new variety'. There is some truth in this, but one man's 'improvement' is often only seen as a slight difference by another and, with a group of plants so easily propagated as asters, it is more likely that the necessity for commerce to have a steady stream of new varieties to offer year after year was the real cause of such disappearances. Cultivars such as 'Climax' and

'King George', which have appeared in nursery catalogues for many decades, have outstanding qualities that justify their continued inclusion.

THE NATIONAL COLLECTIONS
Outstanding qualities were also exhibited by Isabel Allen when she decided to gather a complete collection of asters. In the wartime austerity of the 1940s, simple pleasures such as looking over a low wall at a colourful garden could bring blessed relief from dismal day to day life. On a balmy September day in the Wiltshire town of Devizes, this is just what Isabel Allen experienced as she admired drifts of misty-coloured asters growing in the garden of Mrs Thornley, a little-known yet prolific breeder of Michaelmas daisies. Miss Allen determined there and then to recreate this lovely autumn colour in her own garden, which was attached to a large property near Bristol that she was converting into a residential home for the elderly. (By an odd coincidence, the house was leased from Lord Wraxall, a member of the Gibbs family of Aldenham.) Over the next 50 years Isabel Allen established the largest collection of asters in the British Isles, exceeding the great collection of Aldenham at the end of the nineteenth century.

The National Council for the Conservation of Plants and Gardens (NCCPG) came into being in the 1980s with a remit to assure the future for endangered garden plants, partly by the establishment of National Reference Collections of numerous genera. Isabel Allen's collection of asters was one of the first to be recognized and her devotion to the genus has been continued by The Picton Garden in Colwall, The National Trust at Upton House near Banbury and Temple Newsam garden run by Leeds City Council, where National Collections are presently growing. By this means, the old and otherwise 'non-commercial' species and cultivars of asters are available for the public to see growing alongside the latest introductions.

CUT-FLOWER TRADE
Stock from the collections as well as commercial sources has also been used in the production of new cultivars for the cut-flower trade and the expanding industry that 'manufactures' dwarfed asters for containers. Currently, many millions are propagated each year for large-scale operations in Europe, Israel, the USA,

PLATE IA

New York aster
A. novi-belgii 'Blue Eyes'

New England aster
A. *novae-angliae* 'Rosa Sieger'

Small-flowered
cultivar for cutting
A. *pringlei* 'Monte
Cassino'

Small-flowered
cultivar for gardens
A. 'Ochtendgloren'

All flowers are shown at approximately ½ size

Africa and in New Zealand (where Sandy Cooper has bred many new asters to use in his business). Asters have never ceased to excel as cut flowers since the early days of their hybridization. The main difference is that today's asters, grown specifically for the purpose, cover a far greater area of the earth's surface. Another distinction is that cultivars are being bred solely for cultivation under glass or in polytunnels and such plants are often useless as garden varieties.

As with so many commercial aspects of horticulture, it is Dutch growers who have led the way. Because of their traditional concentration on the A. *novae-angliae* and A. *amellus* groups of cultivars, Dutch and German plantsmen and nurserymen inadvertently helped to revitalize a general interest in asters for gardens. This

Asters *en masse* in The Picton Garden in early October, showing how effective first-year plants can be.

was largely through their promotion of A. × *frikartii* 'Mönch', such a patently good and trouble-free plant that it escaped untainted by the demise of other asters, and A. *amellus* 'Veilchenkönigin' and A. *novae-angliae* 'Andenken an Alma Pötschke', which proved to be bestselling perennials in garden centres and nurseries alike. These European-inspired peaks of popularity managed to keep asters sufficiently in the public eye through the 1960s and 1970s for a revival of interest to become apparent in the mid-1980s.

MEDIA ATTENTION

As far as horticulture is concerned, widespread attention by the media is very much a modern phenomenon. During a significant period in the early 1990s, a number of quality magazines ran feature articles on the various National Collections, almost giving the impression that asters had only recently been discov-

ered. It had been several decades since gardeners had seen massed, autumn floral colour of this nature, and interest grew to the point that Michaelmas daisies were featured by the British national press and 'starred' on television and radio programmes. This great exposure emphasized an already established change in the requirements of the vast majority of the plant-buying public: although people are happy to enjoy the massed colour of Edwardian-style borders in a public display, modern gardens can rarely accommodate such displays, even if they were thought to be desirable. Plants must be adaptable to the gardening styles of the day and asters are diverse enough to stay in the forefront of popular plants.

GARDEN DESIGN

The awareness that asters, like so many other plants, look best in large groups is not new: William Robinson and other plantsmen of his era were the first to translate into garden situations this vision that was witnessed in the wild by the first botanical explorers, such as Douglas and Thoreau.

In current garden design, there is a strong movement towards using herbaceous perennials in plantings that are much closer to nature than those of traditional beds and borders. Small areas of prairie land are being simulated within the bounds of gardens; drifts of perennials run beside meandering streams; large rocks and areas of shale and gravel, once the domain of alpines, now back up groups of taller herbaceous plants; grassland areas are being filled with naturalized plantings. The environs of many new building developments are no longer solely clothed with shrubs; generous groups containing 50 or more perennials of a single species or cultivar are often used to soften the effects of bricks and mortar.

The opportunity of taking herbaceous perennial colour late into the months of autumn is not being overlooked by leaders of the present trend in garden planting such as Piet Oudolf in Holland. Mr Oudolf and several other growers are breeding a new race of asters adapted for the twenty-first century garden. These are cultivars such as 'Herftsweelde' that produce airy sprays of small flowerheads gracing sturdy, self supporting stems arising from clumps which are happy to be left to grow undisturbed for several years. Many asters of much older origin are taking on a new lease of life. The A. cordifolius × A. novi-belgii cultivar 'Little Carlow' is a perfect example of the type of plant in demand today, and there are endless cultivars in the vast A. novi-belgii group capable of being adapted to a new style of planting. The A. lateriflorus, A. ericoides, A. novae-angliae, A. amellus groups and many other individual species, such as Aster oblongifolius, are already in wide use.

ASTERS FOR CONTAINERS

The restricted size of many modern gardens has encouraged a renewed interest in growing plants of all types in containers. Here, too, asters are coming into their own. I am not referring to those produced by large-scale commercial growers to compete with the all-the-year-round chrysanthemum. My interest is in plants produced by traditional and natural methods to fill the late summer and autumn with colourful pots, urns, tubs, troughs, sinks, baths and whatever. The more compact and dwarf cultivars of A. novi-belgii might have been tailormade for this purpose, and I am delighted to note that both amateur and professional gardeners are quickly realizing their potential. Of course, nothing is really new; professional gardeners in Edwardian times grew many asters in containers and these were frequently taken into the great houses of the day for decoration.

Times have changed a lot since the days when Edwin Beckett and Vicary Gibbs grew hundreds of seedling asters in the great kitchen garden at Aldenham. Asters have seen a steady rise in popularity, experienced the humiliation of public rejection and surged back to new horizons. And it says much for the variety of the genus that it has had the resources to meet the changing demands of horticulture.

2

A BOTANY OF ASTERS

Until quite recently, the genus *Aster* belonged to the Compositae family, commonly known as the daisies. Compositae has now been changed to Asteraceae, embracing all the genera that formerly belonged to Compositae, although both names are acceptable.

The daisy family is one of the largest and most widely spread of the plant kingdom. It contains about 1,300 genera and some 21,000 or more individual species, to which can be added a long list of cultivars, making up about one-tenth of the worldwide total of flowering plants. Unlike many other families, where the relationship is not immediately clear to non-botanists, the Asteraceae are easily recognized: daisy flowers invariable look 'daisy-like'.

Apart from *Aster*, other examples of popular genera that belong to the Asteraceae family are *Rudbeckia* (black-eyed Susan, cone flowers), *Helianthus* (sunflowers), *Dahlia*, *Gaillardia* (blanket flowers) and *Helenium* (sneezeweed).

At first glance, a daisy flower looks simple enough – a circular assembly of petals surrounding a central boss of stamens and anthers – but this apparent simplicity is deceptive. What looks like a single flower is really many small, individual flowers grouped together in one head. In daisies, all these flowers combine forces to perform the biological task of a single flower, and it is this composite flowerhead from which the family derived its original name. The clustered head of flowers is more effective than a single flower when it comes to attracting bees and other insects for the purpose of pollination. The pollinators have the advantage of easy access to nectar and pollen, which can be gathered in large quantities.

THE GENUS ASTER

The genus contains more than 250 species. The majority in cultivation worldwide are herbaceous perennials, classified as hardy in the regions where they are popularly grown. A few species are annuals, biennials or shrubs (these do not feature prominently in this book, which deals mainly with the autumn-flowering aster species and cultivars, with a section devoted to earlier-flowering species). Asters are natives of Europe, Asia and North America, with a few in South Africa and South America. The greatest concentration of species is in North America.

ROOTS, SHOOTS AND STEMS

The stems are sometimes scape-like, sometimes leafy and branched, the leaves usually alternate and simple. The lower leaves, which often wither prior to flowering, are stalked; the upper ones are narrower and more-or-less sessile.

A great many herbaceous perennial species of asters form clumps of roots, shoots and stems. Experienced growers can recognize the different species and cultivars by the distinctive characteristics of the plant's growth below ground. Take for example, *A. novi-belgii*. Some of its cultivars exhibit amazingly vigorous growth: within ten months of a spring planting a single shoot of 'Christine Soanes' is likely to give rise to a tangled mass of about forty stoloniferous, underground shoots, many of which are 60cm (24in) or more in length; by contrast, a cultivar such as 'Chequers' might have up to forty shoots but these will be tightly clustered around the base of the previous year's flowering stems and just the odd new shoot will break away and become stoloniferous. Between these two extremes lie

Root systems of various aster species, clockwise from top left: A. *commixtus*, woody and spreading; A. *novi-belgii*, spreading roots with stoloniferous new shoots; A. *cordifolius*, clump-forming; A. *novae-angliae*, woody and clump-forming with vigorous new shoots; A. *amellus*, woody.

all sorts of variations on the theme of producing new shoots in the search for the fresh soil needed to foster healthy growth for the coming season.

Colour and size is another aspect of A. *novi-belgii* shoots. Below a new crop of green leaves 'Dolly' has bright purple-red stems which become paler the further below ground level they are but are never white. The small leaves topping shoots of 'Fellowship' as they emerge above ground are green and bronze tinted, the colour soon fading away down the shoots into white. Some cultivars have fat, robust shoots reminiscent of asparagus, while others can only manage thin, spindly affairs. All this is evidence that the A. *novi-belgii* group of cultivars has drawn many other species into its breeding: one nurseryman was even able to distinguish between the different scents of various cultivars.

THE LEAVES

The botanical definition of aster leaves is 'simple'; the more decorative leaf groupings and forms, such as pinnate or palmate, are not found among the species in the genus. Aster leaves are mainly linear to lanceolate, with ovate and cordate occurring less frequently. In general aster foliage does not merit a high rating for the attractiveness of the individual leaves, but many plants do have a foliar beauty when viewed as a whole. Some cultivars of A. *lateriflorus* are especially worthwhile.

Gardeners might find equal interest in the contrasting sizes of leaves. The broadly ovate foliage on the clumps of A. *macrophyllus* creates a quite different effect to the heather-like sprays of A. *ericoides*, which

A selection of aster leaves drawn to scale.

are well-clothed with neat, linear leaves, some of them minute. Aster leaves growing low on the stems or on basal clumps are usually noticeably larger than those higher up the stems and among the flowering sprays.

Green, in a wide range of shades, is the universal colour. This is tinged with purple in some species, and a few have grey-green leaves.

THE FLOWERHEADS

The solitary or clustered flowerheads are borne in corymbs or racemes. Each flowerhead consists of a central disc of many tiny flowers called disc florets, surrounded by a circle of usually larger flowers called ray florets. The receptacle, by which the florets are attached to the stem, is flat or slightly convex.

The fertile or neuter ray florets, in one or two series, each have one long, flat and usually narrow ray (ligule), which may be bluish, pink or white. To the casual observer the rays appear to be petals; indeed, each ray is a group of petals fused to form a corolla. The number of rays in an aster head can be as few as five in some wild plants to as many as 250 in a modern cultivar such as 'Marie Ballard'. It is normal for the rays to be of one colour giving the flowerhead its overall shade.

The central disc is yellow, orange, brownish or purple (rarely white or whitish) and can contain as many as 300 tiny flowers. These consist of a tubular, 5-toothed corolla, entire anthers and flat, deltoid or lanceolate style branches. The assembly of disc florets is usually circular but in some species and many cultivars is rather irregular (or squashed). Disc florets are bisexual, usually fertile.

THE INVOLUCRE

Leafy, protective bracts surround the rays from below and form what is termed the involucre. The involucre may be tubular, bell-shaped, top-shaped or hemispherical. The bracts, which are various, imbricated and in several series, are referred to as involucral bracts. Sometimes the bracts overlap each other and in other instances they will be set out in a number of rows; some species of Aster have bracts that are much more visually prominent than others.

The involucre as a whole is characteristic of the species and an important aid to the often difficult task of accurate identification.

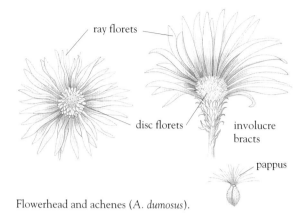

Flowerhead and achenes (A. *dumosus*).

THE ACHENES

The fruiting bodies (achenes) of plants in the Asteraceae family can be mistaken for seeds because of their dry nature and small size. They are more-or-less flat and are ribbed on the margin, with up to four ribs on the face. Each achene contains a solitary seed and does not open when ripe. The apex of each achene usually has few to many pappus (a modified calyx consisting of hairs or bristles), in one or two series. They are elongate, scabrous and white or brownish. The outer ones are often shorter, rigid and scale-like. The purpose of the pappus is to help the distribution of the fruits. Like the involucre, the pappus type is a great aid in identification.

EVOLUTION OF THE DAISIES

In the evolutionary process of flowering plants, the multiple inflorescence, or capitulum, of Asteraceae is regarded by botanists as being highly developed. Genera such as *Magnolia* (Magnoliaceae) and *Gentiana* (Gentianaceae) belong to a more primitive group of plant families having their origins much further back in time than the daisies, which can be rated as comparative newcomers. This might help to explain the bewildering variability within the *Aster* genus, giving rise to a plethora of intermediate forms between different species.

Before the eighteenth century it was quite common practice for plants with flowerheads containing yellow ray florets to be included in *Aster*. Then, in 1752, M. Vaillant, a French botanist, decided it would be advantageous to exclude all yellow-rayed species from the genus. The adoption of this system has worked well since any tendency towards yellow rays among asters is usually thought to be because of a *Solidago* species hybridizing with an *Aster* species. (The odd man out might possibly be *Aster linosyris* but since this rarely has any rays on its flowerheads, it is safe to discount it, although, botanists were concerned about its inclusion in the past and it was variously called *Chrysocoma linosyris* or *Linosyris vulgaris*.)

Many plants formerly classified as *Aster* species have been consigned to other genera, such as *Boltonia*, *Chrysocoma*, *Erigeron*, *Felicia*, *Heteropappus*, *Kalimeris*, *Machaeranthera* and *Olearia*. Some species have been in and out of different genera with indecent rapidity over the years. Therefore, no apology is made for any inclusion in this book of *Aster* species that may have a different generic name in some, if not all, quarters!

A NOTE ABOUT PHOTOPERIODISM

The way in which plants adapt to periods of light and dark is detailed in the work of W.W. Gardner and H.A. Allard carried out in the 1920s, which led to the discovery of photoperiodism. Plants can only flower when they have reached a size sufficient to carry the weight of blossoms and fruit, and have enough food resources to fulfil the needs of reproduction. They use their leaves to gauge the passage of time and to promote reproduction, by measuring the amount of daylight in each 24-hour period. Some plants, including asters, will flower only when the number of daylight hours is below a certain level, and others only flower when levels are higher. Spring- and autumn-flowering asters are termed short-day plants and need something less than 15 hours of daylight length to begin flowering. This fact is very important if one is persuading asters to be in full flowering prime for a show or exhibition.

The ability to control the amount of light by alternating darkness using screening with periods of artificial daylight has enabled commercial growers of cut flowers and pot plants to produce asters for a year-round market.

Aster novi-belgii cultivars – shapes of the flowering sprays.

short-branched

bushy

open

upright or erect

spire or pyramid

PLATE IB

EXAMPLES OF THE DIFFERENT
TYPES OF ASTER

Frikart's aster
A. × *frikartii* 'Mönch'

Blue wood-aster
A. *cordifolius* 'Ideal'

Italian starwort
A. *amellus* 'Nocturne'

All flowers are shown at approximately ½ size

Frostweed
A. *ericoides* 'Pink Cloud'

Calico aster
A. *lateriflorus* 'Horizontalis'

3

NEW YORK ASTER

*A*ster *novi-belgii* has long been accepted as the name for an enormous group of hybrid asters, many of which it would be difficult to identify to the typical species.

The species was first identified and described in Europe in 1687 by Paul Hermann, a German botanist at the University of Leiden in Holland. The specific name means New Belgium, a place that the most diligent searches have failed to find. Seeds for the plants that Hermann raised at the Leiden Botanic Gardens were collected in North America from the area now covered by New York City. This had been a British colony since 1664, before which it was a Dutch settlement known as New Amsterdam. A charitable explanation of Hermann's naming would be that his best stab at a Latin equivalent for New Netherland turned out as *novi-belgii*. If that was the case, it was out of date from the beginning. Linnaeus, who managed to make sense of most other botanical names, somehow let *novi-belgii* slip through the net when he published his *Species Plantarum* in 1753.

Fortunately, New York aster has long been established as the popular name for the native species and the race of cultivars attributed to it. There appears to be a good case for the wider adoption of the name to identify the cultivar group in a way that makes sense to gardeners, as well as being recognizable and pronounceable. **Note**: H=height, F=flowerhead diameter.

ASTER NOVI-BELGII
L. (1753) New York aster
The New York aster grows in usually strong, spreading clumps, with firm, entire or slightly serrate, oval- to linear-lanceolate leaves, 5-15cm (2-6in) long and glabrous. The flowerheads, borne from late summer to mid-autumn on slender, much-branched flowering sprays, have 15-25 violet-blue rays and yellow disc florets. It is a variable plant, and these variants and their descendants have been cultivated since 1710. Moist soil and swamps from Newfoundland to Maine and Georgia, mainly near the coast. Hardy to Z2. H to 1.2m (4ft), F to 5cm (2in).

It was not until well into the nineteenth century that gardeners undertook any hybridization of North American asters but collections of species had been established. With the propensity towards promiscuity of most aster species, it is reasonable to assume that many chance seedlings must have occurred and been noted as different and worth growing.

Records are few and far between. However, it is known that a very large percentage of the New York aster group in existence today are the result of crosses with the smooth aster, *A. laevis*. A first cross between these two species is recognized as *A.* × *versicolor*, although this and its one or two forms remain closer to *A. laevis* in appearance. The other species that greatly influenced New York aster cultivars is *A. dumosus*, a compact and bushy plant. This is not only evident in the great range of popular dwarf cultivars, but can also be seen in the fine leaves and bushy flowering sprays of many cultivars growing 90cm (3ft) or more high. 'Accidental' crosses with *A. cordifolius* cultivars still crop up quite frequently in gardens and many of them look more typical of the New York aster, as we know it, than of *A. cordifolius*.

A. ericoides and *A. lateriflorus* must have made their mark and the vigorous *A. lanceolatus* is also evident in the overall stature, graceful sprays and frankly invasive nature of some cultivars. To a simple gardener, like myself, studying the plants in detail and recognizing features that are primarily characteristic of other species gives sufficient insight into the background of this vast hybrid group. A more scientific investigation with the aid of up-to-date knowledge would, undoubtedly, open the door to some interesting areas that might be relevant to modern plant breeders.

A HISTORY OF BREEDING

As far as is known, the first really great collection of aster species was established at Aldenham in Essex, in the vast and magnificent garden belonging to the Honourable Vicary Gibbs (see page 12). There are no records as to the origins of the many cultivars of asters that originated from Aldenham. We do not know if Beckett set about a deliberate programme of hybridization. The likelihood must be that chance and insects played a large part. After all, if no cultivars are in existence, every seedling from a promiscuous group such as asters will have the potential to be different. But after fifty or more years of selection have produced around one thousand cultivars, the chances of finding a seedling that is different enough to be a 'winner' become quite limited.

We do know that Beckett did not set out to concentrate solely on producing cultivars of A. novi-belgii, let alone a new race of hybrid garden plants: growers at the end of the nineteenth century could hardly have foreseen that in a few years' time asters would become one of the most widely grown herbaceous perennials, a popularity entirely due to the rapid development of a wide range of A. novi-belgii-based cultivars. Old photographs of borders containing asters in the period up to about 1910 show generous groups of the small-flowered asters – arching, foaming sprays, literally awash with tiny, pale-coloured stars – and, here and there, the odd group with large flowerheads and prominent discs, probably standing rigidly at the back of the border, their tall stems hidden by the swirl of little blooms clouding before them. A photograph of a good border of asters in the 1930s or even 1950s reveals the different stature of the plants, in addition to the overwhelming preponderance of large flowerheads. Were colour available for the earlier pictures, the contrast between the pale shades of pre-1914 and the rich tones of the 1950s would be even more marked.

ERNEST BALLARD

One man devoted much of his life to improving and popularizing the cultivars of A. novi-belgii. He was Ernest Ballard, son of Stephen Ballard the civil engineer who worked with Brunel in the construction of the canals, railways and roads that transformed much of Britain in the nineteenth century.

The Ballard family was large, with various members living throughout the Herefordshire village of Colwall where they were landowners, farmers, fruit growers and manufacturers of cider vinegar. Ernest lived at Old Court and was official chemist in the process of vinegar production. He was also a noted amateur botanist, naturalist, photographer and gardener. The beautiful western slopes of the Malvern Hills provided an arcadian setting for all these activities.

Inspired by William Robinson, who was a personal friend, Ernest Ballard planted large drifts of asters in his garden to create a natural haze of soft autumn colours. He quickly discovered that many seedlings produced flowerheads of different colours to the original plants, and judged that there must be tremendous potential to breed varieties with much more definite shades of colour. He purchased, prior to auction, the field known as The Reddings, which lay just across the road from Old Court. Here, on about two acres, he established his aster trial grounds. As he became aware of their commercial potential, the trial grounds were developed into Old Court Nurseries, specializing in the breeding, production and sale of 'New Improved Asters'.

In 1907, the Royal Horticultural Society organized a great trial of some 300 asters of all types, and Ernest Ballard sent specimens of his first great achievement called 'Beauty of Colwall'. This cultivar contained, in its flowerhead, more ray florets than any other aster and was hailed as the first 'double', being the only plant in the whole trial to be awarded a First Class Certificate. Awards came Ballard's way in plenty during the forty or so years during which time he transformed asters from pale little things with small flowerheads into richly coloured stars with rows of ray florets totalling as many as 250 in the like of 'Marie Ballard'.

Ballard had many specific goals in his breeding programme, such as to achieve pure shades of blue, pink and red in the ray florets, a good white, single blooms of shape and substance, doubles and yellows. To achieve the latter, he spent many years crossing asters

PLATE II

A. *NOVI-BELGII* CULTIVARS — WHITE AND PALE SHADES

'Sandfords's White Swan'

'Nursteed Charm'

'Cloudy Blue'

'Albanian'

'Priory Blush'

'Kristina'

'White Wings'

'Blandie'

'Snowsprite'

'Mount Everest'

All flowers are shown at approximately ⅔ size

with *Solidago caesia* and breeding from the progeny to achieve large and shapely flowerheads. His diaries reveal some modest success which tragically came to a sudden end when his small stock of yellows were inadvertently ploughed up during the Second World War to allow for potato planting. In December 1945, an entry in Ernest Ballard's diary is described by him as 'a few tips for anyone who wishes to carry on the work of raising new asters':

> Little or no progress is made by raising seed from known named varieties. If you are to be first and lead, you must raise seedlings from the seed produced by your best unnamed seedlings which will probably be named and put into commerce when stock is sufficient.
>
> By the time you show a new variety you should have raised seedlings from it for a couple of years, and from its ensuing generations. Keep ahead with your own seedlings. Raise seedlings from 'freaks', they nearly always need developing.
>
> If the seed derived from a selected plant does not appear to ripen, always plant what appears dud seed; often some, and sometimes a lot, will germinate.
>
> Plant seed in the first week of February (late winter), under glass – all such will flower first year. Do not discard the poor weakly grown ones or those slow in germination, they are often the best.
>
> Your 'hybridization' exists in your eye, not your forceps and brush. God and nature with the insect world will knock spots off your attempts.

Ernest Ballard was by no means the only breeder of New York asters but he was the undisputed leader in the field. Others followed his path and quite frequently 'refined' his cultivars by obtaining a cleaner colour or better habit of growth. Rarely did they manage to beat him in the introduction of cultivars distinctly different to the many that preceded them.

VICTOR VOKES AND DWARF ASTERS

There was one area of aster breeding which held no great interest for Ballard and that was in the evolution of a range of dwarf cultivars. (A word of warning about the little pots of brightly coloured asters seen each autumn in commercial outlets from market stalls to supermarkets and garden centres. Most of these will have been made dwarf by the use of chemicals and might grow to more than 90cm (3ft) tall the following year.) Although *A. dumosus* was grown in collections, it was thought to be a plant of indifferent quality by the majority of growers, in spite of its compact nature. This makes it all the more odd that Reginald Farrer, a notoriously outspoken writer and critic of the most minor faults in plants, should heap praises in its direction.

Dwarf asters in the *A. novi-belgii* group did not exist until the 1920s, although the gardening public had long sought such plants. None more so than Mr H. Victor Vokes, an official of the War Graves Commission, who was looking for perennial plants to bring autumn colour to the cemeteries in his charge. There were plenty of asters on offer but none of sufficiently sturdy and compact stature to meet his requirements. The only hope was to combine the dwarfness of *A. dumosus* with the colours of *A. novi-belgii* cultivars by deliberate hybridization.

It took Mr Vokes about four years to obtain a viable set of seed and his first dwarf hybrids came into flower in the autumn of 1925 at heights of between 20cm (8in) and 45cm (18in). He waited for a further seven years to build up stocks and test the new cultivars to make sure they retained their compact growth in various types of soil and would flower freely through the variable weather conditions of a British autumn. Many nurserymen saw the commercial prospects for dwarf asters and so this useful race of plants was safely launched.

After Victor Vokes came A.H. Harrison of Gayborder Nurseries in Derbyshire, who in the late 1920s to the early 1950s raised many dwarf cultivars in England, and German growers, such as Heinz Klose, have been responsible for some excellent introductions in this field since the 1960s.

There are a few dwarf cultivars that have not been crossed with, or derived from, *A. dumosus*, and these bear the hallmarks of a scaled-down New York aster. This latter aspect is immediately obvious to anyone who has handled clumps of these asters and seen how distinctly different the new shoots are to those of *A. dumosus*. Ernest Ballard did actually raise two dwarfs – 'Rosebud' and 'Snowsprite' – presumably somewhat by accident. 'Jenny' is the most superb example of a dwarf cultivar of A. *novi-belgii* in this sense (i.e. not having A. *dumosus* in its breeding), although modern exponents of horticultural taxonomy have lumped them all under the same banner.

Meanwhile, the commercial grower's race to better their rival's annual introductions of new aster cultivars was in full swing. The great gardening public had to see new plants at every autumn flower show, where order books would be filled with their requirements for the next season. This occasionally encouraged overproduction of desirable cultivars by dint of using weak, and sometimes unhealthy propagating material. The result was a disastrous decline in the vigour of many previously strong-growing plants.

SANDFORD'S NURSERIES

Ernest Ballard exhibited his asters at flower shows but his trial grounds and nursery comprised row upon row of plants, with no thought of making a display garden. This project was taken on by Sandford's Nurseries of Barton Mills on the borders of Cambridgeshire and Suffolk. Here, several acres were devoted to what must have been the finest formal borders of A. *novi-belgii* cultivars ever seen in the British Isles. Large groupings were planted each spring and many of the taller cultivars were sheared down in late spring and early summer, in order to produce self-supporting sprays and a mass of colour while at a modest height. Sandford's raised a number of cultivars, the best of which, still widely grown, is 'Sandford's White Swan'. The nursery became a garden centre in the 1960s.

BAKER'S (BONINGALE) NURSERIES

Baker's (Boningale) Nurseries of Codsall were near Wolverhampton, close to the heartland of industrial England (possibly close enough for the sulphurous atmosphere in the days before air pollution controls to limit mildew). Tom Reeves was in charge of introducing new aster cultivars to the nurseries and he made an important business deal with Ernest Ballard for the joint marketing of his cultivars after 1948. In the 1960s, Baker's were also fortunate in handling the superb asters raised by Ronald Watts at a time when the latter was head gardener to Mrs Stafford Fawell, near Farnham, Surrey.

Ballard had died in 1951 and Ron Watts had used many of his cultivars to raise plants that, to all intents

and purposes, developed New York asters still further on the Ballard lines of large flowerheads combined with strong, healthy growth. In retirement, Ron retained a large number of asters and his generosity with plant material was instrumental in building up the National Collection.

GAYBORDER NURSERIES

Gayborder Nurseries, another important name in the development of aster cultivars, were founded near Melbourne in Derbyshire early in the twentieth century by a florist called William Sydenham. He emigrated to Australia in the late 1920s selling the nursery to Arthur Herbert Harrison. Mr Harrison raised many A. *novi-belgii* cultivars bearing the Gayborder or Melbourne prefix, as well as the immensely popular 'Winston S. Churchill'. When Mr Harrison retired in 1953 the nursery was bought by Roy Lidsey who continued raising new 'Gayborder' cultivars, and also the commercially successful 'Chequers' and 'Percy Thrower', until he retired in 1974, when the nursery closed.

GEORGE CHISWELL

George Chiswell was born in Colwall. As a young man, he worked in the gardens of a local mansion and in later life moved to the Somerset mining village of Midsomer Norton, where for many years he ran a very successful nursery. He seemed able to turn his hand to growing anything that produced roots and leaves, including herbaceous perennials and anything a little unusual. During the early 1960s he raised many excellent cultivars that followed Ballard lines. Few of his plants were widely distributed because they suffered the misfortune of arriving on the scene at the time of the great decline in the popularity of asters (see page 14). Luckily, some of the best, such as 'Timsbury', 'Gurney Slade' and 'Carlingcott' (all named after villages near his home) survive in the National Collection.

NEW YORK ASTERS WORLDWIDE

A. *novi-belgii* cultivars have never assumed their English importance in the countries of continental Europe or the United States. In the case of the USA this might be due to the wider range of climatic zones encountered and the obvious fact that gardeners have much easier access to a full range of native species, their varieties and cultivars. One or two large mail order

PLATE III

A. *NOVI-BELGII* CULTIVARS –
LAVENDER AND VIOLET SHADES

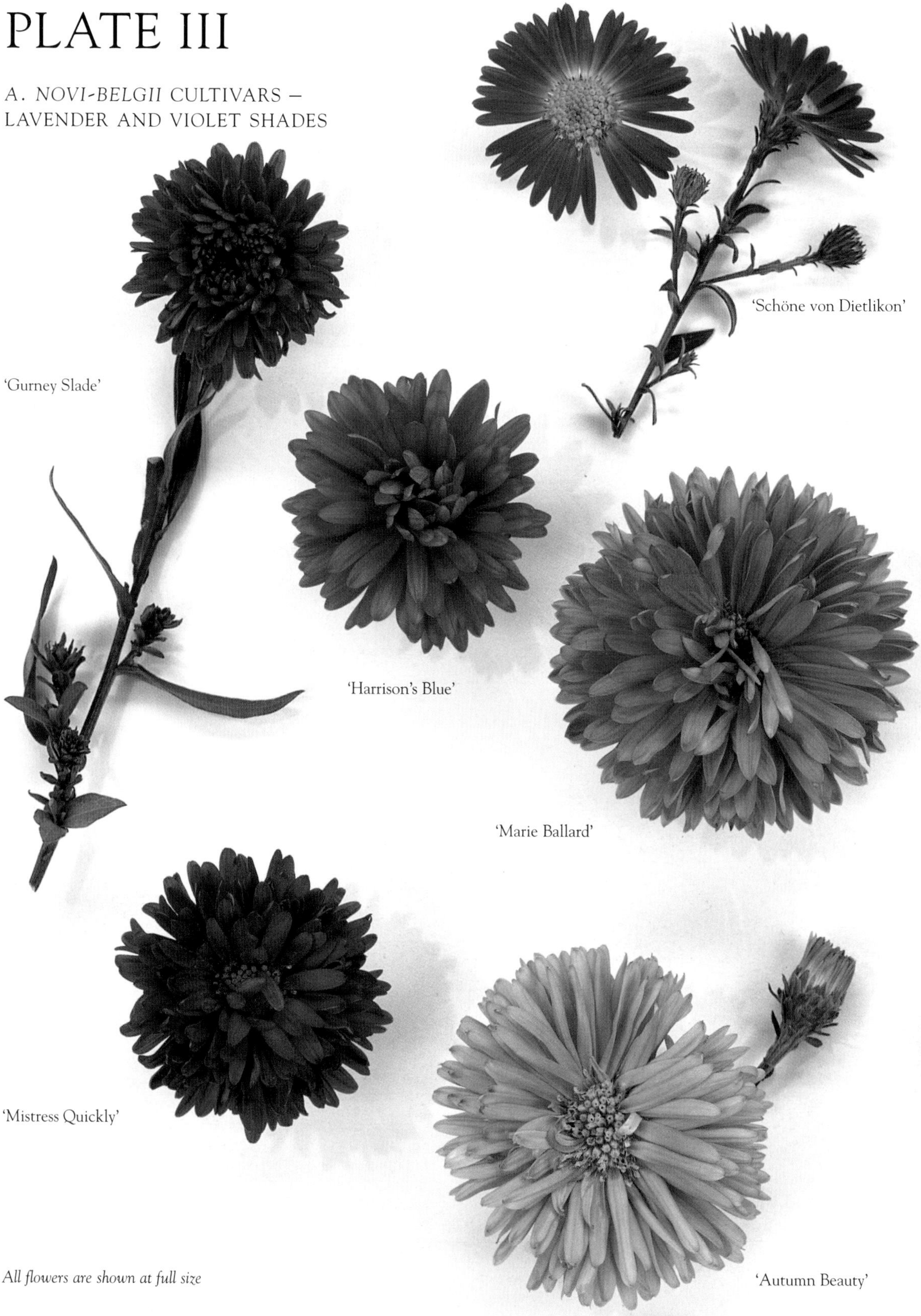

'Schöne von Dietlikon'

'Gurney Slade'

'Harrison's Blue'

'Marie Ballard'

'Mistress Quickly'

'Autumn Beauty'

All flowers are shown at full size

'Sarah Ballard'

'Fair Lady'

'Blue Radiance'

'Blue Eyes'

'Professor Anton Kippenberg'

'Peace'

nurseries did sell some of Ernest Ballard's cultivars but this seems to have been a short-lived enterprise. For once, Dutch nurserymen contented themselves with producing the best of the British cultivars that were suited to their purpose. German breeders have shown more interest in New York asters, with the names of Klose and Foerster being prominent in the raising of very worthwhile cultivars. But Continental European interest has traditionally concentrated upon *A. amellus* and *A. novae-angliae*.

THE FUTURE

Plant breeders such as Piet Oudolf in Holland are working on new aster cultivars containing *A. novi-belgii* for garden planting. Throughout Europe, and in Israel, New Zealand and the USA, larger enterprises are incorporating cultivars of New York asters into their breeding programmes for both cut flowers and containers. Having been at the leading edge of breeding new asters for about a century, British growers seem to have lost interest in the challenge and are content to market the products of other nations.

For any enterprising hybridists there are several lines that it would be useful to follow up in breeding for new cultivars. An immediately obvious boost would be achieved by developing a range of mildew-resistant asters with all the good points of New York asters. Hope must lie in going back to *A. laevis* and its mildew-resistant cultivars such as 'Calliope'. The old and still widely planted 'Climax' is also reasonably resistant as are the shorter-growing 'Little Man in Blue' and 'Remembrance'. New England (*A. novae-angliae*) and New York asters have no recorded hybrid and may be presumed incompatible, but 'Kylie' is the result of a cross between *A. novae-angliae* and *A. ericoides*, and *A. ericoides* will readily mate with *A. novi-belgii*. Is it possible for the mildew-resistance of the New England aster to be passed on to the New York aster by this route? The field is open for a time-consuming task that might well be undertaken by a devoted amateur grower.

Observation over a long period has led me to believe that some cultivars of *A. novi-belgii* are less attractive than many others to the tarsonemid mite. A detailed scientific study might be worthwhile and could precede another line of breeding. The dwarf cultivars ought to provide a lucrative area for some far-sighted hybridizer. If a range of colours could be introduced into plants matching 'Jenny' for quality of growth and size of flowerheads, the scope for garden bedding plants and containers would be immense.

CULTIVATION

A. novi-belgii cultivars are an extremely varied group of tough, herbaceous perennials, capable of adapting to a wide range of growing conditions. In the garden they can be used to provide small patches of colour or a massed display. Some cultivars might be grown for the express purpose of providing flowers for picking; others might be used for decoration in containers.

Before setting off on the challenge of growing an aster, or any other plant, the first task is to acquire the initial stock. As with any commodity the availability of a plant is reliant on existing demand being sufficient to justify its being stocked. At one stage in the development of asters for garden planting, long before anyone had heard of a garden centre, a number of commercial nurseries produced catalogues that contained several closely printed pages of asters. A few specialist growers listed hundreds of varieties. Sadly, there are now fewer specialists, but a reasonably large number of sources do offer a limited range of asters. Where To Buy Asters (p.156) gives information on the best suppliers and other ways in which to obtain plants.

Seed from *A. novi-belgii* cultivars might well be available in abundance. However, assuming successful germination, the resultant seedlings will not faithfully reproduce the parent plant, and in most instances will bear little or no resemblance to it. Seed strains are offered in a few catalogues but they mostly seem to be very mixed and the same can be said about the end result when the plants come into bloom. The time and trouble required to germinate seed and grow on thousands of seedlings can only be justified if large quantities are needed for massed planting schemes where a natural effect is called for, unless, of course, you are undertaking a breeding programme, modest or large, in the search for new cultivars.

The majority of New York asters are not at all difficult to grow, but it is an unfortunate truth to say that they are extremely easy to grow badly as they do need a certain amount of attention throughout their growing season to achieve good results during the autumn flowering period.

SITE AND SOIL

In common with most other plants, the overall siting and soil conditions have great influence on the growth of A. novi-belgii cultivars. An ideal site is open (not overhung by trees or shrubs) and exposed directly to about six or seven hours of sunlight – at least from mid-morning until mid-afternoon. The hours of sunlight are especially critical from the end of midsummer until the end of mid-autumn, in other words, from bud formation and through the flowering period. I have grown the same cultivars in both east-facing and south-facing borders. The results in the latter are without exception notably superior, the distinction being especially marked in a wet year. A north-facing site, even if open and well lit, is less than ideal, although some of the early-flowering cultivars will grow quite successfully here. Try to avoid close proximity to walls and hedges as these hamper air circulation, making it easier for mildew spores to settle, and the plants invariably suffer from dry soil conditions.

Due to their very mixed parentage, the cultivars will tolerate an extremely wide range of soils and will even survive in the most extraordinary rubbish. But tolerance and survival are not the objective when the ambition is to grow a plant in such a way as to encourage it to display at the peak of its capabilities.

Asters can grow perfectly on both sandy and clay soil. The former requires more work to ensure the retention of moisture and plant food by the regular addition of properly composted organic material and irrigation in dry summers; clay soils have to be caught at just the right moment for cultivation and planting, since they are often too wet or too dry to be easily worked. Quite a few cultivars will produce good flowering sprays in very heavy clay but will produce smaller clumps of new shoots than the same plant growing in lighter soil. This is likely to be of concern for gardeners trying to keep slugs away from the new shoots because these pests seem to be most numerous in wet clay soils. In the wild A. novi-belgii is most likely to be found growing in rather moist, acid soil. In gardens, its cultivars will give better results if the soil is slightly alkaline to allow for a more effective use of plant foods.

SOIL PREPARATION

New York aster root systems are shallow, not penetrating much beyond 15cm (6in), so there is no need to get rich compost down to a great depth. Planting a whole bed or border of asters, as opposed to a few groups among shrubs or other perennials, might make a difference as to when the soil can be prepared. If possible do this during the winter, either by hand or mechanical cultivator. When making regular use of a rotary cultivator it is important to break the 'pan' of soil lying at the cultivation depth every couple of years. This problem is likely to be more pronounced on clay soils. I am not the least bit old-fashioned when it comes to making use of up-to-date innovations in the garden, but for most serious digging purposes in the ordinary garden a really good spade and fork are the investment of a lifetime: they are cost effective, environmentally friendly and provide the finest form of exercise you could wish for. A stainless steel digging spade might seem like an extravagance, but had you turned as much Herefordshire clay as myself you would see it as a very welcome Christmas present.

As with any planting, it pays to pick out every bit of perennial weed and weed root during preparation. This is especially important if any asters are to be left in situ for several years: it could be argued that the less noxious weeds will do little harm if your plants are going to be lifted annually. In addition to the appearance of bad workmanship, weeds of any sort will rob your plants of food and might well harbour pests and diseases; sow thistles, groundsel and dandelions play hosts to mildew and rusts, which can easily spread to the asters.

ORGANIC ADDITIVES

It is fortunate that mushrooms are such an important commercial crop in Britain, and are likely to remain so in the foreseeable future. One of the best moves of my gardening life was in changing to the use of spent mushroom compost in the preparation of borders and patches of ground for asters. It is much more consistent and easier to handle than farmyard manure, and I think it produces a planting bed of a better texture in both light and heavy soils. If the mushroom compost is fresh from the growing sheds, I like to stack it for twelve months in the open air, before use. This gets rid of excess lime and any minor crops of mushrooms (some gardeners might see the latter as a disadvantage). Incidentally, and rather to my surprise, mushroom compost treated in this way has proved a successful growing medium for such fussy plants as Meconopsis grandis and

PLATE IV

A. NOVI-BELGII
CULTIVARS — PINK SHADES

'Sheena'

'Coombe Margaret'

'Christine Soanes'

'Mary Deane'

'Coombe Gladys'

'Chatterbox'

'Elizabeth Hutton'

'Fellowship'

'Heinz Richard'

'Lady Frances'

'Sterling Silver'

'Rosebud'

All flowers are shown at full size

M. × sheldonii. Unless your soil is extremely alkaline, the lime content will not be a problem for most asters, so you can use it fresh if more convenient.

For ornamental garden use, I believe that all fresh farmyard or stable manure needs stacking for a year before use. Its ability to create the right texture in your soil is worth far more than any direct feed value. Plants gain their nourishment very readily if their root systems are in good order, as a result of careful soil management.

Many other soil conditioners are available, including excellent products from recycled sewage and household waste. Garden compost ought to be wonderful material, and sometimes is, but there is rarely enough of the finished product. The stack of unmade compost always seems enormous yet the few wheelbarrow loads of the 'good enough to eat' humus-rich material cover very little ground.

Very light soils may benefit from a moisture-retaining layer of compost just below root level to prevent them becoming overdry in the summer months. When used as directed, rockwool can be applied as a conditioning material in most types of soil, and could aid the preservation of moisture in sandy loams.

PLANTING

The best displays of *A. novi-belgii* cultivars can only be produced as a result of considerable effort on the part of the grower. The aim is to grow a vigorous young plant from one shoot and go on to develop a single large flowering spray on it. This can only be achieved if beds and borders or groups of plants are lifted and completely replanted every year. Plants for cut-flower production will similarly give the best quality when grown in this way, the main difference being that if smaller sprays are required the shoot will be 'stopped' at an early stage in its growth ensuring that each plant produces several sprays.

Under normal circumstances, plants grown for garden display must not be stopped and the flowering sprays from un-stopped plants are likely to be the most satisfactory for cutting for domestic use, one such spray often being sufficient to fill a vase. Nearly all New York asters are good as cut flowers, although some are rather better than others. The various cultivars have many different shapes of flowering spray, the glory of which can only be appreciated when they have been allowed to develop naturally. (A list of the best cultivars for cutting is on page 152.)

My own borders of New York asters are replanted every spring and are entirely made up of cultivars planted in groups of up to twenty single-shoot plants from 7-10cm (3-4in) pots. Each flowering spray is supported by a bamboo cane, inserted in such a way as to be hidden by the foliage. This virtually guarantees an even display of flowers. Another important factor is that these initially small plants develop so quickly and so vigorously that they will produce, from their clumps, a larger crop of strong, healthy new shoots for propagation purposes than could be achieved by using divisions. Small, pot-grown stock can be safely planted up to the end of late spring and still give a good display in the autumn. In fact all, except the very dwarf cultivars, will give the best results in all respects when grown in this way. Even if the cultivar is not a prolific producer of new shoots, just a single healthy shoot rooted and established in a small pot will form a superior flowering spray to the several thrown up by divisions. However, the less work-intensive method of dividing clumps, is quite suitable in gardens where just the odd group or two of asters are used for late colour in mixed borders. (Superior cultivars for this purpose are listed on p.153.)

Open-ground plants need to be lifted, divided and replanted during early spring, or even late winter if the weather is suitable and depending upon whether single offsets or split clumps are being used. If you are working with offsets, the early part of mid-spring is likely to be right, but everything must be judged according to prevailing weather conditions. Stock produced in containers of larger sizes, up to 30cm (12in) in diameter, can be planted out in the summer for autumn flowering or can even be put in as space fillers at flowering time. These larger plants can also be set out in autumn and winter as a temporary measure prior to splitting them in the spring. If desired, cultivars of modest growth can be left in to flower again the next autumn, provided the ground has been properly prepared.

SPACING YOUNG PLANTS FROM SMALL POTS

Small pots of New York asters will contain one strong new shoot, possibly more if they have been 'stopped'. They look best in groups, so it does not matter if they are planted fairly close together. Plant in groups of uneven numbers (3, 5, 7 and so on). Make sure your

The production of young plants of A. *novi-belgii* cultivars. Clockwise from top left: a year-old clump, with shoots suitable for propagation, is lifted in late winter; (left) a shoot is removed from the clump and (right) the leaves and stem are shortened, ready for potting up; the shoot is inserted into a 7.5cm (3in) pot of compost; trays of young plants are grown on in polytunnels in early spring; plants are selected for planting out in late spring; the pot is removed revealing a healthy root system.

plants are deep in the soil; I usually bury several centimetres of stem when planting. Use a hand trowel and firm the plants just enough to keep them upright (see the advice on watering below).

Try to judge the spaces between the various groups to be wide enough to prevent the shoots from running into each other during the winter. Dwarf cultivars, up to about 40cm (16in) tall, can be spaced as wide apart as 45cm (18in) if they are strong growers and you are sure of growing each plant well, otherwise come down to 30cm (12in) and let them clump up. The latter spacing is also about right for small growers such as 'Rosebud'. Even the really vigorous, spreading cultivars such as 'Little Pink Beauty' and 'Lilac Time' do not want to be too far apart, because there will be insufficient flowering sprays to produce sufficient massed colour effect in relation to the green, new shoots on the clumps. Cultivars above about 40cm (16in) and below 90cm (3ft) in height can be spaced 30-60cm (12-24in) apart,

according to the form of the flowering spray. In other words, really bushy cultivars like 'Cecily' ought to be wider apart than plants of a cultivar with compact sprays, such as 'Gayborder Royal'. Similar spacing can be applied to most cultivars growing up to about 1.2m (4ft) tall, as the taller sorts are usually not especially bushy. There is no need to give wider spacing than 60cm (24in) for giants such as 'Mount Everest' or 'Anita Ballard' when they are planted in groups of single shoots. I plant most of my own plants even closer together than the 'ideal' and still get good results.

DEALING WITH CLUMPS

The best way of dividing established clumps of New York asters is the traditional way, which is not the quickest way. Lift clumps in early spring and shake or poke the soil off. Most cultivars will have two different types of new shoots. Clustered around the woody central area, with the remains of the flowering stems, will

PLATE V

'Winston S. Churchill'

A. *NOVI-BELGII*
CULTIVARS —
RED TO PURPLE SHADES

'Jenny'

'Peter Chiswell'

'Helen Ballard'

'Brightest and Best'

'Lisa Dawn'

All flowers are shown at approximately ¾ size

'Dusky Maid'

'Pride of Colwall'

'Thundercloud'

'Fuldatel'

'Prunella'

'Janet Watts'

'Guardsman'

be fairly small and frequently rather weak shoots; unless you are desperately short of better material, these will be discarded. The second type of shoot will be stoloniferous, running away from the centres of the clumps with varying vigour according to the cultivar. Many of these will look lush and healthy, with white lengths of stem tipped by a green shoot, the leaves of which should not be fully expanded, and lots of brand new, fibrous roots. Select the required number from the best of these shoots and cut them off so that you have root, stem and leaf shoots as a complete little plant – frequently called an Irishman's cutting or an offset – up to 15cm (6in) long, depending on the cultivar.

Replant these offsets in groups each about 15-30cm (6-12in) apart according to the vigour of the cultivar and its height. Make sure each one is planted deeply, with the roots set straight down and not sideways and just the leaves above ground. Both dwarf and tall cultivars can be treated in the same way.

Some cultivars make up clumps that are tightly packed with shoots, few or none of which are stoloniferous. I suspect these to have species such as A. cordifolius and A. ericoides in their background. The tight and frequently rather woody clumps can be split into smaller sections of 6-10cm (2½-4in) diameter.

Flowering asters are typically sold in 2-litre pots.

WATERING

Although I am fortunate enough to garden on the Malvern Hills, near the spring line in Colwall, where Malvern Water is bottled, our actual rainfall is quite low, the bulk of the rain-bearing weather-fronts from the South-West having deposited their water on the Welsh hills. However, like many other parts of Britain we are now experiencing a very variable climate; the spring months can be either hot and dry, cold and dry, warm and wet or cold and wet; in some years, the same goes for all the seasons.

To grow A. novi-belgii cultivars to the highest standards you must be prepared to irrigate your crop when necessary. Permanent systems in aster borders are likely to be awkward because of the need to replant each year. But, a 'leaky hose' on the soil surface, weaving among the groups is both efficient and economic in use. Sprinklers are effective if they can be directed on to plants needing water without wasting too much on pathways and so on; however, they become less useful as the summer progresses and the aster leaves become more abundant making it difficult to achieve an even distribution of moisture to the root systems. In some years water is needed at flowering time to make the blooms last longer and, at this stage, using a sprinkler for long periods will damage the flowerheads.

WHEN TO WATER

Unless the season is wet, I make it a rule to 'puddle' in every plant at the end of the day's planting. I do not overfirm the soil as I plant, but allow a generous watering with a watering can or a carefully used hosepipe to settle the earth around the roots. This flooding is usually enough to see the young plants through to the stage where their roots are growing strongly and their stems and leaves are strengthening and enlarging. Occasional, light use of a sprinkler or leaky hose will keep the ground moist if wind and sun are drying it out too rapidly, but be careful not to flood the soil again.

Once the young plants are completely settled, mulching will conserve natural or applied moisture. The need for further irrigation will depend solely on there being enough rainfall to keep the asters growing strongly. It is also worth remembering that modern systemic fungicides against mildew attack work more efficiently if the plants are drawing an adequate supply of water, and fertilizers applied in powdered or granular

Careful cultivation of A. *novi-belgii* 'Snowsprite' (p.70) is rewarded with good quality flowerheads.

A. *novi-belgii* 'Autumn Rose' (p.51) is free-blooming and colourful at the end of the flowering season.

form will need moist soil if they are to be of benefit to the plants.

If your asters have a spindly, thin-leafed appearance in midsummer, you can be pretty sure that they need some water: they ought to be thick, lush and rich green by then. Watering is likely to be beneficial at the end of late summer, when the majority of cultivars are fattening their flower buds. After cold, sometimes misty, mornings the days of early autumn can be sunny, hot and dry. If this situation follows on from a dry late summer there is little doubt that watering while asters are in bloom will prolong their flowering season and improve their quality.

KEEPING ASTERS UPRIGHT

It is unfortunate that, when grown with skill and love to a state of perfection, New York asters above 60cm (24in) tall are more likely to need support than those plants given less attention. Their large flowering sprays will be top heavy and quite incapable of withstanding the first blasts of wind accompanying the autumn equinox. Asters left as clumps will be self supporting to a degree, or at least able to take advantage of neighbouring plants, but even here some caution is advisable. Experience has taught me that you can bring a wonderful clump of asters into glorious flowering while early autumn retains the warm, balmy days of summer, then, overnight, a gale will sweep in and dash everything to the ground. What a task it is, having to rush out early the next day with armfuls of stakes, bundles of string and a heavy heart. Take my advice on the subject of staking: adopt a 'belt and braces' policy.

BAMBOO CANES

In my main borders of New York asters, any cultivar taller than 'Remembrance', which reaches 50cm (20in), is staked with a single 1.2m (4ft) bamboo cane to each plant. The canes are put in place once the young plants are safely established and have about 20cm (8in) of growth. When viewed from the front of the borders, the canes are behind the plant they are supporting. Soft, three-ply jute string is used to loop the plant stems to the canes and is placed between the leaves to avoid tying them back to the stems. Canes of 1.2m (4ft) will only be about 1.1m (3½ft) above ground level at most, but this will easily support cultivars of about 1.3m (4¼ft) tall and anything higher can have canes 1.5m (5ft) or taller added to the grouping when the plants have grown tall. Five taller canes, often fewer, are enough for my groups, after some tricky work with large loops of jute around each spray. Careful placing among the exuberant growth will make all this work invisible. The number of ties per stem depends very much upon the characteristics of particular cultivars, three or four being sufficient for most.

When the flowering buds have been formed, the sprays have reached their full height. At this time it is a good idea to remove the tops of any canes still standing prominently above the sprays, so that the whole border presents a more pleasing appearance. If all of this seems like too much work, there are alternatives.

PEASTICKS

One of the finest methods of supporting asters, and, indeed, any other sort of herbaceous perennial, are the traditional twiggy sticks or brush, cut from hazel bushes and often known as peasticks. A border staked in this way by an experienced gardener is a veritable work of art and looks neat and tidy from early spring onwards. The sticks are cut to a height appropriate to each group of plants and are pushed into the soil around the edges of the groups. When freshly cut, they are pliable and can be arched over the plants and woven to make a twiggy framework for the shoots to grow through. By midsummer the result is a border of perennials giving every appearance of being self-supporting.

OTHER TYPES OF SUPPORT

Proprietary aids to hold plants up can be found in all sorts of guises, such as wire rings of various diameters, Y-shaped stakes and inverted L-shaped stakes which can be linked together in an endless range of patterns. The latter are not cheap but they are long lasting and ideal for asters because they have long supporting legs and can give plenty of height. The Y-stakes are good in more informal settings where just a few sprays need to be kept in place, such as where groups of asters are among shrubs and have been skilfully placed to allow the shrubs to carry much of the burden. Another use for this sort of staking is where plants are growing close to paths and lawn edges and need to be kept off them.

STAKING FOR CUT FLOWERS

Life tends to be easier if you are growing some New York asters for the sole purpose of having cut flowers.

The several means of supporting the sprays all have the advantage of being less troublesome than staking plants in the pleasure garden.

On a small scale, set out the young plants in rows about 1m (3ft) apart. Get some strong stakes about 45cm (18in) taller than the tallest of the cultivars; the wooden variety should have a top of 6-10cm (2½-4in) diameter. Drive the stakes into the ground at either end of the rows and at about 2m (6ft) intervals along the rows. If the rows are fairly short the stakes within the rows can be slightly lighter in weight than those at the ends. Having got the stakes in it is an easy matter to run strong string or plastic-coated wire either side of the plants. As the flowering sprays develop in height tie some loops between each opposing line of string or wire to prevent the sprays from slipping lengthways. Add as many lines as are needed to keep the sprays supported as they become taller throughout the summer. When cutting the flowering sprays pull them downwards, out of the lines of wire or string: attempting to hoist them up will damage the side branches.

Another way of supporting cut-flower asters is by using plastic plant support mesh. This looks just like a roll of stock fencing and its width must match that of the rectangular bed in which the young asters are planted. To allow for easy access to the crop from either side, 1.5m (5ft) is likely to be quite wide enough and can accommodate five rows of plants. The mesh is laid horizontally and has to be well secured to stout stakes, set at regular intervals. It is carefully moved upwards to keep pace with the increasing height of the plants.

MAJOR PESTS AND DISEASES

When the early breeders of A. *novi-belgii* cultivars evolved their new race of garden flowers thoughts of producing plants with resistance to pests and diseases were very much secondary to the new-found joys of larger and more brightly coloured flowerheads and various forms of flowering sprays. In fact, literature from the early years of the twentieth century indicates little evidence of concern for plant health in the case of asters. Later years saw an inclination to the 'spray it or burn it' method of disease control.

Although all chemicals legally available to amateur growers are now subject to rigorous procedures to ensure their safety during correct application, modern gardeners are very much aware of the need for carefully controlled use of pesticides in particular, and many are disinclined to grow plants that need a spraying programme to keep them healthy. Fortunately, there are many asters that are not frequently subjected to attack by bugs or fungi, but gardeners who wish to stick strictly to the pathway of organic cultivation are advised to look to groups other than the New York aster. Experience has taught me that even the most careful attention to good cultivation cannot guarantee these to be healthy. Even if everything else is well, there will always be the need for a regular spraying programme to prevent mildew from attacking the foliage.

There are a few cultivars that have proved to have some resistance. I hesitate in naming them because so much depends upon the prevailing conditions in a particular garden in a given year, so the list given on page 154 carries with it the strong proviso that it is a personal selection of plants that have proved themselves in my own garden over a period of forty years.

POWDERY MILDEW
(*Erysiphe cichoracearum*)

Mildew has two distinct phases. Usually the first sign is a white powdery coating spreading over the leaves; the early stages of this can be found as small patches on the undersurface of the leaf, but this is often missed. If unchecked, the fungus will distort the leaves which will then die. As the fungus matures, it produces spores in massive quantities and these are dispersed over a wide area by the slightest breeze. Under the right conditions, one mildewed aster might be sufficient to infect a whole border.

The fungus enters its second phase in autumn when it forms dark, pinhead-like fruitbodies which are attached to the dried leaves. These live through the winter months and will be the source of infection of young aster shoots in the spring.

It is a strange truth that few gardeners would readily deny themselves the pleasure of growing roses, which they will happily spray to prevent all sorts of ills, yet the same people will admire the beauty of a border of New York asters but proclaim to their friends that they could not possibly grow them because of the need for spraying. *A. novi-belgii* cultivars are far from being the only garden plants easily disfigured by mildew, and one of the best preventive measures is to ensure the health of other susceptible genera such as *Rosa*, *Spiraea*,

Aster mildew on the leaf of an A. *novi-belgii* cultivar.

Monarda and *Phlox*. The complete elimination of weeds such as groundsel, dandelion and sow thistle will also greatly reduce the numbers of mildew hosts. However, these and many other weeds have an irritating habit of hiding behind shrubs or among clumps of perennials where their filthy habits go unnoticed until it is too late.

The key to having New York asters with the beautiful rich green foliage of which they are capable is to do the plants well and spray while they are healthy and growing vigorously. Do not wait for mildew to become apparent. Growing the plants each year from single shoots and cultivating them to the highest standards will undoutedly help to stave off attack by any form of disease, but it cannot provide the same level of insurance as a regular programme of preventive spraying.

Until the development of Benlate, there were several very smelly and messy methods of controlling mildew that involved spraying sulphur-based products on the plants at the first signs of infection. Benlate was very effective until its withdrawal in the early 1990s. Copper-based sprays have long been in use, but only became effective in the control of mildew in asters when it was possible to apply them by means of a low volume, fan-assisted sprayer. This is still a method suited to asters cultivated under glass or polythene. The great breakthrough came with the introduction of safe-to-use systemic fungicides such as those based on propiconazole and bupirimate with triforine. It is now possible to carry out preventive spraying at several stages during the growing season so that the plants will build up some resistance to infection. Up to the present time, I have had the best results from products based on propiconazole. Products of different chemical origin are available and standard advice is to use two types within a spraying programme to avoid the risk of immunity being acquired by the infective organism. Sprays of systemic function are likely to be less effective if the plants are very root dry or growing sparsely.

Many New York aster cultivars, particularly the earlier-flowering ones such as 'Ada Ballard' and 'Margery Bennett', produce large numbers of their new shoots, including stoloniferous ones, in the autumn. Sometimes quite a large amount of leafy growth is made and a few short flowering sprays may be thrown in for good measure. All this tends to happen as the main crop of flowerheads are going over and well beyond the time when one would expect to be applying preventive sprays of fungicide. However, this crop of new shoots is especially vulnerable to attack by mildew and must be dealt with in the autumn to avoid endless trouble in the spring. The plants will not be harmed if the shoots are cut off at ground level, either before mildew appears or as soon as the first signs are evident. If desirable flowering sprays have been formed, preventive application of fungicide is worthwhile.

Occasionally, there might be a reason for taking young shoots and potting them in the autumn to overwinter in a frame or greenhouse. Even if they appear clean when potted, they always seem to become mildewed and must be sprayed. Shoots propagated during the normal late winter to spring season rarely show any signs of mildew but it is advisable to spray them once when the pots are well filled with roots and new growth is advancing above. Having done this, I have never found it necessary to spray newly planted-out stock until their roots and shoots are well developed in early summer, but again it depends entirely upon the prevailing circumstances in a garden and the brand of spray used. The strength and frequency of application will be clearly stated on the container and it is vital that these and any other instructions are strictly adhered to, in order to achieve the most effective disease control combined with the observation of every aspect of safety. Working as directed, continue spraying up to the stage when the flowerheads of individual cultivars begin to show colour.

However diligent one has been about the prevention of mildew infection during the growing season, there will always be the danger of the disease striking as flowering comes to an end, from spores drifting in from areas outside the garden. If this happens the best solution is to cut off all the growth and get it shredded and composted.

MICHAELMAS DAISY WILT
(*Phialophora asteris*)

Michaelmas daisy wilt is a soil-borne fungus that lives in the root clumps of asters. Its mycelia inhabit the lower parts of the stems preventing the upward movement of moisture and plant foods in the sap, and they produce a poisonous substance that eventually kills the leaves and stems. The first sign of trouble is usually noticed when some of the leaves appear pale and droughted, and close inspection might reveal discol-

This withered flowering spray of an *A. novi-belgii* cultivar shows the damage caused by an attack of aster wilt.

oration at the base of the flowering spray stems. Later the leaves will turn yellow then brown, firstly from the base of the spray. Often only one or two stems rising from a clump of asters will be affected but on occasion the whole clump will suffer.

If only a very few stems on a clump have to be pulled out, the remainder might well produce enough flowering sprays for the season and the clump can be dug up and destroyed in the autumn. Fortunately, if plants are produced by the single shoot method and well cultivated they are likely to be less vunerable to this disease. However, if the single flowering spray of single-shoot plants is infected the only course is to remove the entire plant.

Clumps attacked by *Phialophora* will react by bursting forth with large numbers of new shoots which give every appearance of being strong and healthy. Because the disease will almost certainly infect a new generation of stock, affected plants must not be used for propagation – except in one circumstance. If you have only one plant of a cultivar that would be difficult to replace, dig it up and pot it, after cutting off and destroying the diseased stems. Late in the following spring take some softwood cuttings from the tips of the new shoots when they are well clear of the soil level. When rooted, these can be potted on ready for planting out early in the spring of the next year. Such plants are usually perfectly healthy.

Commercial growers have access to effective soil sterilants such as Dazomet and other chemical controls, which are not available to amateurs because of hazards associated with their application. They can also employ straightforward steam soil sterilization. This ensures that new stock you may purchase from a reputable grower will be quite healthy. Much to the annoyance of my chemical suppliers, I have found that beds treated with Dazomet will grow healthy asters for about three years before further treatment is needed. But I remind you that these are intensively planted beds that have been on the same patch of ground for nearly 100 years, probably a situation that would be encountered by few amateur growers.

As is the case with so many soil-borne plant ailments, wilt is likely to be more troublesome in gardens where asters are being grown intensively, with little or no opportunity for crop rotation. The latter is always an option in mixed herbaceous borders and when asters

The destruction of budding flowerheads on this plant is evidence of tarsonemid mite infestation.

are grouped with shrubs. Following an outbreak of the disease, the next season's asters can be planted in a different place only a few feet away and this often suffices to prevent reinfection. If you are among the few really unlucky gardeners whose asters are infected year after year, the only hope is to grow plants in containers. Provided clean stock is used and the plants are not potted in garden soil, they will be fine. I have planted mature asters, on the point of flowering, into patches of ground troubled by wilt, and they have remained healthy. However, I always take the precaution of not using them for propagation.

MICHAELMAS DAISY OR TARSONEMID MITE
(*Tarsonemus pallidus*)

Michaelmas daisy mites, which are not visible to the naked eye, are creamy-white and are usually found in leaf sheafs and flower buds of asters. Damaged stems have rough brown scars where the mites have been grazing and this causes stunted growth. If the pest is unchecked the flowers will not develop properly and will turn into rosettes of small, green leaves instead of opening into colourful ray florets.

No mention of this insidious pest attacking asters is found in books written before 1950, but it was, and still is, an important pest of strawberries. It may have been a coincidence but our own asters were not troubled until there was a large increase in the acreage of a nearby commercial strawberry farm. Being caught unawares, the first sign we noticed was that many plants of the cultivar 'Freda Ballard' had flowering

The compact and brightly coloured A. *novi-belgii* cultivar 'Dolly' (p.56).

observation revealed several instances of an unknown predator in hot pursuit of *Tarsonemus pallidus*.

Amateur gardeners should look for any distorted shoots and leaves when cultivars start to regrow in the spring months. Stock propagated from offsets and raised under cover should be carefully checked because the first signs of attack are likely to be seen as damage to the young stems. Infested shoots can be removed from outdoor clumps and burned. Young, single-shoot plants will need to be sprayed with a suitable contact insecticide at the recommended rate of application. Any clumps remaining in borders should also be sprayed. Make sure that the spraying is repeated at the correct interval to catch the next hatch of mites (normally 10 to 14 days). If tarsonemid mite is troublesome in your area it is advisable to carry out the same spraying schedule in midsummer, when the pests are likely to be at their most active.

Do remember that insecticides and acaricides must be handled and used with great care and in accordance with the manufacturer's directions. It is quite possible that sprays available to amateur gardeners may not be adequate to deal with heavy infestations of Michaelmas daisy mites, in which case badly affected plants might as well be dug up and burned because they will have few, if any, flowers and the mites could be carried through to the next year in the clumps.

sprays of normal size but had either failed to form any flower buds or had large numbers of distorted buds. A considerable amount of expert examination was needed before the culprit was discovered. It was not very long before other large-scale growers of asters were experiencing infestations. The tarsonemid mite problem had become so widespread by the early 1960s that many of the magnificent borders of asters previously seen in large gardens were consigned to a place in the history books.

As far as commercial growers are concerned, several effective acaricides are available making control of tarsonemid mite a relatively straightforward procedure that can be carried out before the public buy their plants. Kelthane emulsion has been used successfully for many years, and more recently Dynamec has proved to be efficient on both indoor and outdoor crops. Research into natural biological controls might be worthwhile: in field tests of Dynamec, microscopic

OTHER PESTS AND DISEASES

In comparison to those mentioned above, other problems of New York asters seem relatively minor and mostly need to be dealt with as they arise as opposed to being routinely prevented.

Black Root Rot is caused by the fungus *Thielaviopsis basicola* and is first noticed by yellow mottling of aster foliage. Plants can become stunted and their flower buds will be deformed or abortive. The disease seems most prevalent in plants growing in cold, damp climates where the soil is extremely alkaline. The best preventive measures involve the development of a good soil structure combined with adequate drainage and high fertility. Some control can be achieved with fungicide used as a root drench.

Foot Rot or Collar Rot is the result of activities by the widespread fungus *Phytophthora cryptogea* whose spores have the ability to survive the winter months. Young shoots will show signs of blackening and will rot off at the base. Early treatment with a suitable fungicide ought to prevent the spread of the disease.

Rusts are caused by several genera of fungi which manifest themselves as brownish or reddish foliar discoloration. Many rusts are specific to a particular plant species and may live on only one part of that plant, such as the stem or leaf. Species of *Puccinia* and *Coleosporium* are the most common causes of rusts among herbaceous perennial plants; *Coleosporium senecionis* is frequently evident as orange-red pustules on the leaves of groundsel and has been found on aster leaves. The obvious method of preventing any rust problems in asters is to eradicate seedlings of groundsel as soon as possible. If careless cultivation has allowed any infection, removal of the appropriate aster leaves and spraying with a fungicide will rectify matters.

Aphids (*Aphididae*) or greenfly cause direct damage to the soft growing tips of asters and, more importantly, are among the main carriers of viral diseases. I have rarely experienced notable aphid damage once plants of *A. novi-belgii* are established in the garden: young plants in glasshouses and polytunnels are more at risk, and some of the spring- and summer-flowering species, such as *A. alpinus*, can be infested. Many types of insecticide, such as sprays based on pirimiphos-methyl or heptenophos along with many others, are effective and will readily deal with this problem and, under cover at least, some growers have great success with biological controls.

Cuckoo spit or froghopper is frequently to be seen on the soft shoots of young asters growing under cover and less often in the garden. The 'spit' surrounding the little insect is made up from the sap of the plant, and malformation and wilting can result from infestations that have been tolerated. Few chores are more satisfying than removing the culprits between thumb and forefinger or blowing them and their mess away with a strong jet of water. A more restrained approach involves the use of an insecticide based on dimethoate.

Slugs and snails are fond of new aster shoots and can cause serious problems with young plants, which, by the nature of things, have few spare shoots. Clumps will undoubtedly be grazed in the winter and early spring months but most asters are so tough and vigorous that replacement shoots easily outpace the most voracious of molluscs. I have used the usual types of slug pellets for years and have not witnessed damage to

any wildlife other than the targets. When used in the open garden, one good blitz in the early spring seems to be very effective.

Vine weevil (*Otiorhynchus sulcatus*) The adult beetles feed at night through warm periods of the summer months and the ragged edges seen on some of the lower leaves of asters can be attributed to their activities. It is rare for such damage to be of importance; the real danger with vine weevils is presented by their grubs which love to overwinter in container pots of nursery stock and feast upon the roots of many plants.

Sedum and *Heuchera* are among their favourite herbaceous perennials and they appear to dislike the roots of most asters, but this does not prevent their loving parents from giving them a home in pots of asters during the early autumn. Overwintered pots ought to be shaken out and inspected carefully in the late winter when any maggots can be removed. They are plump and white with brown heads, about 1.25cm (½in) long and contain a lot of white juice which pops out in a very satisfactory fashion when they are squashed. This is done to protect other plants in the garden which can easily be destroyed by this pest. Biological controls, such as nematodes in the genus *Heterorhabditis*, are very effective under the right climatic conditions and the soil around vulnerable plants can be drenched with chemicals based on HCH or pirimiphos-methyl.

PROPAGATION

Native aster species primarily reproduce themselves through forming large quantities of seeds which are distributed by the winds. Most also spread the growth of their clumps by means of stoloniferous shoots which make new root systems and can take up plant food from fresh soil.

The only sensible reason for raising seedlings of *A. novi-belgii* cultivars is in the search for new varieties. If you are doing this try to collect the fluffy seedheads on a dry, sunny day and store them directly in brown paper bags. If time allows during the winter, it is a good idea to separate the achenes from the pappus, selecting only plump examples of the former, on the basis that they ought to contain fertile seed. The practical purpose behind undertaking this fiddly task is simply to use up less space when sowing the seeds. The best germination will come from seeds sown in a frost-free greenhouse in late winter. The seedlings can be pricked out into trays, hardened in coldframes and either lined out directly into a patch of garden in mid- to late spring or grown on in pots if more convenient. Most plants grown in this way will flower in the same autumn. Any promising ones must be grown for a further two years or more to assess their long-term habit of growth, constitution and other qualities as garden plants. Good results can be obtained by sowing seed in a coldframe but fewer plants are likely to be advanced enough to flower in the first year.

To create new stock of existing cultivars one can choose between dividing clumps, planting offsets, potting up single shoots or taking soft cuttings. I am convinced that the most healthy and vigorous plants are produced by the careful selection of single shoots from the stolons during late winter. Such shoots need be no longer than about 7.5cm (3in) including small leaves or buds, stem and a few new roots. They must always be taken from the outer edges of the clump and the whitish or purple-tinted section of stem must be plump and flexible, and not at all woody. Some cultivars are so strong that their shoots will be larger; others will only make new shoots towards the bases of the old flowering stems. Allow for this sort of variation and select only the best-looking material available. Insert just one shoot into each 7.5cm (3in) pot of compost, label it accurately and place the pots in an unheated greenhouse, polytunnel or coldframe. The absence of artificial heat is essential to ensure sturdy plants; to further this aim, as soon as a large enough root system is established in the pots and the weather is suitable, stand the young plants outside or open the frame lights. Plants thus grown can be set out in the garden in mid- to late spring or used for planting up containers.

A GENERAL NOTE ABOUT POTTING COMPOSTS

A. *novi-belgii* and most other members of the genus are not the most demanding of plants when it comes to choosing a suitable potting compost. The majority of proprietary brands and gardeners' own mixtures appropriate to the various stages of their growth are suitable. Fresh potting compost is essential; never repot plants into the mix from the previous year's pots or containers, even if it has been freshened up with a new batch.

My ambition for many years was to hit upon a compost suited to all the species and cultivars of asters in my collection – from shoots in small pots through to plants established in large containers. Experts will be quite likely to dismiss the idea as impossible. If so, I can only suggest they visit Colwall to see the results obtained from the following simple formula. For a total volume of 100 litres of compost, mix together 70 litres of medium-grade spaghnum peat, 20 litres of sterilized fibrous loam and 10 litres of Cornish grit (or similar fine, sharp grit of neutral ph). To this add 60gm (2oz) of Osmocote® 8-9 month slow-release fertilizer and 36gm (1¼oz) of magnesium lime (dolomitic lime).

Peat-free composts using a range of materials from coir to reclaimed sewage residue are readily available and are certainly good for the production of young plants. Composts based on the traditional John Innes formula, with loam as the chief ingredient, are perfectly acceptable if proper attention is paid to feeding the plants growing in them.

Cultivars of A. *novi-belgii* need a final potting compost that does not drain too rapidly and most other asters are happiest with fairly generous amounts of summer moisture. It is easy enough to control how moist a pot-grown plant is through the winter months. Asters being brought on in containers for a flowering display will benefit from additional feeding with a balanced liquid fertilizer from early summer onwards. Just before flowering, say in the early part of late summer, it is best to change to a feed with a higher ratio of magnesium, such as a tomato fertilizer. Nothing fancy is required but many gardeners take some pride in their own feed mixes or routines and a little experimentation can do no harm.

CULTIVARS OF ASTER NOVI-BELGII

The cultivars of A. *novi-belgii*, New York asters, are the plants most people instantly recognize as Michaelmas daisies and they can be found in flower from late summer until late autumn. Here in Colwall, the vast majority of them are at their best in the weeks either side of Michaelmas Day, 29th September. Most cultivars can be relied upon for a good display of flowerheads for something like three weeks. Well-grown plants of certain cultivars, such as 'White Wings', can look attractive for much longer if enough time can be spared to deadhead the flowering sprays.

FLOWERING PERIODS

Early-season cultivars start to open their flowerheads in late summer and early autumn. The clean pink heads of 'Anita Webb' are outstanding at this time; 'Bewunderung' provides a good show of heather colouring; and the blue shades are well represented by cultivars such as 'Plenty' and 'The Sexton'. 'Alice Haslam', with pale purple-red rays, grows into neat, little mounds of colour and is one of the few dwarf cultivars to flower early in the season.

Mid-season is at the end of early autumn and into mid-autumn. This period contains many of the best-quality cultivars, such as 'Marie Ballard', 'Jenny', 'Chequers' and 'Lady in Blue'.

Late season covers mid- to late autumn, and this is when numerous cultivars with deep richly coloured rays are notable. 'Helen Ballard' is an outstanding purple-red of near faultless form, 'Harrison's Blue' and 'Davey's True Blue' both have tremendous depth of colour. Paler shades are also present with the classically shaped blooms of 'Fellowship' and 'Timsbury' which open into light pink glory.

Truly late autumn-flowering cultivars are fewer in number and tend to have flowerheads of lesser individuality than those that open earlier in the season. But any flowering colour is to be welcomed with sincere appreciation at this time of year and 'Autumn Rose' creates one of the brightest displays; and the lavender-blue heads of 'Queen Mary' and 'Blue Gown' are usually the last of the asters with large flowerheads to grace the garden.

KEY TO DESCRIPTIONS

The cultivar name is followed by the name of the raiser/introducer (I) and date of introduction where known. Heights (H) are based on the plants I have grown from single shoots in the garden in Colwall.

Most of the cultivars are 'double' in the sense that their flowerheads contain several rows of ray florets. Therefore only those with more than the average number of rays are described as being double. Cultivars with more or less one row of rays are called single. Flowerheads 2.5-3.5cm (1-1½in) across are classed as small; medium-sized flowerheads are in the region of 4.5cm (1¾in) across; and large flowerheads are in excess of 5cm (2in) across. The shape of the flowering sprays is an essential element in the overall attraction of a particular cultivar and sprays have a limited number of formations (see p.21).

'Ada Ballard' (Ballard 1952)
Flowerheads lilac-blue, large, double, very early (late summer). Sprays strong, open-branched. Clumps vigorous, tight. Good for borders and cutting. Although inferior to 'Marie Ballard' in colour and the form of the flowerheads, 'Ada Ballard' has much stronger flowering stems and broader, rather more attractive foliage. Quite successful if the clumps are undivided for two or three years. H1m (40in).

'Albanian' (Simmons)
Flowerheads white, moderately large, double, mid-season. Sprays sturdy, open-branched. Clumps strong, tight. Good for borders and cutting. 'Albanian' can be safely rated as an outstandingly good cultivar with flowerheads of a respectable size and good shape. In bud these are distinctly yellow and when fading with

A. *novi-belgii* 'Algar's Pride' (p.50) has large flowerheads reminiscent of A. × *frikartii* 'Mönch'.

age show little, if any, of the mauve-pink discoloration commonly associated with white cultivars. The foliage is dark green and contrasts well with the purity of the flowerheads. H1m (40in).

'Alderman Vokes'
Flowerheads rich mauve-pink, single, early. Sprays rather weak and shapeless. Clumps small. Suitable for borders. A cultivar of historical interest. H80cm (32in).

'Alert'
Flowerheads rich purple-red, double, mid-season. Sprays erect and bushy. Clumps compact. Borders and containers. H30cm (12in).

'Alex Norman' (A.H. Harrison)
Flowerheads pale mauve-pink, medium, single, early. Sprays compact and upright. Moderate clumps. Borders and cutting. H90cm (36in).

'Algar's Pride' (photograph p.48)
Flowerheads lavender-blue, large, single, late. Sprays stiff with the branches forming an open pyramid. Clumps strong. Borders. The narrow rays of the flowerheads are neatly and formally set around small discs creating an overall appearance of A. × frikartii 'Mönch'. Grown from annual division as single shoots, the sprays can reach full potential. When left for two or three seasons, the stems are often shorter and congested, forming a large mound of growth, but no less attractive. H1.5m (5ft).

'Alice Haslam' (A.H. Harrison c1958)
Flowerheads pale red, small, single, early (late summer). Sprays much branched into compact domes. Clumps neat. Good for borders and pots. Usually the first of the dwarf cultivars to come into bloom. Small shoots and leaves are evidence of the influence of A. dumosus. H25cm (10in).

'Alpenglow' (P. Picton 1956)
Flowerheads deep, heather-purple, small, double, mid-season. Sprays compact with short branches. Clumps weak. Borders and cutting. H80cm (32in).

'Anita Ballard' (E. Ballard before 1935)
Flowerheads pale lavender-blue, medium, early. Sprays strong and large with branches forming a pyramid. Clumps vigorous and spreading. Borders and cutting. Ernest Ballard described the colour as 'an exquisite, wistful shade of soft china-blue'. H1.5m (5ft), but a well-grown group can send stems up to 1.8m (6ft) tall and will need secure supports.

The very early flowering A. *novi-belgii* 'Alice Haslam' has a compact, domed habit.

'Anita Webb' (P. Picton 1962)
Flowerheads rosy pink, medium, early (often late summer). Sprays sturdy, branching into neat pyramids. Clumps strong and spreading. Borders and cutting. The sprays are notable for their fine shape when grown from single shoots. The rays are an especially clean colour. H1m (40in).

'Anneke'
Flowerheads deep mauve-pink, small, single, mid-season. Sprays branch into mounds. Clumps strong. Borders. H35cm (14in).

'Apollo'
Flowerheads white, small, single, mid-season. Sprays branch into mounds. Clumps moderate. Borders. H30cm (12in).

'Apple Blossom' (E. Ballard 1952)
Flowerheads very pale pink, medium, single, late. Sprays not strong; branches short and upright. Clumps modest and rather weak. This is a useful cultivar for cut flowers because of its light colour and neat sprays, but it is susceptible to wilt and therefore tiresome if grown as a border plant. H1m (40in).

'Arctic'
Flowerheads white, large, single, mid-season. Sprays strong with open branches. Clumps strong. Borders and cutting. H90cm (36in).

'Audrey'
Flowerheads mauve-blue, mid-season. Sprays branch into mounds. Clumps strong. Borders. Not one of the cleanest colours by modern standards and somewhat prone to wilt. Still popular with many amateur gardeners – perhaps they have an 'Audrey' in their family circle! H30cm (12in).

'Autumn Beauty'
Flowerheads lilac-blue, large, double, mid-season. Sprays strong with sturdy, open branches. Clumps vigorous, tight. Borders and cutting. Shapely flowerheads are packed with rays making them very double. Similar to many of the Ballard cultivars and very like 'Ada Ballard' but later into flower and with more hints of pink in the more numerous rays. H1m (40in).

'Autumn Days' (Bees Nurseries)
Flowerheads pale mauve-pink, large, early. Sprays moderately strong; open-branched. Clumps modest. Borders. H60cm (24in).

'Autumn Glory' (H.C. Elsdon, I by Baker's Nurseries)
Flowerheads bright red-purple, large, late. Sprays rather weak; open-branched. Clumps not strong. Borders. The rays tend to twist and are irregularly placed around a large assembly of golden disc florets. Not for a perfectionist but showy when the flowering season is dry. H1m (40in).

'Autumn Rose' (photograph p.41)
Flowerheads mauve-pink, medium, single, very late (usually mid-autumn into late autumn). Sprays strong and well supplied with fairly tightly packed, upright branches. Clumps strong and tight. Borders and cutting. The flowering period alone would make 'Autumn Rose' a truly desirable cultivar and the fact that it is really colourful makes it a 'must-have'. H1.2m (4ft).

'Baby Climax'
Flowerheads pale lilac-blue, small, single, very late (end of mid-autumn). Sprays strong with comparatively short branches forming a pyramid. Clumps vigorous. Borders and cutting. In spite of the name, this is not a compact version of the famous 'Climax' (see page 54). Useful for late garden colour and flowers for cutting. H75cm (30in).

'Beauty of Colwall' (E. Ballard 1905)
Flowerheads lilac-blue, medium, double, mid-season. Sprays rigid, branching into a pyramid. Clumps strong. The Royal Horticultural Society held a trial of over 300 aster cultivars in 1907 and 'Beauty of Colwall' was

the only one to be awarded a First Class Certificate. Probably the very first cultivar with sufficient ray florets to be termed a double. H1.35m (4½).

'Beechwood Challenger' (W. Wood c1936)
Flowerheads purple-red, medium, mid-season. Sprays sturdy with open branches. Clumps moderate. Borders and cutting. H1m (40in).

'Beechwood Charm' (W. Wood c1937)
Flowerheads deep pink, small, single, late. Sprays stiff, well-branched and bushy. Clumps vigorous, spreading. Borders and cutting. Probably the best of the existing Beechwood cultivars. H1m (40in).

'Beechwood Rival' (W. Wood c1938)
Flowerheads purple-red, medium, mid-season. Sprays strong with upright branches. Clumps moderate. Borders and cutting. H80cm (32in).

'Beechwood Supreme' (W. Wood c1935)
Flowerheads deep pink, medium, late. Sprays moderate with open branches. Clumps strong, tight. Borders and cutting. H1m (40in).

'Bewunderung' (Zur Linden)
Flowerheads purple-pink, medium, early. Sprays sturdy with short branches. Clumps strong. Borders. H90cm (36in).

'Blandie' (E. Ballard 1945; photograph p.52)
Flowerheads white, medium, mid-season. Sprays moderately stiff with numerous upright branches. Clumps strong. Borders and cutting. Named after Ernest Ballard's second wife, who was a Miss Bland, and undoubtedly the finest white cultivar he raised. The rays are noticeably cream-coloured in bud and do not exhibit too much mauve discoloration as they age. The foliage is rich green. The sprays can be heavy and good support is needed. Parent of many good cultivars. H1m (40in).

'Blauglut' (H. Klose 1980)
Flowerheads light violet, medium, early. Sprays strong with open branches. Clumps vigorous. Borders. H90cm (36in).

'Blue Bouquet'
Flowerheads lavender-blue, medium, late. Sprays strong, branching into a bushy mound. Clumps strong, spreading. Borders and pots. This cultivar has larger flowerheads with sturdier and more weather-resistant rays than many others in the dwarf range. H40cm (16in).

'Blue Boy'
Flowerheads mauve-blue, small, single, mid-season.

A. *novi-belgii* 'Blandie' (p.51) has white flowerheads, preceded by cream buds, in generous sprays ideal for picking.

Sprays bushy and branching into low mounds. Clumps vigorous, spreading. Borders and pots. H15cm (6in).

'Blue Danube'
Flowerheads deep lavender-blue, medium, single, early. Sprays strong with upright branches. Clumps vigorous, tight. Borders and cutting. H1.2m (4ft).

'Blue Eyes'
Flowerheads rich lavender-blue, medium, single, mid-season. Sprays strong with numerous upright branches. Clumps strong, tight. Borders and cutting. Similar in most respects to 'Blue Danube'; both represent the best in this colour group. Good if undivided for several years. H1.35m (4½ft).

'Blue Gown' (Thornely)
Flowerheads lavender-blue, large, single, very late. Sprays moderate with open branches forming a pyramid. Clumps strong. Borders and cutting. Said to have been bred from 'Climax' (see page 54) and certainly

bears similar broad, firm leaves of rich green. Although the rays are longer (creating a flowerhead of greater diameter), they are fewer in number and slightly twisting, leaving a rather ragged effect – as opposed to the more refined 'Climax' flowerhead. 'Blue Gown' usually flowers in late autumn and easily justifies planting for that reason alone. H1m (40in).

'Blue Lagoon'
Flowerheads violet-blue, large, mid-season. Sprays sturdy with short branches forming a broad mound. Clumps moderate, compact. Borders and pots. One of the few deep colours at this height. H50cm (20in).

'Blue Patrol'
Flowerheads deep lavender-blue, large, mid-season. Sprays strong with open branches. Clumps strong. Borders and cutting. H1m (40in).

'Blue Radiance' (Baker's Nurseries *c*1958)
Flowerheads light lavender-blue, large, single, mid-season. Sprays rather weak with few branches. Clumps moderate, compact. Good for 'spot' locations and large containers. Very narrow rays are grouped around a small disc in a large flowerhead of near-perfect formality. The sprays fall and twist at every opportunity and need constant attention to keep them upright. The single flowerheads are often over 50cm (2in) across and are an unusually clean shade of blue. When well grown it is an extremely effective cultivar, well worth the extra effort. H90cm (36in).

'Blue Whirl' (I. Allen)
Flowerheads pale lavender, medium, single, late. Sprays moderately sturdy with open branches. Clumps strong. Borders. The rays are whirled in a 'Catherine wheel' effect. H90cm (36in).

'Bonanza'
Flowerheads purple-red, medium, mid-season. Sprays branched into a mound. Clumps strong. H45cm (18in).

'Boningale Blue' (Baker's Nurseries *c*1963)
Flowerheads deep lavender, medium, double, mid-season. Sprays stiff with open branches. Clumps moderate. Borders and cutting. H90cm (36in).

'Boningale White' (Baker's Nurseries *c*1963)
Flowerheads white, medium, double, early. Sprays strong with upright branches. Clumps strong. Borders and cutting. H90cm (36in).

'Bridesmaid'
Flowerheads bright mauve-pink, medium, single, late.

Sprays strong with crowded branches. Clumps vigorous. Borders and cutting. H1.4m (4½ft).

'Brightest and Best' (E. Beckett, I by Wells before 1918)

Flowerheads rich bright purple-pink, large, double, mid-season. Sprays stiff with short, congested branches. Clumps moderate. Borders, containers and cutting. Vivid colour from a cultivar requiring little staking. H75cm (30in).

'Cameo' (I by Baker's Nurseries 1963)

Flowerheads bright, mauve-pink, medium, double, late. Sprays sturdy with short, upright branches. Clumps small. Borders, containers and cutting. The numerous rays are congested to make an unusually double flowerhead for a cultivar in this height range. H50cm (20in).

'Cantab'

Flowerheads pale lavender, single, late. Sprays branch

into spreading mounds. Clumps vigorous. Borders. Although the sprays are short they can be flattened by very wet weather. This possible failing apart, 'Cantab' is invaluable for late colour. H30cm (12in).

'Cantonese Queen' (M. Park, I by Monksilver Nursery 1997)

Flowerheads purple-blue, large, disc florets brown, mid-season. Sprays open-branched. Clumps vigorous. Borders. The real attraction of this cultivar is that its leaves are strongly suffused with yellow throughout the growing season. H60cm (24in).

'Carlingcott' (L.G. Chiswell c1965)

Flowerheads lilac-blue, small, double, mid-season. Sprays sturdy with bushy branches. Clumps strong. Borders and cutting. One of a series of cultivars named after the former mining villages located south of Bath, Somerset. The strain was developed from Ballard cultivars and exhibits a similar robust habit. The flowerheads are well supplied with rays and are not overlarge, making them proof against wet weather. H90cm (36in).

'Carnival'

Flowerheads purple-red, medium, double, early. Sprays strong with open branches. Clumps strong. Borders and cutting. H90cm (36in).

'Cecily' (I. Allen)

Flowerheads very pale mauve-blue, medium, single, late. Sprays branch into generous mounds. Clumps vigorous, spreading. Borders and containers. Still looks good when the clumps have not been lifted for two or three years. H50cm (20in).

'Charles Wilson'

Flowerheads pale purple-red, small, single, late. Sprays strong with bushy branches. Clumps vigorous. Borders. H1m (40in).

'Chatterbox' (Baker's Nurseries)

Flowerheads pale pink, large, mid-season. Sprays branch into generous mounds. Clumps strong, tight. Borders and containers. One of the most popular dwarf cultivars with larger than average flowerheads for this height range. Often successful if undivided for several years. Said to have been named after the raiser's young granddaughter, who undoubtedly was one! H35cm (14in).

'Chelwood' (L.G. Chiswell)

Flowerheads lilac-pink, large, double, mid-season. Sprays strong; branches open. Clumps vigorous. Borders and cutting. H1m (40in).

The combination of a deep colour and large flowerheads make A. *novi-belgii* 'Blue Lagoon' an unusual dwarf cultivar.

A. *novi-belgii* 'Coombe Radiance' produces unusually large and bright flowerheads for an end of season cultivar.

'Chequers' (R. Lidsey, I by Gayborder Nurseries *c*1953)
Flowerheads rich violet, medium, mid-season. Sprays compact with upright, bushy branches forming neat mounds. Clumps small. Borders and containers. One of the best looking cultivars in this height range, the deep colour of the rays beautifully offset by bright yellow disc florets. Narrow foliage and small shoots indicate the influence of A. *dumosus* in the parentage. H60cm (24in).

'Choristers' (P. Picton 1959)
Flowerheads white, medium, single, early. Sprays sturdy with short branches. Clumps moderate. Borders and cutting. H90cm (36in).

'Christine Soanes'
Flowerheads rose-pink, large, single, early. Sprays strong with bushy branches. Clumps vigorous. Borders and containers. The rays are a good, solid colour, possibly not enhanced by prominent discs but the overall effect is worthwhile. H50cm (20in).

'Climax' (E. Beckett *c*1906)
Flowerheads lavender-blue, large, single, late. Sprays strong with short branches forming a tall spire. Clumps strong, spreading. Borders and cutting. The flowerheads are perfectly formed with a happy balance between the neat, pale yellow disc and the clean-

coloured rays. Broad, rich green foliage could indicate the influence of A. *laevis*. 'Climax' is one of the oldest cultivars still to be widely planted and its position at the back of a border or in a large floral arrangement is justly earned. H1.35m (4½ft).

'Cloudy Blue' (E. Ballard *c*1910)
Flowerheads very pale, violet-blue, large, single, early. Sprays weak with open branches. Clumps vigorous, spreading. Borders. H1.4m (4½ft).

'Colonel F.R. Durham' (H.V. Vokes 1933)
Flowerheads purple-blue, large, mid-season. Sprays strong with open branches. Clumps small. Borders and cutting. H1m (40in).

'Coombe Delight' (R. Watts 1963)
Flowerheads pink, large, double, mid-season. Sprays sturdy with open branches. Clumps strong. Borders and cutting. H90cm (36in).

'Coombe Gladys' (R. Watts 1960)
Flowerheads deep pink, large, single, late. Sprays strong with open branches. Clumps moderate. Borders and cutting. Narrow rays on a large flowerhead create a distinctive appearance. H90cm (36in).

'Coombe Joy' (R. Watts 1963)
Flowerheads purple-red, medium, mid-season. Sprays sturdy with upright branches. Clumps strong. Borders and cutting. H1m (40in).

'Coombe Margaret' (R. Watts 1960)
Flowerheads pale pink, large, double, mid-season. Sprays strong with upright branches. Clumps moderate. Borders and cutting. Long, quilled rays, generously packed on to a shapely flowerhead exceeding 5cm (2in) across, make this cultivar as desirable as the better known 'Fellowship' (see page 57). It is also usually a more robust grower than 'Fellowship' in heavy soils. H90cm (36in).

'Coombe Pink' (R. Watts 1963)
Flowerheads deep pink, medium, mid-season. Sprays sturdy; open branches. Clumps strong. Borders and cutting. H1m (40in).

'Coombe Queen' (R. Watts 1963)
Flowerheads deep pink, medium, double, mid-season. Sprays compact with upright branches. Clumps strong. Borders and cutting. H80cm (32in).

'Coombe Radiance' (R. Watts 1963; photograph p.1)
Flowerheads bright purple-red, medium, single, late. Sprays strong with short, upright branches. Clumps compact. Borders and cutting. With its neat sprays and

bright colour this cultivar is a useful addition at the end of mid-autumn. H1m (40in).

'Coombe Ronald' (R. Watts 1962)
Flowerheads deep purple-pink, large, double, mid-season. Sprays strong with open branches. Clumps vigorous. Borders and cutting. A substantial cultivar of good quality very much in the mould of the popular breeding of the 1950s and 1960s. H1m (40in).

'Coombe Rosemary' (R. Watts 1962)
Flowerheads rich heather-purple, medium, double, mid-season. Sprays sturdy with open branches. Clumps strong, tight. Borders and cutting. Probably the finest of the Coombe prefix cultivars, being a neat grower with good, dark foliage and very freely produced, shapely flowerheads. H90cm (36in).

'Coombe Violet' (S.C. Fawell 1954)
Flowerheads deep violet-blue, medium, late. Sprays not strong with few, upright branches; notably tall and narrow. Clumps neat. Borders and cutting. A good deep colour. Needs adequate support and seems prone to tarsonemid mite damage. H1.2m (4ft).

'Countess of Dudley' (H.V. Vokes before 1935)
Flowerheads mid-pink, small, single, late. Sprays branch into low mounds. Clumps compact. Borders and containers. Other dwarf cultivars exhibit more quality but this is one of the last to flower. H25cm (10in).

'Court Herald'
Flowerheads rosy lilac, small, late. Sprays branch into strong mounds. Clumps vigorous and spreading. Borders. H40cm (16in).

'Crimson Brocade' (Baker's Nurseries 1950)
Flowerheads bright purple-red, medium, single, late. Sprays stiff; branches much divided. Clumps neat. Borders and large containers. H90cm (36in).

'Dandy' (A.H. Harrison, I by Gayborder Nurseries)
Flowerheads pale purple-red, small, single, early. Sprays sturdy with short, upright branches. Clumps compact. Borders and containers. A neat little plant often flowering well in late summer. H45cm (18in).

'Daniela' (H. Klose 1991)
Flowerheads lilac, medium, double, late. Sprays branch into low, compact mounds. Clumps small. Borders and containers. Perhaps not the most free-flowering of dwarf cultivars but very short and very late flowering. Flowering is improved if tarsonemid mite can be controlled. H20cm (8in).

A. *novi-belgii* 'Coombe Rosemary' is a free-flowering and sturdy cultivar, the best to be raised by Ron Watts.

'Daphne Anne' (E. Ballard before 1950)
Flowerheads mauve-pink, medium, double, mid-season. Sprays compact with upright branches. Clumps moderate. Borders and cutting. H90cm (36in).

'Dauerblau' (K. Foerster 1950)
Flowerheads lilac-blue, small, single, mid-season. Sprays sturdy with short branches. Clumps compact. Borders and cutting. Produces very neat sprays for cutting and is successful if undivided for several years. H90cm (36in).

'Davey's True Blue' (V.G. Davey 1960)
Flowerheads deep purple-blue, medium, late. Sprays strong with upright branches. Clumps strong, tight. Borders and cutting. A distinctive colour that is certainly one of the richest on the scene in mid-autumn. H1.2m (4ft).

'David Murray' (G. Murray)
Flowerheads pale mauve-pink, large, single, early. Sprays stiff with open branches. Clumps compact. Borders and cutting. H90cm (36in).

'Dazzler' (E. Ballard before 1936)
Flowerheads bright purple-pink, small, single, late. Sprays strong; branches bushy. Clumps vigorous. Borders, containers and cutting. The large, well-branched sprays are abundantly covered with brightly coloured heads. Young plants grown from late spring cuttings of

soft tips will make a lovely show in mid- and late autumn containers. H1m (40in).

'Destiny' (Baker's Nurseries c1957)
Flowerheads lilac-blue, large, single, mid-season. Sprays strong with open branches. Clumps strong. Borders and cutting. H1m (40in).

'Diana' (raised before 1939)
Flowerheads lilac, small, single, late. Sprays branch into mounds. Clumps strong and spreading. Borders. Not in the first rank of dwarf cultivars. H30cm (12in).

'Diana Watts' (R. Watts 1963)
Flowerheads mauve-pink, medium, double, mid-season. Sprays sturdy with open branches. Clumps strong. Borders and cutting. H1m (40in).

'Dietgard'
Flowerheads bright pink, small, single, late. Sprays branch into neat mounds. Clumps strong, compact. Borders and containers. Free-flowering late in the season, this cultivar always looks good in containers. H35cm (14in).

'Dolly' (photograph p.46)
Flowerheads bright purple-pink, small, mid-season. Sprays lax with upright branches. Clumps compact. Borders and cutting. Needs to be provided with good support. H90cm (36in).

'Dusky Maid' (Baker's Nurseries)
Flowerheads deep purple-pink, large, double, late. Sprays strong with open branches. Clumps strong. Borders and cutting. A rich colour getting close to the purple-red range; substantial and shapely flowerheads. H1.2m (4ft).

'Elizabeth'
Flowerheads light lavender-blue, medium, mid-season. Sprays compact with open branches. Clumps neat. Borders and cutting. H90cm (36in).

'Elizabeth Bright' (E. Ballard 1934)
Flowerheads mauve-pink, small, single, mid-season. Sprays compact with bushy branches. Clumps small. Borders. H70cm (28in).

'Elizabeth Hutton' (P. Picton 1962)
Flowerheads pink, medium, mid-season. Sprays stiff with upright branches. Clumps strong. Borders and cutting. A distinctly clean shade of pink, derived from the old cultivar 'Irene'. H1m (40in).

'Elsie Dale'
Flowerheads deep purple pink, medium, single, mid-season. Sprays bushy with short branches. Clumps

Effective in a large container, A. *novi-belgii* 'Eva' makes a richly coloured, compact plant.

strong, tight. Borders and cutting. Narrow rays and small disc florets. H80cm (32in).

'Elta'
Flowerheads bright mauve-pink, small, double, late. Sprays strong with short, upright branches. Clumps compact. Borders and cutting. H90cm (36in).

'Erica' (E. Ballard 1952)
Flowerheads heather-purple, medium, single, early. Sprays strong with bushy branches. Clumps vigorous, spreading. Borders and cutting. One of the most robust cultivars and still a good performer if not divided frequently. H1m (40in).

'Ernest Ballard' (E. Ballard 1950, I by Picton)
Flowerheads rich purple-pink, large, double, mid-season. Sprays strong with open, rather thin branches. Clumps small, not strong. Borders and cutting. The flowerheads are enormous, being some 5.5cm (2¼in) across, and the rays twist and are somewhat irregularly set around a prominent array of pale yellow disc florets.

This spectacular cultivar was named after Ernest Ballard after his death. H1.2m (4ft).

'Eva'
Flowerheads deep purple-pink, medium, single, late. Sprays bushy with short branches. Clumps compact. Borders and cutting. H80cm (32in).

'Eventide' (E. Ballard 1950)
Flowerheads deep lavender-blue, large, double, early. Sprays strong with upright branches. Clumps vigorous. Borders. A successful cultivar which spawned many similar. The flowerheads are over 5cm (2in) across and often exhibit an elongated array of disc florets, which detracts from their appearance for cut flowers. Usually one of the first to be infected by mildew. H1m (40in).

'F.M. Simpson'
Flowerheads purple-blue, large, single, mid-season. Sprays strong with open branches. Clumps compact. Borders and cutting. H90cm (36in).

'Fair Lady' (P. Picton 1960)
Flowerheads bright lilac-blue, small, double, mid-season. Sprays compact with bushy branches. Clumps strong, tight. Borders and cutting. Masses of flowerheads create quite heavy sprays but they are unaffected by wet weather. H90cm (36in).

'Faith' (I. Allen)
Flowerheads deep lavender-blue, large, mid-season. Sprays compact with upright branches. Clumps strong. Borders. H75cm (30in).

'Fellowship' (Sandford, I by T. Carlile 1955)
Flowerheads pale pink, large, double, late. Sprays strong with long branches. Clumps small, thin. Borders and cutting. The rays are slightly quilled and generously fill a very well-shaped flowerhead of some 5.5cm (2¼in) across. Quite superb if picked and used as specimen flowers. Not one of the strongest growers where clumps of new shoots are concerned, but this does not prevent it from being one of the most popular asters raised since 1950. H1m (40in).

'Flamingo' (P. Picton 1967)
Flowerheads pale purple-pink, large, double, mid-season. Sprays weak with open branches. Clumps compact. Borders and cutting. Quilled rays and large flowerheads make this similar to 'Fellowship' but the rays are of a deeper shade. Susceptible to verticillium wilt. H80cm (32in).

'Fontaine' (E. Ballard 1952)
Flowerheads deep pink, medium, single, mid-season.

Sprays lax with bushy branches. Clumps neat. Borders. H75cm (30in).

'Freda Ballard' (P. Picton 1959)
Flowerheads bright purple-red, large, double, early. Sprays strong with upright branches. Clumps strong, tight. Borders and cutting. Robust habit and rich colour but the flowerheads lack the refinement of the later flowering 'Helen Ballard' (see page 58). Tarsonemid mite damage can be a problem. H90cm (36in).

'Fuldatal' (H. Klose 1971)
Flowerheads deep heather-purple, large, late. Sprays sturdy with upright branches. Clumps moderate. Borders and cutting. One of the best cultivars in this colour range for mid-autumn flowering. H1m (40in).

'Gayborder Blue' (A.H. Harrison, I by Gayborder Nurseries)
Flowerheads light violet-blue, medium, early. Sprays strong with open branches. Clumps strong. Borders and cutting. H90cm (36in).

'Gayborder Royal' (A.H. Harrison, I by Gayborder Nurseries)
Flowerheads lilac-blue, small, double, late. Sprays stiff with short, upright branches. Clumps small. Borders and containers. H70cm (28in).

'Gayborder Splendour' (A.H. Harrison, I by Gayborder Nurseries c1963)

A. *novi-belgii* 'Fellowship' has among the largest flowerheads in this group. The generous sprays are good for cutting.

A. novi-belgii 'Heinz Richard' is a strong-growing and brightly coloured dwarf that is showy in a container.

Flowerheads deep purple-pink, large, double, mid-season. Sprays strong with open branches. Clumps vigorous. Borders and cutting. H90cm (36in).

'Glory of Colwall' (E. Ballard before 1930)
Flowerheads pale lilac, medium, double, mid-season. Sprays strong with upright branches. Clumps vigorous. Borders and cutting. H1.2m (4ft).

'Goliath' (Thornely)
Flowerheads lilac-pink, large, single, late (often end of mid-autumn). Sprays stiff with short, open branches forming a spire. Clumps strong. Borders and cutting. Very graceful sprays. H1.2m (4ft).

'Grey Lady' (E. Ballard 1920)
Flowerheads very pale violet, large, double, mid-season. Sprays sturdy with open branches. Clumps moderate. Borders and cutting. The flowerheads of this cultivar are almost white with just a hint of colour. H90cm (36in).

'Guardsman' (G. Shepheard-Walwyn 1956)
Flowerhead purple-red, medium, double, mid-season. Sprays very sturdy with short, bushy branches. Clumps vigorous. Cutting and large containers. A very compact, brightly coloured cultivar of strong and reliable growth. H80cm (32in).

'Gulliver'
Flowerheads pale heather-purple, small, single, mid-season. Sprays branch into neat mounds. Clumps strong. Borders and containers. H45cm (18in).

'Gurney Slade' (L.G. Chiswell 1966)
Flowerheads purple-blue, medium, double, mid-season. Sprays strong, neat with upright branches. Clumps strong. Borders and cutting. Well-shaped flowerheads. The name is a village in Somerset. H90cm (36in).

'Guy Ballard' (P. Picton 1960)
Flowerheads deep pink, large, single, early. Sprays weak with thin branches. Clumps small. Borders. Needs good support. H80cm (32in).

'Harrison's Blue' (A.H. Harrison, I by Gayborder Nurseries)
Flowerheads deep violet-blue, medium, double, late. Sprays strong with bushy branches. Clumps compact. Borders and cutting. A good rich colour for mid-autumn. Large sprays of good shape able to withstand inclement weather. H1m (40in).

'Heinz Richard' (H. Klose 1978)
Flowerheads bright purple-pink, large, mid-season. Sprays branch into neat mounds. Clumps vigorous. Borders and containers. One of the most showy dwarf cultivars. H30cm (12in).

'Helen' (R. Watts 1963)
Flowerheads purple-pink, large, double, mid-season. Sprays strong with upright branches. Clumps small with strong shoots. Borders and cutting. Ray florets incurved. H1m (40in).

'Helen Ballard' (P. Picton 1962)
Flowerheads bright purple-red, large, double, late. Sprays of good shape and strong with open branches. Clumps compact. Borders and cutting. The rays are formally arranged around bright golden disc florets. The foliage is deep green. H1m (40in).

'Herbstfeuer'
Flowerheads purple, small, mid-season. Sprays branch into mounds. Clumps strong. Borders. H30cm (12in).

'Herbstfreude'
Flowerheads bright pink, large, mid-season. Sprays

branch into low mounds. Clumps vigorous. Borders and containers. H30cm (12in).

'Herbstgruss Von Bresserhof' (Pötschke via Walter 1956)
Flowerheads pink, small, single, early. Sprays branch into mounds. Clumps strong. Borders. H40cm (16in).

'Herbstpurzel' (E. Benary via Walter)
Flowerheads lavender, small, mid-season. Sprays branch into low mounds. Clumps strong. Borders. H30cm (12in).

'Hilda Ballard' (E. Ballard 1938)
Flowerheads pale mauve-pink, large, early. Sprays strong with open branches. Clumps vigorous. Borders and cutting. Dark stems and broad leaves of a rich green set off the flower sprays of this cultivar. H1m (40in).

'Ilse Brensell' (H. Klose 1985)
Flowerheads lilac-pink, medium, single, mid-season.

A. *novi-belgii* 'Hilda Ballard' is an early-flowering cultivar with strong sprays of dark foliage.

Sprays branch into low mounds. Clumps compact. Borders. H30cm (12in).

'Irene' (E. Ballard 1952)
Flowerheads deep pink, small, single, late. Sprays strong with short branches. Clumps strong, tight. Borders and cutting. H1m (40in).

'Isabel Allen' (P. Picton 1993)
Flowerheads pink, small, single, mid-season. Sprays strong with bushy branches. Clumps vigorous. Borders. H1m (40in).

'Janet McMullen' (G. Murray 1950)
Flowerheads lilac-pink, large, double, mid-season. Sprays strong with open branches. Clumps small. Borders and cutting. H1m (40in).

'Janet Watts' (R. Watts 1964)
Flowerheads purple-red, large, single, mid-season. Sprays strong with upright branches. Clumps strong. Borders and cutting. H1m (40in).

Named after Ernest Ballard's daughter-in-law, A. *novi-belgii* 'Helen Ballard' is a superb purple-red cultivar.

A winner everywhere, A. *novi-belgii* 'Jenny' has to be the perfect dwarf for borders and containers, as well as cutting.

'Jean' (E.C. Simmonds and Sons *c*1947)
Flowerheads violet, small, double, late. Sprays sturdy with short branches only slightly inclined towards mounding. Clumps small, weak. Borders and containers. A dwarf cultivar with much broader foliage than most others. Usually not very free-flowering but useful for flowers in mid-autumn. H45cm (18in).

'Jean Gyte' (A.H. Harrison, I by Gayborder Nurseries before 1926)
Flowerheads lilac, large, single, early. Sprays strong with upright branches. Clumps moderate. H1-1.2m (40-48in).

'Jenny'
Flowerheads bright, purple-red, large, double, mid-season. Sprays sturdy with short branches. Clumps small. Borders, containers or cutting. Undoubtedly, one of the finest dwarf cultivars with compact, miniature sprays of large flowerheads. Very much a cultivar of

A. *novi-belgii* without much influence of A. *dumosus* being evident. There are doubts as to the authenticity of the name: a cultivar called 'Jenny' was raised by Harrison before 1926 but the plant currently in cultivation did not appear until the mid 1960s. 'Royal Ruby', introduced by Blooms Nurseries of Bressingham, Norfolk in about 1966, is identical to the plant now sold as 'Jenny'. H40cm (16in).

'Jollity'
Flowerheads pink, large, early (often end of late summer). Sprays lax with open branches. Clumps small. Borders or cutting. Must be well supported. H90cm (36in).

'Julia' (Baker's Nurseries 1956)
Flowerheads light pink, large, single, mid-season. Sprays strong with long, open branches. Clumps vigorous, spreading. Borders. H1.2m (4ft).

'Karminkuppel' (K. Foerster)
Flowerheads deep purple-pink, small, double, mid-season. Sprays sturdy with upright branches. Clumps strong. Borders and cutting. H90cm (36in).

'Kassel' (H. Klose 1968)
Flowerheads light purple-red, medium, mid-season. Sprays branch into mounds. Clumps strong. Borders. H40cm (16in).

'King of the Belgians' (before 1916)
Flowerheads pale violet, small, double, mid-season. Sprays strong with short branches forming a spire. Clumps strong. Borders and cutting. H1.3m (4½ft).

'King's College'
Flowerheads purple-blue, large, mid-season. Sprays sturdy with open branches. Clumps compact. Borders and cutting. H90cm (36in).

'Kristina'
Flowerheads clear white, medium, late. Sprays branch into mounds. Clumps strong. Borders and containers. Dark green foliage. One of the most reliable of the white-flowered dwarf cultivars. H30cm (12in).

'Lady Evelyn Drummond' (H.J. Chaplin, I by Lyall 1954)
Flowerheads violet-blue, large, double, mid-season. Sprays sturdy with erect branches. Clumps strong. Borders and cutting. H1m (40in).

'Lady Frances' (P. Picton 1968)
Flowerheads deep mauve-pink, large, double, mid-season. Sprays strong with upright branches. Clumps strong, tight. Borders and cutting. A cultivar with the

A. *novi-belgii* 'Lisa Dawn' (p.62) is a compact plant with early-season, richly coloured flowerheads.

robust growth so typical of many Ballard varieties. Close to the well-known 'Patricia Ballard' but later flowering, deeper in colour and with more erect sprays. H1m (40in).

'Lady in Blue' (A. Perry, I by T. Carlile c1955)
Flowerheads lavender-blue, medium, mid-season. Sprays with fine branches forming wide mounds. Clumps strong, tight. Borders and containers. One of the most successful dwarf cultivars, this displays a perfect combination of the influence of A. *novi-belgii* in the size and colour of the flowerheads and A. *dumosus* in their quantity and the fine-foliaged, compact nature of the plant. Almost guaranteed to put on a good show. H30cm (12in).

'Lady Paget' (A.H. Harrison, before 1930)
Flowerheads bright purple-pink, medium, single, late. Sprays strong with bushy branches. Clumps vigorous. Borders and cutting. H1m (40in).

'Lassie' (Sandford, I by T. Carlile c1955)
Flowerheads pale pink, large, double, early. Sprays strong with upright branches. Clumps strong. Borders and cutting. Starts to flower in early autumn and can continue for a whole month making the task of dead-heading worthwhile. H1m (40in).

'Lavender Dream' (L.G. Chiswell c1960)
Flowerheads lilac-blue, large, double, mid-season. Sprays sturdy with open branches. Clumps strong, tight. Borders and cutting. H90cm (36in).

'Lawrence Chiswell' (L.G. Chiswell c1960)
Flowerheads bright and deep purple-pink, small, double, mid-season. Sprays lax with short branches. Clumps compact. Borders, cutting and large containers. One of the richest colours, with neat sprays that are better with some support. H75cm (30in).

'Leuchtfeuer' (H. Klose 1972)
Flowerheads light purple-red, medium, early (often at the end of late summer). Sprays strong with upright branches. Clumps compact. Borders and cutting. H1m (40in).

'Lilac Time'
Flowerheads lilac, medium, single, late. Sprays branch into large mounds. Clumps vigorous, spreading. Borders. A truly tough plant which can be useful in poor soil. H40cm (16in).

'Lisa Dawn' (photograph p.61)
Flowerheads dusky purple-red, medium, single, early. Sprays sturdy with bushy branches. Clumps strong, open. Borders and containers. Prominent golden discs contrast beautifully with the deep colour of the rays. Always in flower at the end of late summer, this cultivar tends to trickle on for weeks without being smothered in bloom at any one time. This makes dead- heading essential if the plants are growing in containers. H45cm (18in).

'Little Boy Blue' (E. Ballard c1920)
Flowerheads violet-blue, medium, late. Sprays branch into mounds. Clumps vigorous. Borders and containers. H40cm (16in).

'Little Man in Blue' (E. Ballard 1935)
Flowerheads lavender-blue, medium, single, late. Sprays branch into mounds. Clumps vigorous, spreading. Borders and containers. A cultivar with much broader foliage than others in this height range. H35cm (14in).

'Little Pink Beauty' (G. Shepheard-Walwyn 1959)
Flowerheads bright mauve-pink, large, mid-season. Sprays branch into mounds. Clumps vigorous, spreading. Borders and containers. An extremely free-flowering cultivar making wide mounds of colour. H35cm (14in).

'Little Pink Lady' (E. Ballard before 1922)
Flowerheads mauve-pink, large, single, late. Sprays branch into mounds. Clumps vigorous, spreading. Borders and containers. A softer colour than 'Little Pink Beauty'. H40cm (16in).

'Little Pink Pyramid' (A.H. Harrison, I by Gayborder Nurseries c1950)
Flowerheads purple-pink, medium, single, mid-season. Clumps vigorous, spreading. Borders and containers. H45cm (18in).

'Little Red Boy' (W. Woods and Son c1946)
Flowerheads pale purple-red, small, single, mid-season. Sprays stiff with fine, bushy branches. Clumps small. Borders and containers. Notable for its broad, well-branched sprays which carry flowerheads over a very long period without the need for deadheading. Suscep-

A. *novi-belgii* 'Little Pink Lady' is one of the oldest dwarf cultivars and has surprisingly bright flowerheads.

tible to verticillium wilt in most garden soils but this should not be a problem in containers. H45cm (18in).

'Little Treasure'
Flowerheads deep purple-pink, small, single, late. Sprays branch into low mounds. Clumps neat. Borders. The flowerheads are easily spoiled by wet weather. H25cm (10in).

'Lucy'
Flowerheads pale purple-red, small, single, early. Sprays branch into rather upright mounds. Clumps small. Borders. H40cm (16in).

'Mabel Reeves' (Baker's Nurseries c1957)
Flowerheads purple-pink, large, double, early. Sprays strong with upright branches. Clumps strong. Borders and cutting. H1m (40in).

'Madge Cato'
Flowerheads pale lilac-blue, large, double, late. Sprays strong with open branches. Clumps strong and tight.

Borders and cutting. Almost white with a hint of colour; beautifully formal flowerheads. H90cm (36in).

'Malvern Queen' (P. Picton c1960)
Flowerheads deep purple-pink, large, double, mid-season. Sprays sturdy with short, open branches. Borders and cutting. Often wrongly named 'Malvern Castle'. H80cm (32in).

'Mammoth' (E. Ballard 1929)
Flowerheads lilac, large, single, mid-season. Sprays strong with open branches forming a spire. Clumps small. Borders and cutting. H1.3m (4½ft).

'Margaret Rose' (H.V. Vokes, I by Barr's)
Flowerheads purple-pink, small, mid-season. Sprays branch into low mounds. Clumps small. Borders. H35cm (14in).

'Margery Bennett' (P. Picton c1966)
Flowerheads bright deep purple-pink, large, double, early. Sprays not strong; open-branched. Clumps compact. Borders and cutting. Needs support for the rather heavy sprays. Among the brightest colours around in late summer and early autumn. H90cm (36in).

'Marie Ann Niel'
Flowerheads deep violet-blue, medium, double, mid-season. Sprays strong with open branches. Clumps strong, tight. Borders and cutting. One of the better cultivars in this colour range. H1m (40in).

'Marie Ballard' (E. Ballard, I by P. Picton 1955)
Flowerheads clear lavender-blue, large, double, mid-season. Sprays sturdy with short, open, branches. Clumps strong, tight. Borders and cutting. The flowerheads are fully 5cm (2in) or more across and can hold about 230 rays in perfect formation; indeed this cultivar cannot be bettered for long-lasting, well-shaped flowerheads, and they are as near to 'true blue' as those of any autumn-flowering aster. The disc florets are not visible until the heads age. Not the most perfectly shaped spray because the branches are gathered near to the top and the base shoots tend to become rather tall during the flowering period; however, the latter produce flowerheads after the main spray has finished (albeit of lesser quality). Surprisingly, good when not divided for two or three years with smaller, stronger sprays and smaller flowerheads. Raised by Ernest Ballard just before his death and named after his second wife. H1m (40in).

'Marie's Pretty Please'
Flowerheads lilac-blue, small, early. Sprays sturdy with

A. *novi-belgii* 'Marie Ballard' is an all-time favourite with perfectly formed double flowerheads of an exceptional colour.

upright branches. Clumps compact. Borders. A cultivar that fails to match the promise of an interesting name. H90cm (36in).

'Marjorie' (before 1935)
Flowerheads lilac-pink, small, single, late. Sprays branch into low, tight, mounds. Clumps small. Borders. Not free-flowering. H25cm (10in).

'Marjory Ballard' (P. Picton 1994)
Flowerheads purple-pink, medium, early. Sprays strong with open branches. Clumps strong. Borders and cutting. H90cm (36in).

'Mary'
Flowerheads lavender, medium, mid-season. Sprays sturdy with open branches. Clumps compact. Borders and cutting. H90cm (36in).

'Mary Deane' (R. Watts 1987)
Flowerheads bright purple-pink, large, double, late. Sprays strong with open branches. Clumps small with

A. *novi-belgii* 'Norman's Jubilee' produces large, pale pink flowerheads on compact plants.

unusually large shoots. Borders and cutting. Broad foliage indicates the presence of 'Climax' as the seed parent of this fine cultivar, which has a long flowering season and is resistant to wet weather. H1.2m (4ft).

'Melbourne Belle' (A.H. Harrison, I by Gayborder Nurseries c1950)
Flowerheads pink, large, single, mid-season. Sprays strong with bushy branches. Clumps strong. Borders and cutting. Noted for a beautifully shaped flowerhead, contrasting with the majority of modern cultivars, which are largely double. H90cm (36in).

'Melbourne Magnet' (A.H. Harrison, I by Gayborder Nurseries c1950)
Flowerheads pale violet-blue, large, double, late. Sprays strong; open branches. Clumps vigorous. Perfect form flowerheads just tinged with colour. H90cm (36in).

'Michael Watts' (R Watts 1964)
Flowerheads pale pink, medium, mid-season. Sprays

sturdy with open branches. Clumps compact. Borders and cutting. H90cm (36in).

'Mistress Quickly' (W. Wood and Sons c1954)
Flowerheads rich violet, medium, early. Sprays sturdy with upright branches. Clumps compact. Borders and cutting. Rays of a warm colour nicely contrasted by prominent golden discs; small sprays. H90cm (36in).

'Mittelmeer' (H. Klose 1977)
Flowerheads lavender, small, mid-season. Sprays branch into mounds. Clumps strong. Borders. H30cm (12in).

'Mount Everest' (E. Ballard, before 1930)
Flowerheads white, large, single, mid-season. Sprays sturdy with many upright branches, forming a graceful pyramid. Clumps strong. Indispensable for the back of borders and large flower arrangements. Small discs and very 'clean' rays that do not exhibit too much mauve colouring as they age. H1.65m (5½ft).

'Mrs Leo Hunter'
Flowerheads heather-purple, large, mid-season. Sprays strong; upright branches. Clumps compact. Borders and cutting. H1m (40in).

'Nesthäkchen' (Pötschke via Walter)
Flowerheads purple-pink, small, late. Sprays branch into tight mounds. Clumps compact. Borders. H25cm (10in).

'Newton's Pink'
Flowerheads purple-pink, medium, double, mid-season. Sprays sturdy with bushy branches. Clumps small. Borders and containers. H45cm (18in).

'Niobe' (H.V. Vokes before 1935)
Flowerheads white, small, single, late. Sprays branch into congested mounds. Clumps very small, weak. Small borders or rock gardens. Rarely flowers well. H15cm (6in).

'Norman's Jubilee' (Bees Nurseries c1985)
Flowerheads pale pink, large, early. Sprays branch into mounds. Clumps compact. Borders and containers. Almost identical to the better-known 'Chatterbox' but at least two weeks earlier into flower. H40cm (16in).

'Nursteed Charm' (Thornely)
Flowerheads pale mauve-pink, medium, mid-season. Sprays strong with open branches. Clumps vigorous. Borders and cutting. H1.2m (4ft).

Magnificent in its own right, A. *novi-belgii* 'Peace' (p.66) was an important development in modern cultivar breeding.

'Oktoberschneekuppel' (K. Foerster)
Flowerheads white shaded with pink, medium, mid-season. Sprays sturdy with bushy branches. Clumps strong. Borders. H80cm (32in).

'Orlando' (P. Picton 1954)
Flowerheads purple-pink, large, single, mid-season. Sprays strong with short branches. Clumps moderate. Borders and cutting. Well-shaped heads in what quickly became an unfashionable colour. H1m (40in).

'Pacific Amarant'
Flowerheads violet, medium, mid-season. Sprays branch into mounds. Clumps vigorous and spreading. Borders. H50cm (20in).

'Pamela' (R. Watts c1960)
Flowerheads deep mauve-pink, large, double, mid-season. Sprays strong with open branches. Clumps strong. Borders and cutting. Another fine cultivar from this raiser, exhibiting the compact and sturdy growth associated with later Ballard cultivars. H90cm (36in).

'Patricia Ballard' (P. Picton 1957)
Flowerheads bright mauve-pink, large, double, early. Sprays strong with open branches. Clumps vigorous. Borders and cutting. A very reliable and widely grown cultivar with a compact habit of growth. The flowerheads are a good shape and are freely produced. Succeeds well when not divided for several years. H90cm (36in).

'Peace' (E. Ballard 1946; photograph p.65)
Flowerheads lilac, large, double, mid-season. Sprays moderately strong with rather lax branches. Clumps small. Borders and cutting. This cultivar represents one of Ernest Ballard's great advances in aster breeding. He introduced it along with 'Plenty' and 'Prosperity' to celebrate the end of the Second World War. The flowerheads are fully 5.5cm (2¼in) across, with plentiful narrow and rather quilled rays. Very much a forerunner to many other asters with this type of head, such as the ever popular 'Fellowship'. H90cm (36in).

'Percy Thrower' (R. Lidsey, I by Gayborder Nurseries c1958)
Flowerheads deep lavender-blue, large, double, mid-season. Sprays strong with open branches. Clumps strong and tight. Borders and cutting. The ray florets twist to reveal a paler blue reverse, creating a bicolour effect. A good and distinctive cultivar, worthy of being named after this most famous of media gardeners. H90cm (36in).

'Peter Chiswell' (L.G. Chiswell 1962)
Flowerheads bright purple-red, medium, double, early. Sprays sturdy with short, bushy branches. Clumps strong, tight. Borders, cutting and large containers. One of the best cultivars in this colour range for flowers in early autumn. H75cm (30in).

'Peter Harrison'
Flowerheads pale mauve-pink, small, single, early. Sprays finely branched into low mounds. Clumps compact. Borders and containers. H35cm (14in).

'Peter Pan' (H.V. Vokes before 1935)
Flowerheads mauve-pink, small, single, late. Sprays branch into very low mounds. Clumps small. Borders. Not reliably free-flowering enough to live up to its promise but attractive if carefully grown and kept free of tarsonemid damage. H15cm (6in).

'Picture' (Baker's Nurseries 1955)
Flowerheads purple-red, large, single, late. Sprays strong with upright branches. Clumps small. Borders and cutting. H1m (40in).

'Pink Lace'
Flowerheads lilac-pink, medium, late. Sprays with fine branches bushing into mounds. Clumps small. Borders and containers. A once-popular cultivar ousted by the advent of 'Chatterbox', 'Little Pink Beauty' and so on. H35cm (14in).

'Plenty' (E. Ballard 1946)
Flowerheads lavender-blue, large, early. Sprays strong with open branches. Clumps vigorous. Borders and cutting. A good clean colour in the lighter blue shades. H1.2m (4ft).

'Pride of Colwall' (E. Ballard c1951)
Flowerheads heather-purple, small, double, mid-season. Sprays sturdy; short, upright branches; compact. Clumps moderate. Borders and cutting. H90cm (36in).

'Priory Blush' (L.G.Chiswell c1961)
Flowerheads white shaded with pink, small, late. Sprays strong with open, bushy branches. Clumps vigorous, spreading. Borders and cutting. Large, shapely sprays with heads of an unusual colour. H1m (40in).

'Professor Anton Kippenberg' (E. Benary, I by Walter 1949)
Flowerheads lavender-blue, medium, late. Sprays branch into mounds. Clumps vigorous, spreading. Borders and containers. Brightly coloured ray florets are contrasted by prominent golden discs. Quite reliable even if not divided every year. H30cm (12in).

A. *novi-belgii* 'Percy Thrower' is a good-quality plant adorned with large, colourful flowerheads.

'Prosperity' (E. Ballard 1946)
Flowerheads purple-pink, large, early. Sprays strong with open branches. Clumps strong. Borders and cutting. H1m (40in).

'Prunella' (J.E. Todd, I by Baker's Nurseries)
Flowerheads deep purple-pink, large, single, late. Sprays sturdy with bushy branches. Clumps small. Borders and cutting. Richly coloured rays and a small, golden disc. H80cm (32in).

'Purple Dome'
Flowerheads deep heather-purple, medium, mid-season. Sprays strong with bushy branches. Clumps strong, tight. Borders and cutting. The sprays might well be the correct shape but they are a bit tall for most gardeners' perceptions of what constitutes a dome. H90cm (36in).

'Queen Mary' (E. Beckett)
Flowerheads pale lavender, large, single, late. Sprays strong with short, open branches forming a spire. Clumps vigorous, spreading. Borders and cutting. The rays are somewhat thin and openly arranged but any flower at the end of mid-autumn is to be welcomed. Broad foliage indicating the influence of A. *laevis*. H1.2m (4ft).

'Queen of Colwall' (E. Ballard 1922)
Flowerheads lilac-purple, large, mid-season. Sprays weak with few branches. Clumps small. Borders or containers. Effective when flowering but a challenging plant to grow well. H90cm (36in).

'Ralph Picton' (P. Picton 1991)
Flowerheads purple-pink, large, double, late. Sprays strong with open branches. Clumps vigorous. Borders or cutting. H90cm (36in).

'Raspberry Ripple'
Flowerheads bright mauve-pink, medium, double, mid-season. Sprays sturdy with upright branches. Clumps compact. Borders and cutting. H90cm (36in).

'Red Robin' (G. Shepheard-Walwyn c1958)
Flowerheads purple-red, small, single. Sprays branch

Large flowerheads at the end of the season are the hallmarks of the compact, bushy *A. novi-belgii* 'Remembrance'.

into bushy mounds. Clumps compact. Borders. H45cm (18in).

'Red Sunset' (E. Ballard 1950)
Flowerheads dull purple-red, medium, mid-season. Sprays moderately strong with open branches. Clumps are strong and tight. Borders and cutting. H90cm (36in).

'Rembrandt' (P. Picton 1961)
Flowerheads bright purple-pink, small, double, mid-season. Sprays strong with short, upright branches. Clumps small. Borders and cutting. H90cm (36in).

'Remembrance' (H.V. Vokes before 1935)
Flowerheads lavender-blue, large, late (often the end of mid-autumn). Sprays sturdy, branching into mounds. Clumps strong. Borders, containers and cutting. Much larger heads than normal for a cultivar in this height range, freely produced on fine-foliaged, bushy growth. H50cm (20in).

'Reverend Vincent Dale'
Flowerheads deep heather-purple, medium, mid-season. Sprays strong with upright branches. Clumps small. Borders and cutting. H90cm (36in).

'Richness'
Flowerheads bright heather-purple, small, double, mid-season. Sprays strong with short branches. Clumps vigorous, tight. Borders and cutting. One of the best cultivars in this colour range. Capable of looking good even if not divided for several years. H90cm (36in).

'Robin Adair'
Flowerheads lilac, large, single, early. Sprays strong with open branches. Clumps strong. Borders and cutting. H1m (40in).

'Roland Smith' (Baker's Nurseries c1956)
Flowerheads purple-pink, medium, double, mid-season. Sprays sturdy with open sprays. Clumps moderate. Borders and cutting. H90cm (36in).

'Rose Bonnet'
Flowerheads pale lilac-pink, large, double, late. Sprays branch into mounds. Clumps compact. Borders and containers. Certainly in the top range of dwarf cultivars. Free-flowering with heads of a good size and colour. H35cm (14in).

'Rosebud' (E. Ballard before 1950)
Flowerheads pale pink, small, double, mid-season. Sprays sturdy with short, upright branches, very compact. Clumps small. Borders, containers and cutting. One of a select group of dwarf cultivars known to have no allegiance to *A. dumosus*. The little flowerheads are also unique in being so tightly packed with rays that the disc florets are hidden. Not one of the strongest growers but easy to keep going if given reasonable attention. H30cm (12in).

'Rosemarie Sallman' (Sallman)
Flowerheads pink, medium, mid-season. Sprays branch into mounds. Clumps moderate. Borders and containers. H30cm (12in).

'Rosenwichtel' (Zur Linden 1969)
Flowerheads deep pink, medium, late. Sprays branch into low, compact mounds. Clumps vigorous, spreading. Borders and containers. Robust cultivar of low stature; bright colour in mid-autumn. H25cm (10in).

'Royal Ruby' (A. Bloom, I by Bressingham Nurseries c1966)
This plant appears to be identical to the cultivar sold as 'Jenny' (see page 60).

'Royal Velvet' (A. Bloom, I by Bressingham Nurseries c1953)
Flowerheads violet, small, double, late. Sprays sturdy with bushy, upright branches; compact and elegant. Clumps small. Borders and cutting. This cultivar seems more susceptible to drought conditions and/or a shortage of plant food than most cultivars. This is usually manifested by yellowing or browning of the foliage, which can easily be mistaken for verticillium wilt. H90cm (36in).

'Rozika' (Janos Vizi 1985)
Flowerheads lilac-pink, very small, single, late. Sprays branch into congested mounds. Clumps small. Borders and containers. Usually appears reluctant to flower freely, probably as a result of tarsonemid mite damage. H15cm (6in).

'Rufus' (P. Picton 1956)
Flowerheads purple-red, medium, single, mid-season.

Large, shapely flowerheads and bushy dwarf growth make
A. *novi-belgii* 'Rose Bonnet' good for borders and containers.

Sprays strong with bushy branches. Clumps vigorous, spreading. Similar to the better known 'Winston S. Churchill', but has less brilliance of colour in the rays and a much stronger constitution. H80cm (32in).

'Sailor Boy' (I by Baker's Nurseries c1963)
Flowerheads deep violet-blue, medium, mid-season. Sprays strong with upright branches. Clumps compact. Borders and cutting. H1m (40in).

'Saint Egwin' (I before 1907)
Flowerheads purple-pink, small, single, mid-season. Sprays strong with open branches. Clumps vigorous. Borders and cutting. H1m (40in).

'Sam Banham'
Flowerheads white, medium, single, late. Sprays strong with short, open branches forming a tall spire. Clumps vigorous, spreading. Allied to 'Climax', with similar broad foliage and attractive sprays, but the flowerheads are less well formed. H1.5m (5ft).

'Sandford's Purple' (Sandford Nurseries)
Flowerheads purple-blue, medium, double, mid-season. Sprays strong with upright branches. Clumps strong. Borders and cutting. H90cm (36in).

'Sandford's White Swan' (Sandford Nurseries)
Flowerheads white, medium, double, early. Sprays strong with bushy branches. Clumps strong. Borders and cutting. A vigorous cultivar bearing large sprays. A clean white when first opened, the rays assume purple-pink tints as they age, creating a bicoloured effect. H1m (40in).

'Sarah Ballard' (P. Picton 1972)
Flowerheads lilac-purple, large, double, mid-season. Sprays strong with open branches. Clumps strong, tight. Borders and cutting. H1m (40in).

'Schneekissen' ('Snowcushion') (Benary via Walter 1954)
Flowerheads white, small, single, late. Sprays branch into low mounds. Clumps strong and tight. Borders and containers. This cultivar has distinctive pale green foliage and very compact growth, but is not always free-flowering. H25cm (10in).

'Schöne von Dietlikon' (Frikart)
Flowerheads violet-blue, small, single, mid-season. Sprays sturdy with short, upright branches. Clumps strong, tight. Borders; excellent for cutting with neat and well-shaped sprays. H1m (40in).

'Schoolgirl'
Flowerheads bright mauve-pink, large, mid-season.

A. novi-belgii 'Sheena' has distinctive pink flowerheads.

Sprays strong with open branches. Clumps strong. Borders and cutting. H1.2m (4ft).

'Sheena' (R. Watts c1969)
Flowerheads deep pink, large, double, late. Sprays strong with open branches. Clumps moderate. Borders and cutting. A distinctive cultivar with flowerheads of a good, formal shape and rays in an especially clean shade of pink. H1m (40in).

'Silberblaukissen' (K. Foerster 1956)
Flowerheads pale lavender, mid-season. Sprays branch into mounds. Clumps strong. Borders and containers. H40cm (16in).

'Silberteppich' (Bornimer Staudenculturan 1972)
Flowerheads very pale violet, mid-season. Sprays branch into mounds. Clumps strong. Borders. H40cm (16in).

'Sir Edward Elgar' (P. Picton 1962)
Flowerheads deep purple-pink, large, double, mid-season. Sprays sturdy with open branches. Clumps moderate. Borders and cutting. H90cm (36in).

'Snowdrift' (H.J. Jones c1910)
Flowerheads white, large, mid-season. Sprays strong with open branches forming a pyramid. Clumps vigorous. Borders and cutting. H1.2m (4ft).

'Snowsprite' (E. Ballard before 1935: photograph p.41)
Flowerheads white, medium, double, mid-season. Sprays branch into low, open mounds. Clumps small. Borders and containers. Probably the best-quality flowerheads at this height but needs to be grown well to achieve a good display. H30cm (12in).

'Sonata'
Flowerheads lavender, large, single, mid-season. Sprays strong with open branches. Clumps strong. Borders and cutting. H1m (40in).

'Sophia' (R. Watts 1968)
Flowerheads deep purple-pink, small, double, late. Sprays strong with bushy branches. Clumps strong and tight, suitable for borders and cutting. The neat and well-shaped flowerheads are packed with rays. H90cm (36in).

'**Starlight**' (A.H. Harrison, I by Gayborder Nurseries 1961)
Flowerheads purple-red, medium, single, mid-season. Sprays branch into mounds. Clumps vigorous. Borders and containers. 'Starlight usually flowers over a long period and benefits from regular deadheading. H30cm (12in).

'**Steinebrück**' (Dorn)
Flowerheads white, medium, mid-season. Sprays strong with open branches. Clumps strong. Borders and cutting. H1.2m (4ft).

'**Sterling Silver**' (L.G.Chiswell c1960)
Flowerheads pale mauve-pink, large, double, late. Sprays strong with short, upright branches. Clumps strong. Borders and cutting. One of the best cultivars to bear flowerheads with noticeably incurving rays. Tall, compact sprays. H1m (40in).

'**Sunset**'
Flowerheads bright purple-pink, medium, single, mid-season. Sprays strong with bushy branches. Clumps vigorous. Borders and cutting. H1m (40in).

'**Susan**' (F.E. Dawkins c1948)
Flowerheads mauve-pink, medium, single, late. Sprays strong with short, upright branches forming a spire. Clumps vigorous. Broad foliage. This cultivar looks as if it might well be allied to 'Climax' (see page 60). H1.2m (4ft).

'**Sweet Briar**'
Flowerheads pale pink, large, single, late. Sprays sturdy with short, open branches. Clumps small, not strong. Borders and cutting. The flowerheads are well-shaped and contain delicately coloured rays. Very neat sprays. H80cm (32in).

'**Tapestry**' (E. Ballard 1950)
Flowerheads lilac-pink, medium, double, mid-season. Sprays moderately strong with upright branches. Clumps compact. Borders and cutting. Perfectly formed heads and long lasting when used for cutting. H90cm (36in).

'**Terry's Pride**'
Flowerheads deep purple-pink, large, double, late. Sprays sturdy, branching into mounds. Clumps strong. Borders, containers and cutting. Very robust growth for a cultivar in this height range. Richly coloured heads. H45cm (18in).

'**The Archbishop**' (E. Ballard before 1950)
Flowerheads purple-blue, large, mid-season. Sprays

A. *novi-belgii* 'Sweet Briar' is a charming cultivar with flowerheads of a delicate colour.

strong with upright branches. Clumps strong, tight. Borders and cutting. H90cm (36in).

'**The Bishop**' (E. Ballard before 1940; photograph p.72)
Flowerheads dusky purple, large, single, mid-season. Sprays weak with bushy branches. H80cm (32in).

'**The Cardinal**' (E. Ballard before 1950)
Flowerheads deep purple-pink, large, mid-season. Sprays strong with upright branches. Clumps strong. Borders and cutting. H1m (40in).

'**The Dean**' (E. Ballard before 1950)
Flowerheads deep mauve-pink, large, single, mid-season. Sprays strong with upright branches. Clumps strong. Borders and cutting. H1.2m (4ft).

'**The Rector**' (E. Ballard before 1950)
Flowerheads purple, medium, mid-season. Sprays strong with bushy branches. Clumps strong. Borders and cutting. H1.2m (4ft).

'The Sexton' (E. Ballard before 1950)
Flowerheads lavender-blue, large, early. Sprays somewhat lax with open branches. Clumps compact. Borders and cutting. 'The Sexton' provides a good colour early in the season but must be adequately supported. H90cm (36in).

'Thundercloud'
Flowerheads deep heather-purple, small, double, late. Sprays strong with upright branches. Clumps strong, tight. Borders and cutting. H1.2m (4ft).

'Timsbury' (L.G. Chiswell c1966)
Flowerheads pale pink, large, double, late. Sprays sturdy with upright branches. Clumps strong, tight. Borders and cutting. Formal flowerheads are so well packed with rays that the discs are not seen until the heads age. H1m (40in).

The deep heather-purple flowerheads of *A. novi-belgii* 'Trudi Ann' are produced on plants of a mounding, dwarf habit.

'Tony' (Thornely)
Flowerheads pale lilac, small, double, mid-season. Sprays sturdy, branching into mounds. Clumps strong. Borders, containers and cutting. H70cm (28in).

'Tosca'
Flowerheads purple-pink, large, mid-season. Sprays strong with upright branches. Clumps strong. Borders and cutting. H1m (40in).

'Tovarich' (Thornely 1939)
Flowerheads violet, small, double, mid-season. Sprays sturdy with open branches. Clumps strong. Borders and cutting. H90cm (36in).

'Triumph'
Flowerheads lilac-pink, medium, late. Sprays sturdy

A. novi-belgii 'The Bishop' (p.71) was one of the first of Ernest Ballard's famous 'ecclestiastical' range.

with open branches. Clumps strong. Borders and cutting. Broad, unevenly spaced rays and a prominent disc contribute to a rather 'shaggy' yet pleasing appearance. H1.2m (4ft).

'Trudi Ann'
Flowerheads deep heather-purple, large, mid-season. Sprays branch into mounds. Clumps small. Borders and containers. This plant produces sizeable mounds that are well covered with the colourful flowerheads. H40cm (16in).

'Twinkle' (A.H. Harrison, I by Gayborder Nurseries c1950)
Flowerheads bright purple-pink, small, late. Sprays strong with upright branches. Clumps strong. Borders and cutting. H90cm (36in).

'Victor'
Flowerheads lilac, medium, late. Sprays branch into mounds. Borders. H30cm (12in).

'Violet Carpet'
Flowerheads violet-blue, mid-season. Sprays branch into mounds. Good for borders and containers. H25cm (10in).

'Violet Cushion'
Flowerheads violet, mid-season. Sprays branch into mounds. Good for borders and containers. H30cm (12in).

'Violet Lady'
Flowerheads deep violet, small, late. Sprays lax in habit with short branches. Clumps small. Borders. H90cm (36in).

'Wachsenburg' (Pötschke via Walter 1955)
Flowerheads purple-pink, medium, mid-season. Sprays branch into low mounds. Clumps strong. Borders and containers. H40cm (16in).

'Waterperry' (c1960)
Flowerheads pale mauve-pink, medium, mid-season. Sprays branch into mounds. Clumps strong. Borders and containers. H40cm (16in).

'Weisse Wunder' (K. Foerster)
Flowerheads white, medium, single, mid-season. Sprays strong with short, open branches. Clumps strong. Borders and cutting. H1.2m (4ft).

'White Wings'
Flowerheads white, large, single, mid-season. Sprays sturdy with open, lax branches. Clumps strong. Borders and cutting. Heads are up to 5.5cm (2¼in) across with narrow rays and small disc florets; they are well shaped

and not inclined to show purple tints as they age. Noted for a long flowering season and much enhanced by deadheading. The plants must be well supported. H90cm (36in).

'Winston S. Churchill' (A.H. Harrison, I by Gayborder Nurseries c1950)
Flowerheads bright purple-red, medium, single, mid-season. Sprays sturdy with bushy branches. Clumps small, compact and bushy. Borders, large containers and cutting. Still a good red although the rays quickly fade and twist at their tips, especially in wet weather. H80cm (32in).

'Zauberspiel'
Flowerheads white, medium, mid-season. Sprays strong with upright branches. Clumps strong. Borders and cutting. H1m (40in).

The popular cultivar A. *novi-belgii* 'Winston S. Churchill' has compact bushy sprays of purple-red flowerheads.

4

ASTER LAEVIS

The colourful race of hybrid asters accorded the title of *Aster novi-belgii* cultivars owe a very large percentage of their existence to breeding with *A. laevis* and its cultivars, which used to be popular with gardeners. Records exist for more than 25 such cultivars and it seems logical to suppose that many more must have been raised in the early years of the twentieth century.

Native specimens of *A. novi-belgii* flourish in wet ground and are likely to be unhappy with soils that become too dry in the summer months. On the other hand, *A. laevis* is more likely to be discovered where conditions are fairly dry, such as stony banks, fields and wood edges, and even on sandy ground. It might be a nice thought to assume that the original deliberate cross between the two species had the objective of producing garden hybrids tolerant of a wide variety of growing conditions. The truth is that the cross is much more likely to have had a strong accidental element about it. However it came about, the outcome remains for all to see – hundreds of *A. novi-belgii* cultivars which, although loving moist soil, will survive a dry summer and quickly respond to the smallest amount of water reaching their roots.

ASTER LAEVIS
L. (1753)

The smooth aster grows in strong clumps. The flowerheads are produced in early to mid-autumn on strong, open-branched sprays, often with glaucous or purple stems. They have 15-30 lavender to violet rays and yellow disc florets. The leaves, up to 12.5cm (5in) long, are ovate-lanceolate to lanceolate, thick, smooth and bright green. Variable. Usually in dry soil from Maine to Ontario, Virginia, Alabama, Louisiana, Saskatchewan, Missouri and Colorado. Hardy to Z4. H60-120m (24-48in), F2.5cm (1in).

CULTIVARS OF ASTER LAEVIS
A. laevis cultivars are said to be more resistant to mildew attack than most other asters with smooth leaves. This certainly holds true with the depleted numbers available for planting nowadays. **'Bluebird'**, which is offered in the USA, is said to grow into clumps 1.2m (48in) tall with excellent foliage. *A. laevis* var. *geyeri*, which is also available in the USA, does not suffer unduly from mildew.

'Arcturus' (c1892) Flowerheads deep rosy-lilac, early. Leaves deep green; stems nearly black. Sprays sturdy, open branched, produce flowerheads with moderate freedom. Clumps strong. 'Arcturus' is mentioned by E.A. Bowles as a great favourite in his book *My Garden in Autumn and Winter*. It is probable that many plants offered for sale are being confused with 'Calliope'. H1.2m (48in) or more, F3cm (1¼in).

'Blauhugel' is of more bushy growth than 'Arcturus' with violet-blue rays.

'Blauschleier' (H. Klose 1983) Flowerheads pale blue, end of late summer. H to 1.5m (60in).

'Calliope' (raised in the RHS gardens in Chiswick, London before 1892) Lilac-purple rays, yellow disc florets. F3.8cm (1½in).

It is difficult to claim any special features for the flowerheads unless it is their propensity to be daintily spaced in an open spire and not bunched into a great blob, like so many of the more highly developed aster cultivars. Clumps robustly woody, producing large quantities of purple-tinted shoots that develop into open-branched, strong and wiry flowering sprays with almost black stems. Well-grown specimens can attain 2.1m (84in) in good, not too dry soil conditions and a little less if the ground is poor. Although the leaves are thinly placed compared to many asters they are quite decorative, being thick and waxy and rich deep green. 'Calliope' is undoubtedly the most popular of the cultivars still available and has an appeal recognized by plantsmen everywhere. A 90cm (36in) wide clump, standing among shrubs such as buddleia, looks pleasing long before it comes into flower. In addition to combining with shrubs and the general mix of late summer perennials, it stands well at the back of a large border of asters, and such a position would not mean pushing through the other plants to apply regular doses of fungicide as this cultivar seems to be completely resistant to attack.

Good results come from plants divided into small clumps each year or from single offsets planted in groups. Such annual replanting encourages lush growth and rich foliage colour. However, clumps left to their own devices for several years are entirely satisfactory and look rather more natural when growing with shrubs or in a wild garden situation. 'Calliope' must surely be a prime starting point for some enterprising plant breeder who can see the potential in a new range of mildew-resistant asters possessing similar characteristics to the A. novi-belgii group.

LOST CULTIVARS

There are numerous names to haunt us from the past and remind us of our foolishness in allowing so many garden plants to be permanently consigned to the rubbish heap because 'improved' varieties had been introduced. Of course, it is easy to understand why growers in the early years of the twentieth century were looking for flowering hardy perennials with sufficient impact to compete with annual flowers and, therefore, turned their attentions to the A. novi-belgii group, where

colour and height range were more amenable to manipulation. Today, there are so many gardeners adopting such a wide variety of gardening styles that most cultivated plants are in demand somewhere. A. laevis cultivars, with their undemanding growing needs and overall wild or native look, certainly fit into the large niche being established by the promoters of 'natural' planting schemes. Some cultivars that are no longer available are listed below.

'Cordelia' had small flowerheads with starry, bright-blue rays and disc florets which turned crimson, and was said to be free-flowering with an upright branching habit. H to 1.2m (48in).

'Decorus' was blue, tinged with pink, and had a very bushy habit at only 105cm (46in) tall.

'Noir d'Angen' apparently produced lilac rays. F5cm (2in).

'Vesta' had grey-white rays and very compact, bushy growth. H90cm (36in).

ASTER × VERSICOLOR
(A. laevis × A. novi-belgii)
Willd. 1790

This is a hybrid of garden origin and widely naturalized; however, although successful as a colonizer, it has never enjoyed much popularity with gardeners. Flowering in September and October, it bears violet or white rays and yellow disc florets. The flowering sprays are strong with open branches and often form an attractive spire on purple stems. The clumps are vigorous with ovate leaves. Hardy to Z2. H to 2m (80in), F to 3.8cm (1½in).

The few recorded cultivars all had white ray florets quickly aging to purple-pink. It is unlikely that any are still in existence.

'Antigone' (syn. 'Discolor') had slender flowering sprays. H110cm (42in).

'Charming' had wiry-branched pyramids of growth. H90cm (36in) tall.

5

NEW ENGLAND ASTER

ster novae-angliae belongs to a genus beset with natural promiscuity and, in its native habitat, lives alongside many other aster species. Yet despite the obvious opportunities for interbreeding, the pollen distributors of Mother Nature have rarely activated any process of hybridization in it so it retains, virtually unsullied, its own rather minor variations of height and ray colour.

Gardeners have fared little better than nature in the attempt to persuade the plant to impart to other species some of its good qualities – including resistance to mildew, sturdiness and longevity. After nearly 300 years of cultivation just one successful cross with another species is recorded; current botanical thinking has classified only one natural hybrid, *A. amethystinus*, between *A. novae-angliae* and *A. ericoides*; and the 67 or so listed cultivars would not look very out of place if they were transported to their ancestral North American habitats such as in meadows and thickets and by shores and swamps.

ASTER NOVAE-ANGLIAE
L. (1753) New England aster

This species forms strong, woody clumps, tightly packed with shoots, and erect, hispid, pubescent flowering sprays branching into a corymb towards the top. The leaves are lanceolate to oblanceolate, entire and pubescent. They clasp the stem by an auriculate or broadly cordate base.

Between late summer and the end of autumn, numerous flowerheads cluster at the ends of the branches. They have 40-50 narrow ray florets, which are usually violet-purple but can be pink, reddish or white; the disc florets are yellow. The achenes are pubescent with reddish-white pappus and the involucre is hemispheric with linear-subulate, somewhat unequal, spreading, pubescent and more or less glandular, viscid, green bracts.

Native of Quebec to Saskatchewan, South Carolina, Alabama, Kansas and Colorado. Hardy to Z2. H60-240cm (24-96in), F2.5-4cm (1-1½in).

A. novae-angliae is described in *The New Britton and Brown Illustrated Flora of Northeastern United States and Adjacent Canada* (Gleason, H.A.) as 'one of the most beautiful of the genus' and this sentiment has been echoed by many other observers and recorders of North American flora.

Although the species was introduced to Europe as long ago as 1710, for some reason it has not stimulated the same degree of interest with gardeners as has been achieved by *A. novi-belgii*. Of nearly 70 known cultivars only around 40 are still available to growers today, compared with 300 cultivars of *A. novi-belgii* from an original figure of around 1,000 bred since the nineteenth century. However, while it is true that New England asters have languished in the shadow of their more prolific relatives, discerning gardeners have always admired them for their noble clumps of well-leafed, stout stems and bold display of colourful flowerheads, which can achieve diameters of 5cm (2in) or more; although wild plants are unlikely to exceed a ray floret count of 50, cultivars may have as many as 90.

The pale green to grey-green leaves of the New England aster are slightly hairy and less comfortable to handle than the smooth foliage of the New York aster, but they provide a much less acceptable base for mildew spores to settle on.

IN THE GARDEN

Long-lived and tough, New England asters bring both their own autumn colour, and that of many butterflies, to herbaceous and mixed borders. Associations with various herbaceous perennials producing yellow flowers through a similar season always seem to work exceptionally well. Among my favourite accompaniments are the perennial sunflowers, or *Helianthus*, such as H. 'Lemon Queen'. These are able to match or outgrow the robust stature of the asters, and the citrus to golden shades of their flowerheads provide just the right colour contrast for the, basically, violet and purple flower sprays of the asters. H. 'Lemon Queen' is thought to be a form of *H. microcephalus* and produces an enormous crop of comparatively small, pale yellow flowerheads on a generous number of strong, densely packed, neatly leafed stems, at about 1.5m (60in) tall. It is the toughest and most slug-resistant of all the sunflowers I grow. Species and cultivars of *Rudbeckia*, *Solidago* and *Coreopsis* are other good choices to plant among and in front of *A. novae-angliae*.

One of the finest plants to associate with New England asters looks so similar to them, but with bright yellow flowerheads, that a number of nurserymen in the 1950s trumpeted news of a great horticultural breakthrough. The 'golden asters' are mostly native plants of the south-eastern USA and were formerly neatly contained in the genus *Chrysopsis*; today, we have to fight with *Heterotheca* and *Pityopsis* as well. However, the Maryland golden aster is still *Chrysopsis mariana*. It has a succession of deep yellow daisies on stiff 30-60cm (12-24in) stems and is hardy to Z4. The hairy golden aster, now *Heterotheca villosa*, grows up to 1m (40in) tall and puts on a long season's display of 2.5cm (1in) wide heads. Hardy to Z5.

A. novae-angliae cultivars with pink rays, such as 'Rosa Sieger', can stand behind lavender or violet *A. amellus* or a group of *A. × frikartii* 'Mönch'. The lower-growing cultivars of *A. ericoides* are also invaluable for this all-important foreground planting, which is needed to mask the typically bare and rather unsightly lower portions of the flowering stems of established clumps of New England asters. All cultivars except the bluish shades look lovely behind a clump of Russian sage (*Perovskia atriplicifolia*), which should be hardy to Z6; its grey leaves and graceful spires of soft lavender-blue create a wonderfully hazy effect. Just remember

that the asters are likely to need much more summer moisture than the perovskia, although I have found that they do not object to both food and drink, provided they get dry feet through the winter.

A HISTORY OF BREEDING

In its native environment, the vast majority of *A. novae-angliae* seedlings have violet ray florets. Garden cultivars have been developed from colour variations selected in the wild and further refined by sharp-eyed growers who have spotted trends towards new shades of colour, often several generations before the 'break' was achieved. Strong, definite colours and a more compact habit of growth have been universal objectives. There are now various shades of violet and lavender, pink, purple-pink, red-purple and a good cultivar with white rays; even so, seedlings raised from this mix seem to be dominated by those with violet rays.

In Britain, as the Edwardian era came in with the twentieth century, growers such as Amos Perry and H.J. Jones were the main introducers of new cultivars. The cultivar 'Brilliant' was raised by Amos Perry at his Enfield nursery in 1908 and was said to be an improvement on the previously popular 'Mrs J.F. Rayner', with 'glistening, reddish crimson flowers' at a height of 1.2m (48in). Prior to 1907, H.J. Jones, whose nursery was at Lewisham, raised 'Mrs S.T. Wright', a cultivar still popular today. Barr's of Taplow and Miss R.B. Pole of Lye End Nursery, near Woking, Surrey, carried the patient process of selection further. 'Barr's Pink', 'Barr's Blue' and 'Barr's Violet', all from Barr's in the 1920s, are still available today as is 'Lye End Beauty', which was raised by Miss R.B. Pole during the 1950s.

In the later years of the twentieth century, German horticulturists made the greatest contribution to the development of the New England aster or Rauhblattaster.

A leap forward in making the species more popular came in 1969 when 'Andenken an Alma Pötschke' was introduced. The vivid, almost cerise-red rays of this cultivar easily outshine every other aster in the garden through early autumn, making it quite a challenge to site happily. I like to make use of some good background foliage as a foil. The red-purple shades of some of the *Cotinus* cultivars or forms of *Berberis thunbergii* have proved ideal and will combine beautifully with some silver and yellow foreground planting to create a

PLATE VI

'Mrs S.T. Wright'

'Barr's Violet'

'Barr's Pink'

'Violetta'

'Lou Williams'

'Rubinschatz'

'Septemberrubin'

'Rosa Sieger'

'Quinton Menzies'

'Harrington's Pink'

'Herbstschnee'

'Andenken an Alma Pötschke'

All flowers are shown at approximately ¾ size

truly colour-rich corner. It was not just the bright colour that caught the horticultural market place by storm, the compact 90cm (36in) tall growth was another first, and great bonus point.

'Herbstschnee', with white flowerheads, was introduced by H. Klose in 1981 and has proved to be a most welcome replacement for an earlier Amos Perry introduction. This latter plant, listed in 1938 as 'var. *alba*', was said to be a seedling selected from the wild in North America and growing to a 'stately' 1.8m (72in) tall. 'Herbstschnee' is a much neater 1.2m (48in). The Perry plant must have been lost during the wartime chaos of the 1940s.

Another great stride forward has been made with the introduction in about 1990 of the dwarf cultivar 'Purple Dome', from the USA. The compact stature of this roadside discovery is very unlike any other *A. novae-angliae* I have seen. The possibilities for hybridization with the likes of 'Andenken an Alma Pötschke' or 'Rosa Sieger' open up the prospect of an exciting future for New England asters.

'Harrington's Pink' was collected in the wild and introduced by Perry in the 1940s. Compared to all other asters of whatever species, the rays are a uniquely pure shade of pink and remained unchallenged for nearly thirty years before the more sturdy cultivar 'Rosa Sieger' (with larger flowerheads of a similar colour) came along in the 1970s. Although the graceful form of well-grown specimens of 'Harrington's Pink' cannot be matched, the newer introduction is a better plant for smaller gardens.

'Sayers Croft' is a seedling raised from 'Andenken an Alma Pötschke' by the English plantsman Bob Brown. This new cultivar has taken up the neat stature of its parent and the vibrant tones of the rays have been softened with pink shades.

Warm and rich shades of purple-pink pervade the New England aster group of cultivars in almost the same degree as the ubiquitous tones of violet. 'Lye End Beauty' and 'Quinton Menzies' are well-established favourites, while 'Rudelsburg' offers much brighter colour in approximately the format of 'Barr's Pink'.

It seems strange that the old cultivars with red-purple flowerheads, such as 'Brilliant' and 'Stormcloud', were apparently so little regarded by growers that plants with rays of this colour were not widely available until the introduction of 'Septemberrubin' in the 1950s. Gardeners now certainly show more appreciation of their rich contribution to an autumn border.

The violet and lilac-blue colouring commonly seen with the native species should not be spurned in the garden. Cultivars such as 'Mrs S.T. Wright' and 'Barr's Violet' will make a bold group, and careful association with some yellow-flowered plants from other genera can create a fascinating autumn picture, one that will be brought to life by the clouds of butterflies that seem to home in on asters of this colour.

In spite of the existence of *A. amethystinus*, Ron Watts must have been surprised when his two seedlings from 'Andenken an Alma Pötschke' clearly showed that his hybridizing experiment with *A. ericoides* 'White Heather' had been successful. Obvious characteristics from the two parents are evident in the graceful form of the unique 'Kylie' (the name given to the better seedling). The arching sprays of this plant's tiny, pale purple-pink flowerheads may not be everyone's idea of a showstopper, but the cross must open the door for an enterprising breeder to create a new range of hybrid asters. *A. ericoides* is known to hybridize with *A. novi-belgii*, whereas *A. novae-angliae* will not, but perhaps the resistance to mildew of a cultivar containing elements of the latter species can be bred into the *A. novi-belgii* group.

CULTIVATION

A. novae-angliae can be found in a wide range of sunny locations throughout its Northern American homelands, including in dry soils, but the strongest growing plants will always be discovered growing where the soil conditions are moisture-retentive: specimens up to 3m (10ft) tall have been recorded on the edges of swamps (to date there has been no sign of any intrepid nurseryman offering plants of this height for sale). In the garden, plants will tolerate a wide range of soil conditions, with the best results coming from humus-rich soils that can retain summer moisture. Spring and summer mulching and irrigation will improve growth on very light soils and sustain the plants through periods of drought. Sun is essential for the flowerheads to open fully, and it is noticeable that prolonged cloudy, wet

The strong-growing cultivar *A. novae-angliae* 'Quinton Menzies' (p.87) has deep purple-pink flowerheads.

A. novae-angliae 'Sayers Croft' (p.88) is a good example of the new generation of cultivars in this group.

autumns can disrupt flowering. Many of the older cultivars tend to close their rays in dark or damp conditions and will behave in the same fashion when used as cut flowers. However, most of the more recent cultivars have rays that remain open to face the elements.

DIVIDING

Although New England asters are capable of putting on a good show of flowerheads when left to their own devices for several years, it is advisable to divide the clumps every second year when they are being grown in formal borders. There are various reasons for this. Not least of these is the practical consideration about the size of the clump: after four or five seasons of robust growing, some cultivars might have clumps approaching a metre (yd) in diameter; even those that are smaller will still be woody and very densely packed with shoots and fine roots, making them heavy to dig

up and handle. Another point concerns the natural habit of *A. novae-angliae* to lose the leaves on the lower half of its stems; perhaps worse, they might well hang there shrivelled, brown and dreary for all to see. This even happens with well-tended clumps, hence the need for some foreground planting. However, clumps divided frequently and given every encouragement to grow vigorously will be rather less troubled by this blemishing factor.

I like to get down to the task of dividing my clumps in early spring but the precise time will vary according to the location of your garden. The deciding factor must always be the state of the plants. Choose a day in the early part of the spring when the new shoots are beginning to move but are not making any headway above ground level. Split the clumps into segments of about 15cm (6in) across using two forks or a sharp spade and plant them directly into ground previously prepared with garden compost, spent mushroom compost or matured farmyard manure. Set the divisions out in groups of three, five or more, with each piece about 60cm (24in) from its neighbours. Very tall cultivars will benefit from wider spacing. Give the root system time to get moving and then apply a light dressing of a good, organic fertilizer. After this has been done, the plants can be mulched after spring or early summer rainfall. Additional feeding should not be required until the following winter, when a top-dressing of garden compost or similar material will be sufficient.

When cultivated in settings that are less formal than a traditional herbaceous border, New England asters are capable of maintaining a good display for up to five years without being divided. Once the clumps start to die out in the centre, it is time to lift them. Old clumps create a dry, impoverished area around them, making attention to feeding, watering and mulching desirable.

One little trick to hide the dying leaves on the stems is to pinch out the tips of the young shoots around the perimeter of large clumps, when they are about 15cm (6in) tall. This creates some later and lower growth which helps to mask the inner stems. It is quite possible to pinch (or to stop) all the shoots on a clump: this will make the whole plant shorter and must be done early and once only, otherwise flowering will be delayed for too long.

There is one other important consideration to bear in mind, if you are thinking about leaving some clumps undivided for several years. The various cultivars will respond either by making thicker, wider clumps, with the centres finally dying out or by becoming somewhat stoliferous and spreading out, so that flowering sprays spring up on thin, wiry stems, sparsely spaced, over a wide area of ground.

STAKING

The need to use supports of one kind or another very much depends upon the conditions prevailing in any particular garden. Well-grown plants are likely to carry a generous crop of flowerheads in sprays with plenty of branches – seventy or eighty heads on one spray is possible. These will be heavy but, even so, will be supported by the stems until an hour or two of wet, windy weather strikes the garden in early autumn, when those of us who did not bother to put in some canes or strong, twiggy sticks will be sorry (see pp.41-42 for details on methods of support and staking). Perversely, less well-grown plants and those growing in unfavourable conditions or large clumps deliberately encouraged in natural or wild gardens, will have smaller corymbs of flowerheads, supported by more woody stems and will probably stand up beautifully.

DEADHEADING

In Britain, the species seems to produce vast quantities of fertile seed, so it is important to remove the old sprays in the autumn, before this can scatter around the garden and provide you with a large crop of seedlings the following spring. There is a great temptation to leave such seedlings: be advised that this has been a frequent occurrence in past years and the subsequent swamping of desirable cultivars has resulted in many being lost to cultivation.

PROPAGATION

There may be occasions when large numbers of a particular cultivar, perhaps a newly raised and worthwhile seedling, will need to be produced. The simple, but not necessarily easy, way to do this is to lift the thick, woody rootstock or clump in late winter or early spring and get it up on to a potting bench (the kitchen table will do, if you are allowed to get away with it). Considerable efforts with a cleaver, knife and secateurs will enable you to cut up small sections consisting of the base of old flowering stems, around which are grouped

the new shoots and the newly formed roots. Old woody roots and bits of stem must be carefully cut out and the new root system can be reduced a little – make sections that will fit into 10cm (4in) pots. Once potted, these must go under unheated cover for a few weeks to get the roots well established. They can then be stood out for a while before planting up in mid- to late spring.

The commercial practice of taking soft tip cuttings in late spring and rooting them in a mist unit is definitely an easier method of propagation, if the facilities are available. Plants rooted in this way can be grown in small pots for setting out the next spring and are best if kept in a polytunnel or glasshouse until then. Good ventilation and, possibly, light shading will be needed through the summer, and careful overwintering will be essential to avoid losses. During prolonged spells of frost, I bring out that invaluable commodity 'horticultural fleece'; if the weather is unusually severe money has to be spent on providing fuel for a little bit of heating. Details of suitable potting composts can be found on p.48.

In spring nurserymen supply plants produced from cuttings taken in spring of the previous year. They rarely have plants for sale through the summer and autumn months. Although the roots and new shoots of *A. novae-angliae* cultivars are fine for several months in pots, the flowering sprays produced on pot-grown plants are usually bare-bottomed monstrosities with inferior flowerheads. The best plan is to pinch out all the shoots on a regular basis to keep them low and non-flowering, and obviously, as the sales season progresses, these plants will look less and less attractive to any potential customers. Young plants set in the garden in the spring will make a reasonable amount of growth that year but are unlikely to reach their full glory until the second year. To obtain a better display in the first season, plants can be put in quite close together and replanted the following spring to give them wider spacing.

As you might have gathered, raising plants from seed presents few problems, other than what to do with the surplus. The lazy man's method is to cut some stems bearing heads that have set seed, from the selected cultivars in late autumn. Tie them into loose bundles and place them on a gravelled area in full sun (a heavy stone or two on the lower ends prevent the wind from sending them to your neighbour). Remove the bundles in late winter: you can chop them up for the compost heap. In late spring you will be able to transplant a host of seedlings from the gravel into pots or trays and these can be lined out into the garden in early summer. Most will flower that autumn, thus allowing the ray colour to be assessed. Any other characteristics can only be fairly judged in the second year. Proper gardeners rightly despise this simple plan and sow their more precious seeds in a coldframe. Precious seeds are those produced by painstaking, deliberate crossing of two selected cultivars, with the expectation of achieving better results than would natural chance.

PESTS AND DISEASES

Powdery mildew (see p.43) is not likely to be a serious problem with New England asters. I do not support the widely promoted claim that they do not suffer from attack at all, but there is absolutely no doubt that they have a high degree of resistance and will mostly be free from trouble. In the many years I have spent growing asters I have experienced seasons when the flower beds

A. *novae-angliae* 'Rosa Sieger' (p.88) is a popular cultivar with strong sprays of rose-pink flowerheads.

of A. *novi-belgii* cultivars were completely clean (having been sprayed) yet nearby groups of A. *novae-angliae* suddenly developed white leaves. I now give my New England asters a preventive spraying along with the New York asters. To be fair the spread of the fungus was not usually very great and was quickly cleared up by one or two applications of fungicide. Had I been a non-spraying person growing the plants with shrubs or genera other than asters, there would have been little to worry about.

To date, that microscopic troublemaker, tarsonemid mite (see p.45), does not seem to have developed the right taste buds for A. *novae-angliae*. Old clumps may sometimes be attacked by Michaelmas daisy wilt (see p.44), which will manifest itself by the paling, yellowing, browning and drying off of a few flowering sprays when the buds are still developing. Unless the disease is unusually severe and destroys a high proportion of sprays, it is sufficient simply to pull out the infected shoots and divide the clump before next season, to restore healthy growth.

CULTIVARS OF ASTER NOVAE-ANGLIAE

The cultivar name is followed by the name of the raiser/introducer (I) and date of introduction where known. H = height. Heights are based on established plants; first-season plants may be shorter. Flowering seasons are detailed on p.49.

Most cultivars are 'double' in the sense that their flowerheads contain several rows of ray florets. Therefore only those with more than the average number of rays are described as being double. Cultivars with more or less one row of rays are called single.

Flowerheads 2.5-3.5cm (1-1½in) across are classed as small; medium-sized flowerheads are in the region of 4.5cm (1¾in) across; and large flowerheads are in excess of 5cm (2in) across.

'Abendsonne'
Flowerheads purple-pink, large, mid-season. Sprays strong, compact branches. Clumps vigorous. H1.2m (4ft).

'Alpengluhen'
Flowerheads bright purple-pink, medium, mid-season. Sprays robust, widely branched. Clumps vigorous. H1.8m (6ft).

'Andenken an Alma Pötschke' (Pötschke via Walter 1969) ♈
Flowerheads vivid cerise-pink, medium, mid-season. Sprays sturdy; compact branches. Clumps strong, compact. Justly heralded as a breakthrough in terms of colour and compactness and a popular showstopper in gardens worldwide. The bright colouring of the rays is contrasted nicely by golden discs. The growth is well-clothed with bright green leaves. The flowerheads are some 3.5cm (1½in) across and their rays have a tendency to twist and curl towards the tips. This can sometimes create an effect of premature ageing but it does not really detract from the startling display put on by a group of plants during a sunny flowering season. Indeed, sunshine through the flowering season is possibly more crucial to 'Andenken an Alma Pötschke' than most other New England asters: they all love it but this one truly needs it. If the garden is hit by a long spell of wet weather at flowering time disaster comes in the form of soggy, brown flowerheads and unopened buds. Has parented some good offspring. H90cm (36in).

'Andenken an Paul Gerber' (Gerber via Hagemann 1950)
Flowerheads deep purple-pink, large, late. Sprays strong; compact branches. Clumps strong. H1.5m (5ft).

'Barr's Blue' (Barr's Nurseries before 1939)
Flowerheads purple-blue, medium, early. Sprays sturdy; wide branches. Clumps strong. This must be the most universally planted cultivar, its generous clumps having been split and passed from neighbour to neighbour for many decades. Usually stands well without much need for stakes. H1.2m (4ft).

'Barr's Pink' (Barr's Nurseries c1920)
Flowerheads rosy-lilac-pink, large, mid-season. Sprays robust; wide branches. Clumps vigorous. The rays curl and are unevenly placed to give a slightly ragged, but still pleasing, effect. The whole head is enhanced by a prominent boss of disc florets taking up a large share of the 5.5cm (2¼in) overall diameter. H1.5m (5ft).

'Barr's Violet' (Barr's Nurseries)
Flowerheads violet-blue, medium, early. Sprays strong; compact branches. Clumps strong. The rays are slightly deeper and sharper in colour than those of 'Barr's Blue'. H1.2m (4ft).

'Brilliant' (A. Perry 1908)
Flowerheads bright purple-red, large, mid-season.

White flowerheads make A. *novae-angliae* 'Herbstschnee' (p.86) a unique plant in the New England aster group.

Sprays strong with compact branches. Clumps strong. H1.3m (4½ft).

'Christopher Harbutt' (K. Harbutt 1993)
Flowerheads purple-blue, large, mid-season. Sprays sturdy, compact branches. Clumps strong. Bright yellow disc florets. H1m (40in).

'Constanze'
Flowerheads violet-blue, large, late. Sprays robust; wide branches. Clumps strong. Support needed in case wet weather weighs down the exceptionally tall stems. Useful at the back of large borders. H1.8m (6ft).

'Crimson Beauty' (Barr's Nurseries c1920)
Flowerheads rich, purple-red, small, late. Sprays wiry, needing support; short branches. Clumps moderately strong, spreading if left undivided for several years. Dark green leaves. Golden disc florets always make a pleasant combination with the dusky-red rays. A cultivar of very similar appearance to the more recently

A. *ericoides* **x** A. *novae-angliae* 'Kylie' produces graceful flowering sprays bearing quantities of small flowerheads.

introduced 'Septemberrubin'. However, the spring shoots are a totally different shape and come from more open clumps. Probably the best cultivar in this colour range for planting in wild gardens. H1.4m (4½ft).

'Festival'
Flowerheads light purple-blue, medium, mid-season. Sprays strong; wide branches. Clumps robust. H1m (40in).

'Forncett Jewel' (J. Metcalf 1992)
Flowerheads purple-red, large, mid-season. Sprays sturdy; wide branches. Clumps strong. H1m (40in).

'Harrington's Pink' (Harrington, I by Perry's Nurseries 1943) ♔
Flowerheads clear light rose-pink, small, late. Sprays wiry, inclined to be lax and needing support; branches short. Clumps moderately strong. Still the most pure shade of pink to be found among autumn-flowering asters. This cultivar was discovered growing wild in south-western Quebec by Millard Harrington. It was introduced to the British Isles in exchange for a rare fern. H1.5m (5ft).

'Hella Lacey' (A. Lacey)
Flowerheads light violet-blue, large, mid-season. Sprays strong. Clumps strong. H1.2m (4ft).

'Herbstflieder' (H. Klose 1988)
Flowerheads lilac, large, mid-season. Sprays strong; wide branches. Clumps robust. H1.2m (4ft).

'Herbstschnee' (H. Klose 1981; photograph p.85)
Flowerheads white, medium, mid-season. Sprays moderately strong with compact branches. Clumps strong. As far as I am aware, this is the only white-rayed form of A. *novae-angliae* presently in cultivation, although other names have cropped up over the years – 'Variety Alba' was listed by Amos Perry in 1938 and was stated to be a selected wild plant from North America, while 'Bianca' was catalogued by T. Huber in 1987. 'Herbstschnee' has flowerheads 3.5cm (1½in) across with rays that may not be as strikingly white as those of some A. *novi-belgii* cultivars, but most of the latter age into varying shades of purple-pink, whereas those of 'Herbstschnee' die off decently into brown obscurity. The foliage is light green. Each well-branched spray should carry about 70 flowerheads. H1.2m (4ft).

'Honeysong Pink' (A.J. Summers, I by Carroll Gardens)
Flowerheads rich pink, large, mid-season. Sprays strong. H90-120cm (36-48in).

'Kylie' (R. Watts 1990) ♔
(A. *novae-angliae* 'Andenken an Alma Pötschke' × A. *ericoides* 'White Heather')
Flowerheads pale pink, very small (1cm/½in across), late. Sprays wiry, lax, arching with short branches forming a spire. Clumps strong. A unique cultivar; presently the only recorded hybrid between cultivars of these two species. Lasts well when used for cutting. To avoid any confusion it should be stated that the plant was named after Kylie Macdonald, a granddaughter of the raiser. H1.2m (4ft).

'Lachglut' (H. Klose 1988)
Flowerheads salmon-red, large, mid-season. Sprays strong; branches wide. Clumps strong. H1.5m (5ft).

'Lil Fardell' (I before 1907)
Flowerheads deep mauve-pink, large, mid-season. Sprays robust; wide branches. Clumps strong. H1.8m (6ft).

'Lou Williams' (J. Williams 1995)
Flowerheads rich purple-red, large, late. Sprays strong; short branches. Clumps compact. Broad rays, in heads up to 5.5cm (2¼in) across, are marginally less brightly coloured than either 'Crimson Beauty' or 'Septemberrubin' because twisting reveals a paler reverse.

Nonetheless, they are well-contrasted by golden discs. The sprays are virtually self-supporting and stronger than other cultivars of this colour, making it an effective plant for the back of large borders. H1.8m (6ft).

'Lye End Beauty' (R.B. Pole c1958)
Flowerheads bright purple-pink, medium, mid-season. Sprays strong with compact branches. Clumps vigorous. A cultivar of rich colour which can always be relied upon where large clumps are required to stand undisturbed for several years and still retain a compact appearance. H1.4m (4½ft).

'Lye End Companion' (R.B. Pole)
Flowerheads purple-blue, medium, mid-season. Sprays strong; wide branches. Clumps strong. H1.35m (4½ft).

'Mrs J.F. Rayner' (before 1900)
Flowerheads rosy-purple-pink, large, mid-season. Sprays robust with compact branches. Clumps strong. A favourite in its day. H1.2m (4ft).

'Mrs S.T. Wright' (H.J. Jones before 1907)
Flowerheads lilac, large, mid-season. Sprays robust; wide branches. Clumps vigorous. Somewhat grey-green leaves. Probably the best of the older cultivars still grown, and popular for a reliable display of flowerheads to attract late butterflies. H1.5m (5ft).

'Mrs S.W. Stern'
Flowerheads light violet, large, mid-season. Sprays strong; wide branches. Clumps strong. One among several cultivars to have rays of a colour typical of wild plants of A. novae-angliae and the majority of the seedlings that appear in gardens. H1.2m (4ft).

'Pink Parfait'
Flowerheads rosy-pink, large, mid-season. Sprays are moderately strong with compact branches. Clumps compact. H1.2m (4ft).

'Purple Cloud'
Flowerheads purple-blue, large, mid-season. Sprays robust, wide branches. Clumps vigorous. A cultivar with stronger growth than many others of this height but support is needed to prevent wet weather weighing down the heavy sprays. H1.8m (6ft).

'Purple Dome' (R. Seip, I by Lighty and Simon c1990)
Flowerheads violet-purple, small, very late. Sprays branch into low mounds about 60cm (24in) across. Clumps strong, compact. Rich green leaves. This uniquely compact plant was spotted growing on a roadside in Pennsylvania. I find that it needs to be planted where every ray of sunshine will be of benefit; this means that the soil in the site becomes bone-dry in the summer and, therefore, success will only be within grasp if sufficient water is applied to keep the earth reasonably moist. Flowerbuds should tantalisingly dot themselves over the dark green growth and quietly sit there waiting for the sun to shine at the end of mid-autumn. Although never carried in the same numbers as other New England asters, their splash of colour lasting into late autumn is very welcome. 45cm (18in).

'Quinton Menzies' (photograph p.81)
Flowerheads deep purple-pink, medium, mid-season. Sprays strong; compact branches. Clumps strong. Similar good characteristics to 'Lye End Beauty', but just a shade deeper in the colour of the rays. H1.4m (4½ft).

'Red Cloud'
Flowerheads bright purple-pink, medium, mid-season. Sprays strong; wide branches. Clumps strong. H1.4m (4½ft).

A. novae-angliae 'Rubinschatz' (p.88) is a deep purple-pink cultivar and was raised in Germany.

'Rosa Sieger' (K. Foerster, I by Hagemann 1971; photograph p.88)
Flowerheads rose-pink, large, mid-season. Sprays strong with compact branches. Clumps strong. A cultivar of sturdy growth producing showy flowerheads with rays of an unusually clean shade of pink. A popular plant that deserves the place it has in so many gardens. H1.2m (4ft).

'Rosette'
Flowerheads pink, medium, early. Sprays strong; wide branches. Clumps strong. H1.2m (4ft).

'Rose Williams' (J. Williams 1992)
Flowerheads purple-pink, small, mid-season. Sprays wiry with short branches. Clumps vigorous. H1.2m (4ft).

'Rubinrot' (Marx 1986)
Flowerheads light purple-red, medium, late. Sprays strong with compact branches. Clumps strong. H1.20m (4ft).

'Rubinschatz' (K. Foerster 1960; photograph p.87)
Flowerheads deep purple-pink, medium, mid-season. Sprays strong; compact branches. Clumps strong. Produces neat sprays of warmly coloured flowerheads with deep golden discs. H1.3m (4½ft).

'Rudelsburg' (Pötschke, I by Walter 1964)
Flowerheads bright purple-pink, large, mid-season. Sprays sturdy with wide branches. Clumps strong. The brightly coloured rays surround deep yellow disc florets, the latter very soon assuming maroon tints. H1.1m (3½ft).

'Sayers Croft' (R. Brown 1991; photograph p.82)
Flowerheads purple-pink, large, mid-season. Sprays sturdy; branches compact. Clumps strong. A seedling from 'Andenken an Alma Pötschke' inheriting its good qualities of habit with rays of a more subtle shade. Seems less vulnerable to wet weather than its parent. H1m (40in).

'Septemberrubin' syn. 'September Ruby' (E. Benary, I by Walter 1951)
Flowerheads rich purple-red, large, mid-season. Sprays strong; short branches. Clumps compact. Dark green leaves. As with many cultivars of New England aster, the golden disc florets of this cultivar are a prominent feature and combine well with the dark-coloured rays. H1.3m (4½ft).

'Stormcloud' (I before 1925)
Flowerheads light purple-red, large, late season. Sprays

The deep violet-purple flowerheads of A. *novae-angliae* 'Violetta' enrich the later part of the flowering season.

strong; branches wide. Clumps vigorous. I can remember Ernest Ballard growing this cultivar when I was a boy. He, probably rightly, considered its great height an impediment to the prospects of good sales. I have a vivid memory of looking up at this stately plant in great awe. H1.8m (6ft).

'Treasure'
Flowerheads light violet, large, mid-season. Sprays strong with widespreading branches. Clumps vigorous. H1.4m (4½ft).

'Violetta' (H. Klose 1985)
Flowerheads deep violet-purple, small, late. Sprays somewhat lax and in need of support; short branches. Clumps compact. Just about the deepest coloured cultivar to date. Not always as free-flowering as most cultivars. H1.5m (5ft).

'W. Bowman' (c1898)
Flowerheads violet-purple, large, late. Sprays strong, widely branched. Clumps vigorous. H1.5m (5ft).

6

SMALL-FLOWERED ASTERS

Before *Aster novi-belgii* cultivars were bred in such abundance, by far the greatest number of asters in gardens and collections were those species, and their cultivars, that bore graceful, many-branched sprays misted with clouds of tiny star-like flowerheads, each only 13mm (½in) or less across.

The following extract from *The English Flower Garden* by William Robinson, the tenth edition of which was published in 1907, reveals which asters were popular, how they were grown, and what Robinson thought of them:

Aster (Starwort, Michaelmas Daisy) – Hardy perennial plants of much beauty and variety. There is quiet beauty about the more select starworts, which is charming in the autumn days, and their variety of colour, of form, and of bud and blossom is delightful. For the most part starworts are regardless of rain or cold. Less showy than the Chrysanthemum, they are more refined in colour and form. Even where not introduced into the flower garden, they should always be grown for cutting; and they are excellent for forming bold groups to cover the bare ground among newly planted shrubs. Nothing can be more easy to cultivate. The essential point is to get the distinct kinds, of which the following are among the best that flower in early October – *Aster amellus, acris, cassubicus, turbinellus, chapmanii, versicolor, pulchellus, cordifolius, elegans, reevesii, discolor, laxus, horizontalis, ericoides, shortii, multiflorus, dumosus, curtisii, laevis, longifolius, coccineus, sericeus, novae-angliae, novi-belgii, puniceus* and *vimineus*. Every year adds to our autumn blooming plants, and a choice of starworts may be made by autumn visits to collections. As yet gardeners seldom look at general effects – at the whole of things. The flowers are so dear to them that the garden, as a picture, is left to chance, and hence there is so much ugliness and formality in gardens, to those at least who regard the robe as more than the buttons. Some years ago starworts were rarely seen except in bundles in botanic gardens. Since the hardy flower revival, they have become more frequent in collections, but as yet they have made no important place in gardens generally, and we may often still see them tied in bundles, though the effective way of grouping is so clear and simply carried out. The bad effect of staking and bundling may be wholly got rid of, if the plants were supported and relieved by the bushes, and their flowers massed above them here and there. Asters dwarfer than the shrubs among which we place them, are not less valuable, as they help to give light and shade and to avoid the common way of setting plants to face as if they were so many bricks. This is not the only way of growing these hardiest of northern flowers, but it is a charming one, and it lights up the garden with a new loveliness of refined colour.

Of recent years many seedling forms have been raised and named, but in no case are these as good as the best of the wild species, such as *amellus, acris* and *cordifolius*.

Robinson's choice of asters was much more limited than that available to modern gardeners, who can reap

PLATE VII SMALL-FLOWERED ASTERS

A. 'Little Carlow'

A. *ericoides* 'Blue Star'

A. *ericoides* 'Pink Cloud'

All flowers are shown at approximately ½ size

A. 'Photograph'

A. *ericoides* 'Golden Spray'

A. *lateriflorus* 'Prince'

A. *cordifolius* 'Chieftain'

A. cordifolius 'Chieftain' (p.95) grows unusually tall and has flowerheads of a good lavender-blue colour.

the benefit of an additional ninety years of plant breeding. The asters of his day fitted well into the fashion for mass-planting. His vision took the use of plants from the realm of rigid formality into a new era of natural gardening. Designers such as Gertrude Jekyll wielded the form and colour of plants just as a painter might use the colours from a palette, creating seasonal pictures within the bounds of a garden. In the years of recovery after the First World War, considerable numbers of large gardens declined and vanished. Their place on the gardening stage was taken over by a mushrooming of small villa gardens, tended after working hours by their owners. There was no longer space to spare for plants grouped in dozens. Three or five might be the new maximum and, frequently, just one plant had to be capable of making a bold enough statement to justify its place in the garden. As if by some grand design, the new race of A. *novi-belgii* cultivars, being introduced by

plant breeders such as Ernest Ballard, were readily available to meet the growing demand. Small-flowered asters declined in popularity to the point where only enthusiasts and large collections kept the stocks going. Typical hardy plant catalogues through the 1930s featured pages of the A. *novi-belgii* group, a number of A. *amellus* and A. *novae-angliae* cultivars and just a mere handful of A. *ericoides*, A. *cordifolius* and the like.

A resurgence in awareness of the beauty and usefulness of small-flowered asters came in two stages. The first stage was engendered by the international interest in the art of flower arranging, which seemed to take off in the 1950s and 1960s. The floral artists wished to make use of these delicate cloudy sprays in their autumn arrangements and were dismayed to discover a lack of them in florists' shops. Consequently, as with a great many other herbaceous perennial plants of value to them, they found that they had to grow their own plants. When other gardeners saw such glorious plants as A. *cordifolius* 'Silver Spray' and A. *ericoides* 'White Heather' associated with perennials and shrubs, the second stage of revival was ignited and people came to realise that the ideas of Robinson and Jekyll could be scaled down to the new gardening styles, which evolved throughout the 1970s and 1980s. Collections such as the original one started near Bristol in the 1940s by Miss Isabel Allen, and the more recent National Trust collection at Upton House near Banbury in Oxfordshire, have played an important role in keeping the 'primary' range of asters in the public eye and in providing material for propagation.

IN THE GARDEN

The limited size of average modern gardens means that just one well-grown plant of a cultivar such as A. *ericoides* 'Pink Cloud' will make a sufficiently generous display. In truly confined areas A. *lateriflorus* 'Prince' and A. *sedifolius* 'Nanus' will bring some autumn colour and have attractive mounds of foliage throughout the summer. All of these types of asters combine well with roses, often blooming to coincide with a late crop of flowers on recurrent varieties of the latter, and certainly looking lovely with any fruit and foliage colour in addition to generally enlivening the rose garden at the end of the season. I have used the tall growing A. *cordifolius* 'Chieftain' to good effect with a sizeable bush of the lovely *Rosa* × *odorata* 'Mutabilis' behind and around it. 'Chieftain' has also seen good service with the lower branches of the climbing rose 'New Dawn' helping to support its tall spires. Groups or odd plants of asters can be used among shrubs and it is worthwhile remembering that the cultivars of *A. cordifolius* are tolerant of partial shade. Mixing with larger-flowered asters or other herbaceous perennials such as *Anemone × hybrida* cultivars will come naturally. I have seen a bed of hardy fuchsias enhanced and softened by groups of *A. ericoides* cultivars. This soft billowing of tiny stars can look quite startling when associated with a background of *Chamaecyparis lawsoniana* cultivars. The warm golden foliage of 'Lanei' or 'Winston Churchill' is perfect behind *A*. 'Hon. Vicary Gibbs' or the classical, graceful sprays of *A*. 'Photograph'. Some of the sombre greens and blue-greens of conifers will be viewed with renewed interest if they have a foreground plume of pale-coloured stars.

The autumn-flowering monkshood, *Aconitum carmichaelii* 'Arendsii', towers up to more than 1.8m (6ft) in damp soil. Its rich deep blue hoods are quite magnificent in their own right, but plan to have the stout spires zooming up through clouds of *A. cordifolius* 'Elegans' or *A. ericoides* 'Hon. Vicary Gibbs', and you create an even more dramatic picture. In a sunny, well-drained spot, *Euphorbia dulcis* 'Chameleon' will have colour in its warmly purple-bronzed leaves in the autumn and, if the spot is not too dry, *A. ericoides* 'Golden Spray' will stand gracefully beside it. Another good aster to associate with purple-foliaged plants is the carpeter called 'Snow Flurry', which has tiny, dazzling white flowerheads. This aster has very heather-like foliage and does not look at all out of place growing among autumn-flowering callunas.

Silver leaves are my favourite for creating a bit of height behind a mat of 'Snow Flurry', and *Lavandula lanata* takes some beating in this respect. It has late-season flowers too and even tolerates our damp winters when planted in stone and gravel.

Few of the asters in this group are likely to be unhappy in containers since they mostly have fairly compact root systems. Cultivars of *A. cordifolius* will be the most difficult to grow well in pots because of their preference for moisture and coolness, a lack of which will result in discoloured leaves, if nothing worse. The one very strange exception is *A. cordifolius* 'Chieftain', the tallest of the lot. I have often grown this in large containers for shows and have produced plants of 2.4m (8ft) tall that are in flower for nearly two months and have beautiful foliage. *A. pringlei* 'Monte Cassino' and its offspring are perfect subjects for containers, as are most of the cultivars that have been specially developed for the cut-flower trade. One of my favourites is *A. ericoides* 'Golden Spray', partly because it looks attractive for ages before the buds actually open up.

The *A. cordifolius* × *A. novi-belgii* cultivar 'Little Carlow' looks superb in a large container and is possibly even more useful when produced in the following way. If you have an established plant of 'Little Carlow' (you should have at least one, it is a brilliant garden plant) take some softwood cuttings from the growth tips in mid-spring. When these have rooted, which should not take long, plant them into small pots and grow them on in a glasshouse, polytunnel or coldframe. In mid-autumn each little plant will produce a shapely spray of flowerheads at a height of about 20cm (8in). Before the heads open you can plant up all sorts of containers for house or patio decoration. You can even use the little plants to liven up the last of your containers of summer annuals. Remember to put the young plants under cover for the winter if you wish to preserve them for planting in the garden in the spring. The *A. ericoides* group hybrid 'Ochtendgloren' can be grown in the same way if pink flowerheads are desired, as can *A. cordifolius* 'Elegans', which forms a shapely spray of nearly-white flowerheads.

(See p.48 for details of potting composts.)

ASTER CORDIFOLIUS
L. (1753) Blue wood-aster, bee-weed

Aster cordifolius is among the few members of the genus to be tolerant of a little shade. It can be found growing in clearings of woods and thickets from southern Canada and the northern United States to northern Georgia in the south, and westward with less frequency. As with so many Northern American species, the plants are variable in height, leaf form and colour of the inflorescence. Medicinal uses for *A. cordifolius* in its native land appear to have been limited to the production of an aromatic nervine, said to be preferable to valerian in many cases. The inhabitants of Maine were tempted to use the heart-shaped leaves as 'greens'; the plant is known as tongue in that state.

The leaves are typically thin, dull green and slightly hairy. They are slender-stemmed and heart-shaped on the lower sections of the main stems. Examples of the species growing in gardens, and most of the cultivars, are about 1.2m (4ft) in height, although wild plants are said to range between 30cm (12in) and 1.5m (5ft) and 'Chieftain' is capable of exceeding this.

The flowering sprays have rather thin, wiry stems and short branches forming graceful spires. The sprays arch slightly when the flowerheads are open and ideally need support to prevent wet weather from weighing them down. The usual diameter of a flowerhead is only 13mm (½in) and there are rarely more than 10 rays, with some cultivars having 15; these are coloured pale violet-blue to lavender and near white. The disc florets are invariably pale yellow when the heads open but quickly become purple.

CULTIVATION OF ASTER CORDIFOLIUS

Woody bases of the old flowering stems are retained on the clumps through the winter months and the latter become very dense and hard over a period the three years. There is no need to divide plants more frequently and they may even be left for a little longer without any deterioration in vigour or quality of flower production. Eventually you will have to tackle the task of division. This should be done early in spring as the shoots are just showing above ground.

Split the clumps into sections of between 10-15cm (4-6in) across. Although it is quite feasible to split them down to one or two shoots, plus new root growth, at the base of an old flowering stem, there is no point in the exercise unless you need to propagate large numbers of new plants. Better results are obtained from larger pieces. The traditional spade and fork, or two-fork method will work but I prefer to get the clumps on a bench and set to work with a cleaver or substantial knife. This way, with a strong wrist and a minimal amount of skill, less of the lush, brittle shoots will be destroyed. Redundant woody sections of root and old stems can be cut out during this operation. The best commercial method of propagation is by taking soft cuttings of spring growth and rooting them under mist. Young stock produced in this way must be grown in pots, under cover, for planting out in the following spring. A. cordifolius responds well to a humus-rich soil

and it is worth the effort of achieving this state in your flower beds before new plants are introduced.

Cultivars of A. cordifolius have always been popular in collections because of their grace and freedom of flowering. Resistance to attack by mildew and generally easy-going requirements for cultivation, including the ability to tolerate a little shade, make them desirable plants for modern-day gardeners. Do remember that shade means a light dappling from deciduous trees: dense cover from evergreens like holly and yew will be too much, especially in winter. Also, in most shaded areas, some extra attention will need to be paid to keeping the plants sufficiently moist during the growing season. Although the plants are tough enough to survive in dry soils, their foliage is almost sure to be badly discoloured and the flowering sprays will be a sad reflection of their possible glory.

Sprays of A. cordifolius last well when picked, and add to many an autumn arrangement collected from the garden. However, professional flower growers avoid this lovely range, solely due to the inclination of the disc florets to change colour rapidly from cool creamy yellow to purple shades.

There never have been large numbers of cultivars in circulation and it is quite difficult to find any major areas of distinction between several of those being grown today. It is sad that we have lost Edwin Beckett's 'Paragon', raised before 1910; this was said to be 'a beautiful variety, rich blue flowers produced in the greatest profusion, graceful and very attractive'. The 'Elegans' offered now differs from the original pre-1900 description, when it was said to have pale pinkish-lavender flowerheads, and seems to resemble more closely the even older A. cordifolius 'Albulus' with nearly-white rays. Even if it has acquired an incorrect name over the decades, the cultivar remains outstandingly attractive and late-flowering. 'Aldabaran', 'Silver Spray' and 'Sweet Lavender' cover the pale lavender shades at up to 1.2m (4ft) in height. 'Chieftain' is a more positive shade of lavender-blue and readily reaches 1.5m (5ft), plus some more when well-grown.

CULTIVARS OF ASTER CORDIFOLIUS

The flowerheads of all these cultivars are 'single' since they contain only one row of ray florets. The majority are about 13mm (½in) in diameter; with some of the stronger-growing cultivars this can rise to about 2cm

(¾in). Most cultivars bloom in mid-autumn; any described as 'late' will flower at the end of this period. Flowering sprays are erect and uncrowded.

H = Height. Heights are based on established plants; first-season plants may be shorter.

'Aldebaran' (E. Beckett before 1910)
Flowerheads pale lavender, late. Sprays erect, wiry with short branches forming a thin spire. Clumps strong, compact. H1.2m (4ft).

'Blutenregen'
Flowerheads lavender. H90cm (36in).

'Chieftain' (photograph p.92) ♔
Flowerheads lavender-blue, larger than average, late. Sprays strong with upright branches forming a graceful spire; do not arch. Clumps strong, compact. Leaves broader and more hairy than other cultivars. H1.5m (5ft).

'Elegans' (before 1920)
Flowerheads white, very slightly suffused with pale violet, giving a silvery effect. Sprays strong with upright branches, more dense than others. Clumps strong, compact. The last to be in flower and lives up to its name, even though it is probably the nineteenth-century 'Albulus' having adopted a twentieth-century name. H1.2m (4ft).

'Herbstzauber'
Flowerheads lavender-blue. H90cm (36in).

'Ideal' (before 1915)
Flowerheads pale lilac, thin-rayed, mid-season. Sprays arching with broad branches. Clumps strong, compact. H90cm (36in).

'Novemberblau' (H. Klose 1991)
Flowerheads lavender-blue, small, late. Sprays strong, slightly arching, with upright branches. Clumps compact. H1.2m (4ft).

'Silver Spray' (E. Ballard before 1928)
Flowerheads pale lavender, mid-season. Sprays wiry, arching with short branches. Clumps strong, compact. H1.2m (4ft).

'Sweet Lavender' (E. Beckett before 1910) ♔
Flowerheads lavender, late. Sprays sturdy, arching with upright branches. Clumps compact. H1.2m (4ft).

ASTER CORDIFOLIUS HYBRIDS

Strictly speaking these are hybrids that are close to A. cordifolius in habit. Nursery catalogues used to list them under the heading A. cordi-belgii hybrids, thus neatly defining their origin as crosses between cultivars of these two species. Like so many good garden plants, those in existence today are happy accidents as opposed to being the result of a diligent breeding programme. Grow them in the same way as A. cordifolius except that they need open, sunny positions for the best flowering.

'Little Carlow' (Thornely) ♔
Flowerheads bright lavender-blue, 2.5cm (1in) across, mid-season. Sprays sturdy with upright branches forming a substantial panicle. Clumps strong. Lower leaves broadly lance-shaped, deep green. This is a 'must have' plant for herbaceous beds or mixed planting with shrubs. It also performs well as a cut flower and in large containers. Spring-rooted cuttings will produce a lovely spray of flowerheads in mid-autumn and can be used to liven up tired containers of summer bedding. In the garden, clumps of 'Little Carlow' can become quite

A. cordifolius 'Sweet Lavender' is a lovely cultivar and was raised in the famous gardens at Aldenham, England.

A prominent contender for the position of 'best cultivar', A. 'Photograph' has elegant sprays of small flowerheads.

substantial, about 50cm (20in) across in three years, and will put up a large number of flowering sprays, making the flowering-time plant up to 1.2m (4ft) in diameter. The percentage of A. novi-belgii in this cultivar is, unfortunately, just sufficient to allow mildew to be a problem in some years. Mrs Thornely was a prolific but little heard-of breeder of asters in the 1930s and 1940s, living in Devizes, Wiltshire. Few of her cultivars exist today and we are fortunate that the cultivar that has proved to be her greatest achievement has survived. H1.2m (4ft).

'Little Dorrit' (I. Allen)
Flowerheads bright purple-pink, 2.5cm (1in) across, late. Sprays strong with short branches forming a spire. Clumps vigorous. Leaves lance-shaped, deep green. This cultivar looks as if it must be about eighty percent A. novi-belgii but with smaller flowerheads and more gracefully formed sprays. Unfortunately, it is highly subject to attack by mildew, making diligent preventive spraying essential. H1.2m (4ft).

'Photograph' (before 1920) ♛
Flowerheads clear pale lavender-blue, 15mm (½in) across, late. Sprays wiry and arching gracefully with numerous branches. Clumps rather weak. Leaves at base are broadly oval, those higher on the stems being lance-shaped, pale green. This cultivar represents all the best qualities of the small-flowered asters but lacks a strong constitution. The flowerheads and clumps are close to A. cordifolius in character although the sprays more nearly resemble A. ericoides in form. Good colour, grace, ninety percent immunity from mildew and the late-season flowers are all there to be an asset in borders and containers. The flowerheads are also excellent for cutting, even if commercial growers would find the stems lacking in sturdiness, 'Photograph' exhibits little of the A. cordifolius propensity for purple disc florets. Some tasteful staking is needed to protect the sprays from damage. Unfortunately, slugs seem very inclined to feast on the meagre crop of succulent young shoots

each spring and will have to be dealt with. I usually keep a plant in a pot to overwinter in a frame, as a safeguard against losing a cultivar that modern breeders have yet to match. H1m (40in).

'September Mist' (P. Picton 1994)
Flowerheads white shaded pale violet, 15mm (⅝in) across, disc florets pale yellow, quickly turning purple. Sprays sturdy with short branches forming an erect spire. Clumps compact. Lower leaves broad and heart-shaped. H1.2m (4ft).

ASTER ERICOIDES

L. (1753) White heath aster, frost-weed aster

Vigorous, compact clumps with linear to linear-lance-shaped leaves, up to 6cm (2½in) long and sturdy, bushy-branched sprays from early to late autumn. Flowerheads consist of 15-25 white rays, sometimes tinged violet or purple-pink, with yellow disc florets. Dry soil from Maine to Ontario, Florida, Minnesota and Missouri. Hardy to Z3. H30-90cm (12-36in), F to 13mm (½in) across.

CULTIVATION OF ASTER ERICOIDES
In general, the cultivars of A. *ericoides* are among the least demanding of the genus in the garden. They will live happily in one spot for years without being divided, and are more tolerant of dry conditions through the summer than most other autumn-flowering asters. The plants make generous, graceful mounds of delicate colour to enliven the later days of autumn, and provide flower-arrangers with a wealth of material. All except the very tallest are extremely beautiful in pots and other containers, and have another advantage: plants in containers can be placed in a sunny situation through summer and early autumn and can then be used to brighten a shady spot when in flower.

Although one or two of the weaker growing cultivars, such as 'Esther', will need a degree of cosseting, most of this group is tailor-made for the 'plant-it-and-forget-it' gardener. However, good cultivation will reward the grower with superior results: for the finest displays, divide the clumps every three or four years in early spring and replant into well-prepared soil. The flowering sprays should be largely self-supporting, with perhaps a bit of help from neighbouring perennials and shrubs. Mildew is unlikely to be a major problem, but

having experienced occasional difficult years, I do the minimum amount of preventive spraying.

CULTIVARS OF ASTER ERICOIDES
The flowerheads of all the cultivars are 'single' with only one row of ray florets. The majority have about 20-25 ray florets and rarely exceed 13mm (½in) in diameter. Most cultivars bloom in mid-autumn; described as 'late' will flower at the end of this period. Flowering sprays are either erect or arching and are usually well-branched and crowded with flowerheads.

H = Height. Heights are based on established plants; first-season plants may be shorter.

'Alaska' (Bittner)
Flowerheads white. Sprays arching and open-branched. Clumps compact. H1m (40in).

'Blue Star' (H.J. Jones before 1920) ♔
Flowerheads lavender, 13mm (½in) across, late. Sprays

A. *ericoides* 'Esther' (p.98) is a useful plant of short stature but needs careful cultivation for good results.

A. *ericoides* 'Golden Spray' gets its name from its remarkable golden disc florets.

sturdy with many fine branches, making the overall spray bushy. Clumps strong. The best cultivar in this colour range still retaining obvious qualities of the type species. H90cm (36in).

'Blue Wonder'
Flowerheads purple-blue, 18mm (¾in) across, very late. Sprays upright, wiry with short branches. Clumps small, weak. Foliage very fine. Usually flowers in late autumn and is best cultivated under cover. H1.2m (4ft).

'Brimstone' (before 1925) ♱
Flowerheads crisply white rayed, 13mm (½in) across, with prominent golden disc florets, emerge from yellow buds. Sprays strong and erect with branches forming a spire. Clumps compact. Leaves bright green, rather more rounded than many other cultivars. A refined cultivar of good quality. H1.2m (4ft).

'Cinderella'
Flowerheads thinly rayed, white, 13mm (½in) across.

Sprays sturdy with dense, bushy branches. Clumps compact. 'Cinderella' is a good cultivar for growing in containers. H75cm (30in).

'Constance'
Flowerheads white, narrow-rayed, up to 2.5cm (1in) across, late. Sprays wiry, upright with open branches. Clumps small. A graceful, modern cultivar that is very good for cutting. H1m (40in).

'Enchantress' (E. Beckett before 1901)
Flowerheads pale purple-blue aging to white, 13mm (½in) across; disc florets quickly turn maroon, late. Sprays wiry, arching, well-branched into a broad panicle. Clumps compact. H90cm (36in).

'Erlkönig' (Junge 1902)
Flowerheads pale lavender-blue, about 15mm (½in) across, early. Sprays upright with short, open branches in a spire. Clumps strong. H1.2m (4ft).

'Esther' (before 1907; photograph p.97)
Flowerheads pale purple-pink, 18mm (¾in) across, pale yellow disc florets, early. Sprays very strong, crowded with short branches to create a rather heavy pyramid of flower. Clumps small, weak. Unlike other A. *ericoides* cultivars, 'Esther' seems to have more in common with modern cultivars with A. *pringlei* in their breeding, although, in the 1920s, it was catalogued as a cultivar of A. *novi-belgii*. Good winter drainage is essential because new shoots are formed directly on the base of the old flowering stem and are vulnerable to damage from slugs and bad weather. 'Esther' looks best with a small amount of support to keep the heavy flowering sprays off the soil. It is an excellent cultivar for containers and worth the effort of growing it in the garden. Good for cutting. H50cm (20in).

'Golden Spray' ♱
Flowerheads, 13mm (½in) across, thin, white rays, prominent golden disc florets. Sprays wiry, arching, densely branched, creating a good mound. Clumps strong. Good for the garden, containers and cutting. H90cm (36in).

'Herbstmyrte' (K. Foerster)
Flowerheads white-rayed, 13mm (½in) across, prominent yellow disc florets, yellow buds. Sprays upright. H1m (40in).

'Hon. Edith Gibbs' (E. Beckett before 1900)
Flowerheads pale lavender-blue, thin-rayed, 2cm (¾in) across, late. Sprays gracefully arching with open branches. Clumps compact. H1.2m (4ft).

'Lovely'

Flowerheads 13mm (½in) across, with few narrow rays, late. They open light purple-blue and quickly become suffused with pink; pale yellow disc florets perform a similar, quick change to purple-red. The combined effect is of an unusually intense overall colour scheme. Sprays erect, wiry with short, bushy branches. Clumps very compact. Good for containers. H65cm (26in).

'Maidenhood' (before 1908)

Flowerheads white, 13mm (½in) across. Sprays strong, slightly arching with graceful branches. Clumps strong. H90cm (36in).

'Pink Cloud' ♈

Flowerheads pale purple-pink, 13mm (½in) across. Sprays strong and slightly arching with bushy branches. Clumps vigorous. The young shoots in spring are distinctly bronze-red tinted and a little of this colouring is carried on the foliage for the rest of the growing season. The best pink cultivar for garden use. H90cm (36in).

'Schneegitter'

Flowerheads white. Sprays erect with short branches. H1m (40cm).

'Schneetanne' (Junge 1920)

Flowerheads 13mm (½in) across, white rays, golden disc florets, opening from yellow buds, early. Sprays strong with graceful branches. Clumps strong. H1.2m (4ft).

'White Heather'

Flowerheads 18mm (¾in) across, bright white rays, broader and more evenly spaced around the disc than most other cultivars, late. Sprays strong and upright with short branches forming a spire. Clumps strong. Foliage deep green. A superior cultivar when positive white flowers are needed in mid- to late autumn. H1.2m (4ft).

'Yvette Richardson' (photograph p.8)

Flowerheads pale lavender-blue, 2.5cm (1in) across, broad rays, pale yellow disc florets, late. Sprays strong with short, erect branches. Clumps small and not strong. Leaves long, pale green. This plant bears little resemblance to others in the A. *ericoides* groups of cultivars and might well be the result of a cross with A. *novi-belgii*. Very compact and useful at the front of borders or in containers, although some small supports may be required to keep the flowering sprays upright. H45cm (18in).

ASTER PRINGLEI
(A. Gray) Britton (1898) Pringle's aster

This species is of considerable importance to gardeners and commercial growers and is so similar in many respects to A. *ericoides* that inclusion here seems logical.

The plant produces small clumps that are not very strong and bears white flowerheads with yellow disc florets, in mid-autumn. They are in broad panicles on sturdy, slender, upright sprays. At the base of the plant the leaves are oblong to lanceolate; the stem leaves are narrow, linear becoming small and needle-like on the branches. Riverbanks, especially in rocky places, in Massachusetts and Vermont to Wisconsin. Hardy to Z4. H15-60cm (6-24in), F to 18mm (¾in).

Almost always grown as the cultivar **'Monte Cassino'** (Fuss 1983) ♈, this is a plant that might

Shapely sprays of clean white flowerheads make A. *ericoides* 'White Heather' invaluable for picking.

have been exclusively designed for the purpose of flower arranging. Huge numbers are produced commercially under cover in Europe, Israel, New Zealand, the USA and elsewhere, providing florists with a year-round supply of the original 'September flower'. The foliage on the wiry branches of the flowering sprays is so fine and narrow that the starry, white flowerheads appear to be set on sprays of the asparagus fern. The plant is obviously closely allied to A. ericoides but has much stiffer and more slender stems and branches. The clumps are also much weaker than you would expect to find with A. ericoides cultivars (except 'Esther'), with new shoots being formed right at the base of the old flowering stems.

If 'Monte Cassino' is going to be grown in the open garden, the soil will need to light with enough plant food and moisture through the growing season to encourage the production of several good flowering sprays from each clump. Good to sharp winter drainage is essential. I have little success on our Herefordshire clay unless the plants are lifted each autumn and potted for a winter sojourn in a polytunnel or glasshouse. My best examples of 'Monte Cassino' are achieved by planting up a 10 litre (10in) container in the spring, using three plants out of 9cm (3½in) pots. Such containers give a first-class display through mid-autumn and beyond. They can stand outside in a not-too-exposed spot or they can be taken into the house for short periods. If you are sufficiently strong-willed, whole sprays or branches can be cut for flower arranging, thus depriving the floristry trade of considerable income! (I suspect that few, if any, other asters have produced such a large revenue for the horticultural industry.)

Mildew seems to pose few problems where it is possible to grow plants in the open garden but those under cover need some preventive spraying. 'Monte Cassino' is only likely to give of its best as a 'first year' plant, after which the woody clumps can be prised apart if one is bold enough. But the best stock will always come from softwood cuttings rooted in spring and carefully grown on in small pots for planting up some 10-12 months later.

Two more cultivars of A. pringlei are just becoming available to gardeners. 'Phoebe', to 90cm (36in), has mauve-pink rays and 'Pink Cushion', said to grow to only 35cm (14in), has mid-purple-pink rays. One can

safely assume that A. pringlei is involved in many of the burgeoning number of cultivars exclusively produced for the commercial cut-flower market. A few might well be suitable for outdoor garden cultivation but it is unlikely that patented plants will be allowed to escape from a profitable environment into an uncertain marketplace or the hands of green-fingered amateur propagators. (See p.48 for potting composts.)

SMALL-FLOWERED CULTIVARS
The following is a selection of cultivars with small flowers, that are close to A. ericoides in habit. To qualify as 'small-flowered', cultivars have flowerheads that are not more than 4cm (1½in) in diameter; most are much less. The flowerheads are 'single', with one row of ray florets. The majority of cultivars flower at the end of early autmn into mid-autumn; those described as 'late' will be flowering at the end of this period. Habit of growth and form of flowering sprays varies with each cultivar.

H = Height. Heights are based on established plants; first season plants may be shorter.

'Anja's Choice' (P. Oudolf)
Flowerheads white flushed with pale purple-pink, about 4cm (1½in) across, late. Sprays strong with upright branches forming a spire. Clumps strong, compact. Can be left undivided for three or more years and still provide a good display. H1.2m (4ft).

'Blue Star'
Flowerheads lavender, 2.5cm (1in) across, narrow rays, late. Sprays upright, wiry, with short branches. Leaves fine. Clumps compact. One of a series bred for commercial cut-flower production. Capable of making a reasonable display in the garden but must have good winter drainage. H1m (40in).

'Herfstweelde' (P. Oudolf)
Flowerheads lavender, noticeably paling towards the base of the rays, about 3cm (1¼in) across, late. Sprays strong with numerous branches forming an upright pyramid. Clumps strong, compact. Ideal for naturalized planting and suitable for low maintenance where the clumps are left undivided for several years. Also good as a cut flower. H1.2m (4ft).

'Hon. Vicary Gibbs' (E. Beckett)
Flowerheads pale lavender-blue, about 18mm (¾in) across, late. Sprays lax with branches forming a spire. Clumps vigorous. An elegant cultivar which looks as if

Mystery shrouds the origins of A. 'Snow Flurry', one of the outstanding asters of the latter half of the twentieth century.

it might owe some of its origin to A. *cordifolius*. Certainly a good colour and very effective when properly supported. Suitable for borders and cutting. H1.5m (5ft).

'Ochtendgloren' (P. Oudolf) ♔
Flowerheads mid-purple-pink, 2.5cm (1in) across, mid-season. Sprays sturdy with upright, open branches. Clumps strong, compact. Leaves, long, narrow, deep green. Reliable for borders, cutting or containers, long lasting in flower. Makes neat clumps which can be left undisturbed for several years. H1.2m (4ft).

'Pearl Star'
Flowerheads very pale lilac, 2.5cm (1in) across, late. Sprays strong with open branches. Clumps compact. Another of the cultivars bred for commercial cut-flower production. With good winter drainage it is reliable in the garden; very effective in containers. H1m (40in).

'Pink Star'
Appears to be identical in all respects to 'Ochtendgloren'. H1.2m (4ft).

'Poolicht' (P. Oudolf)
Flowerheads white lightly flushed with blue, small, mid-season. Sprays sturdy with open branches. Clumps compact. H1m (40in).

'Ringdove' (before 1920) ♔
Flowerheads, 2cm (¾in) across, pale lavender rays neatly arranged around prominent, creamy-yellow disc florets, late. Sprays strong with upright, open branches. Clumps strong, compact. Leaves long and narrow. A distinctive cultivar of subtle colouring. Good for borders and cutting. H1m (40in).

'Snow Flurry'
Flowerheads 13mm (½in) across, crisply white ray florets and small golden discs, massed. Sprays woody with many short branches. Clumps compact, woody. Leaves fine and small. Looks superb hanging over a dry stone wall or creating the impression of a waterfall among rocks. A sunny position with sharp winter drainage is

essential. Flowering does not start before the latter part of mid-autumn and extends well into late autumn. The growth is so crowded and prostrate that it forms a carpet with the spread of one plant possibly in excess of 60cm (24in). H10-15cm (4-6in). Hardy to Z3.

Since the introduction of this unique and wonderful aster to Britain in 1983, its true origin has been shrouded in mystery. Beth Chatto brought the original material back from a visit to the USA, but neither she nor her plant suppliers can recall where it came from. Plants under the name of A. 'Prostrata' found their way to the 1993 autumn show at Courson in France, where the jury gave it an award for its merit as a garden plant. They also tried to follow up a suggestion that the species involved was A. *diffusus* and that a suitable name for the cultivar would be 'Connecticut Snow Flurry'. However, most modern botanical opinion considers A. *diffusus* as redundant with the species now being known as A. *lateriflorus*. Add to this the obvious fact that 'Snow Flurry' bears little resemblance to any other form or cultivar of A. *lateriflorus* in either its flowerheads or shoots on the base clump and the mystery is continued. The new shoots of asters, formed on the clumps over winter, are unique to each species and cultivar. Those of 'Snow Flurry' are close to A. *vimineus* in all repects, at which point the confusion gets deeper because many authorities have assigned this species to A. *fragilis*. If nothing else, all of this serves to illustrate how difficult it is to decide the true species of asters. The safest course for a gardener, such as myself, is to follow the example of the *RHS Plant Finder* and firmly stick to A. 'Snow Flurry'!

'Snow Star'
Flowerheads 2cm (¾in) across, narrow, brilliant white rays, more numerous than most small-flowered cultivars, late. Sprays strong with wiry, upright branches. Clumps small. Foliage fine, deep green. An outstanding cultivar bred for commercial cut-flower growers but superb for late colour in containers. It has not done well in Colwall as a garden plant, probably needing a drier winter climate. H1m (40in).

ASTER LATERIFLORUS
L., Britton (1826) Calico aster, Starved aster

Formerly called A. *tradescantii*, this species is found from southern Canada down through north-eastern USA to Texas. The flower sprays are wiry and bushy, the lower branches almost horizontal. Late in the season, they produce flowerheads densely set on the upper side of the branches. Often only 13mm (½in), with some cultivars getting up to about 2cm (¾in), they consist of a few dull white rays, mostly only 9-15 in number, which are short with an inclination to recurve, often leaving the disc florets as the most prominent feature. These are pale yellow quickly aging to purple-pink. Calico aster is a reference to the colourful effect produced as they change colour.

The following passage from *The History and Folklore of North American Wildflowers* by Timothy Coffey relates a charming description of the species written on September 14th 1856 by American writer, naturalist and philosopher Henry David Thoreau (1817-1862):

> Now for the *Aster tradescantii*, along low roads, like the turnpike, swarming with butterflies and bees. Some of them are pink. However unexpected these late flowers! You thought that Nature had about wound up her affairs. You had seen what she could do this year and had not noticed a few weeds by the roadside, or mistook them for the remains of summer flowers now hastening to their fall. You thought you knew every twig and every leaf by the roadside, and nothing more was to be looked for there. And now to your surprise, the ditches are crowded with millions of little stars.

The species is still widely grown and is just as worthwhile as any of the cultivars. It is a reliable garden plant which brings a touch of warmer colour among the whites and pale lavender shades prevalent with the late, small-flowered asters. Quite happy if undivided for a number of years and usually sturdy enough to stand without the need for support, it is rarely subject to mildew but if A. *novi-belgii* cultivars are growing nearby some preventive spraying might be advisable, since they are likely to be hosting some spores.

A. *lateriflorus* is capable of growing in both dry and moist soils, in open situations as well as thickets and woodland edges. Wild plants vary between 30cm and 1m (12-40in) tall. Leaves at the base of plants tend to be oval and those on the stems are lance-shaped. They show some bronze-purple colouring in spring and are green thereafter. The clumps are strong and woody and quite compact, especially in the case of the smaller-growing cultivars such as 'Horizontalis' and 'Prince'. Cultivars cover the height range of 40cm to 1.5m (16in to 5ft).

CULTIVARS OF ASTER LATERIFLORUS

A notable feature all A. *lateriflorus* cultivars have in common is the flowering spray with the branches bearing the crowded flowerheads on their upper sides. Another shared feature is the attractive red-purple colouring of the young growth each spring. Some cultivars carry this leaf colour, in varying degrees, through the whole growing season. Combined with the brightly coloured disc florets, this adds to the overall desirability of this race of asters.

All are good and easy-going in the garden, thriving best in fertile soil with summer moisture and a sunny situation. Although the typical species will tolerate shade, the cultivars with the best leaf colour will lose this effect if they are too shaded. Flowering time is through mid-autumn and into late autumn and the sprays are attractive when picked, although, as usual, the dark colouring of the discs does not appeal to commercial cut-flower growers. The compact cultivars make extremely good container plants. There is no necessity to divide the clumps more often than every third year when they can simply be split into smaller sections, discarding any hard wood from the central regions of the clumps. When they are grown as undivided clumps for several years, plants will produce a thicket of flowering sprays capable of standing without support on all but the tallest cultivars. Commercial production of cultivars is best by spring cuttings, made from the tips of the new shoots.

The cultivars are not especially liable to be attacked by mildew if there are no host plants in the vicinity.

Until recently we have been used to growing the species as introduced to Europe in the early nineteenth century, and its diminutive selection 'Horizontalis'. But Eric Smith's 'Prince' has become quite widely grown during the last decade and I am pleased to note the recent introduction of several cultivars from continental Europe to increase the available range.

'Bleke Bet'
Flowerheads 18mm (¾in) across, rays white, disc florets creamy-yellow turning pale purple-pink, late. Sprays

The recently introduced A. *lateriflorus* 'Bleke Bet' has the purple-pink disc florets typical of this group.

strong with open, horizontal branches, the longer of which arch gracefully. Clumps compact. Leaves lance-shaped, larger than typical species, bronze-purple in spring and holding a good amount of colour throughout the growing season. Excellent contrast between the dark foliage and light colouring of the flowerheads. H1.2m (4ft).

'Buck's Fizz'
Flowerheads 13mm (½in) across, rays white, disc florets purple-pink. Sprays have more upright branches than the similar cultivar 'Horizontalis'. Clumps compact. The leaves have good bronze-purple tints. H60cm (24in).

'Daisy Bush' (I by De Bloemenhoek 1993)
Flowerheads 2cm (¾in) across, rays white, disc florets pale yellow. Sprays strong with bushy branches. Clumps strong. Leaves green. H70cm (28in).

'Datschi' (before 1920)
Flowerheads 13mm (½in) across, rays white, disc florets pale yellow and not colouring much as other cultivars. Sprays strong with arching branches. Clumps compact. Leaves deep green. H1.2m (4ft).

'Delight' (before 1902)
Flowerheads 13mm (½in) across, rays white, reflexed,

A. 'Coombe Fishacre' is one of the most richly coloured of the small-flowered asters.

disc florets creamy-yellow. Sprays sturdy with horizontal branches. Clumps strong. H90cm (36in).

'Horizontalis' (before 1892) ♔
Flowerheads 13mm (½in) across, rays white, reflexed, disc florets yellow quickly turning to deep reddish-purple, late. Sprays sturdy with horizontal, spreading branches, bushy and forming mounds. Clumps small. Leaves small and lance-shaped, purple-tinted in spring and dark green by late summer. A wonderfully compact and colourful plant which has enjoyed great popularity for a century. How many other hardy herbaceous perennials can make such a claim? Suitable for borders and containers and also good for cutting. The flowerheads are crowded on the upper sides of the stiff branches and are freely produced. Later flowering than the taller varieties. H50cm (20in).

'Jan' (De Bloemenhoek 1992)
Flowerheads 3cm (1¼in) across, rays white, disc florets

light yellow, both becoming suffused with purple-pink, mid-season. Sprays strong with spreading branches. Clumps compact. Leaves green. Much larger flowerheads than the other cultivars in this group. H80-100cm (32-40in).

'Lady in Black' (De Bloemenhoek 1991)
Flowerheads 18mm (¾in) across, rays white, disc florets yellow turning pale purple-pink. Sprays strong with open, arching branches; main stems deep brown. clumps compact. Leaves bronze-purple in spring and holding their colour well later. Taller and with more open sprays than the typical species. Borders and cutting. H1.3m (4½ft).

'Prince' (E. Smith c1970)
Flowerheads 13mm (½in) across, rays white and reflexed becoming shaded purple-pink with age, disc florets cream turning deep purple-red, late. Sprays sturdy with short, congested branches; main stems purple-brown. Leaves deep bronze-purple in spring and holding their colour throughout the growing season. 'Prince' is good for borders, containers and cutting. H60cm (24in).

CULTIVARS CLOSE TO ASTER LATERIFLORUS

These cultivars are probably a result of crosses with A. ericoides or A. novi-belgii.

'Coombe Fishacre' (c1920) ♔
Flowerheads 18mm (¾in) across, rays pale purple-pink, disc florets pale yellow, very prominent and quickly turning purple-red, mid-season. Sprays strong with horizontal branches. Clumps strong and compact. Leaves green. Borders, containers and cutting. A cultivar of quality providing compact and colourful bushes for a variety of uses. Will thrive on infrequent division and is not especially prone to mildew. H90cm (36in).

(I would love to know the origin of the name: someone told me it was the name of the head gardener who raised the plant. In the late 1940s a seedling from 'Coombe Fishacre', called 'Brightness', was in existence. Apparently it was taller with deeper-coloured and more numerous rays.)

'Plowden's Pink' (Plowden c1981)
Flowerheads 2cm (¾in) across, rays lilac-pink, disc florets yellow turning purple-pink, mid-season. Sprays sturdy with short branches. Clumps small. Borders and containers. H60cm (24in).

7

ASTER AMELLUS AND ASTER × FRIKARTII

Until the end of the sixteenth century, the only aster to be cultivated by English gardeners was the native *Aster tripolium*, sea starwort, which was sometimes called 'Serepia's Turbith'. However, the great herbalist John Gerard was growing the Italian Starwort, *A. amellus*, in his Holborn Physic Garden in 1596. This plant of antiquity was first mentioned in Vergil's *Georgics* more than 2,000 years ago. A certain amount of mystery surrounds the origins of the specific name but there is just a possibility that Vergil named the plant after the River Mella, an Italian tributary of the River Po.

ASTER AMELLUS
L. Italian starwort

Produced from late summer to mid-autumn, the flowerheads have up to 40 ray florets, usually violet-blue, but can be pale to deep purple-pink. The discs are yellow. The flowering sprays, with short branches clustered towards the top, are erect with rather woody stems, and the clumps are woody and compact. Leaves hirsute, lanceolate to obovate. Free-draining, often gravelly, limestone soils on the sunny edges of woods and in open brush in N. Central France and Lithuania, southwards to N. Italy and S.E. Europe, Siberia, Caucasus, Armenia and Anatolia. Hardy to Z5. H30-70cm (12-28in), F to 5cm (2in).

It is a rare plant in the wild, but the cultivars 'Veilchenkönigin' and 'Ultramarine' are close in habit and ray colour to the typical species. Cultivars show much variation in height.

Like so many other plants, *A. amellus* was first cultivated in herb or physic gardens for its supposed curative properties. Columella, a Roman writer of a later period than Vergil actually recommends something he calls 'Amellus' in his book *De re rustica* as a cure for a disease that afflicted bees. In his book *Materia Medica* Dioscorides promotes the use of a plant he calls 'Athenian Aster' in decoctions or poultices as a cure for a variety of inflammations as well as epilepsy and being bitten by a rabid dog. 'Athenian Aster' is recognizable as *A. amellus*.

In the nineteenth century the form var. *bessarabicus* was very popular with its large, rich purple heads on strong 60cm (24in) tall sprays. The tall, violet-rayed 'Cassubicus' and the purple-pink 'Rubellus' are thought to be closely allied to this variety. Because of its overall vigour and long flowering sprays, var. *bessarabicus* has been used in hybridizing: the results are evident in such good cultivars as 'Nocturne' and 'Grunder', the large flowerheads and sprays of which make them invaluable as cut flowers.

At the end of the nineteenth century, Mr H.J. Jones raised 'Charlie' which was said to have compact growth and flowerheads with rays of pink-tinted light blue, but is sadly no longer available. 'Framfieldii', which was in cultivation before 1907, has unusually bushy flowering sprays with thin-rayed lavender flowers in mid-autumn. Several cultivars with pale purple-pink rays were introduced in the 1920s, the best being 'Sonia', raised by a Mr T. Bones. Deeper shades of pink came along when 'Mrs Ralph Woods' was introduced in the 1940s, followed by 'Brilliant' from Thomas Carlile in about 1953. Karl Foerster's later introduction, 'Rosa Erfüllung', is possibly an even better colour and is a compact plant. 'Jacqueline Genebrier' seems to be the only deep, rosy colour readily available and is a little disadvantaged by having long sprays with just a few

PLATE VIII

A. AMELLUS CULTIVARS

'Nocturne'

'Gründer'

'Sonora'

'Veilchenköningin'

All flowers are shown at approximately ¾ size

'King George'

'Brilliant'

'Jacqueline Genebrier'

'Sonia'

'Rosa Erfüllung'

short branches, creating a leggy look. This can be overcome by careful planting that allows the stems to mix in with other plants.

In addition to 'Sonia', T. Bones also raised a number of other good cultivars, including 'Bessie Chapman', a vigorous grower, with large heads of deep lavender rays arranged in two rows, so that a double effect is created in the early stages of blooming, when they hide the disc florets.

The raiser of the cultivar 'La France' is not recorded. It appeared in the Royal Horticultural Society trials of 1925 and was said to have pale mauvish-pink flowerheads of a massive 7.5cm (3in) across. Over the years, lots of seemingly good cultivars have been raised and exhibited but have then been lost. This must partly be due to lack of sales because A. amellus cultivars never achieved the same mass popularity as the new introductions of A. novi-belgii that flooded the market in the 1920s and 1930s.

A. amellus 'King George' was a popular plant for many years before A. × frikartii became well known, and was one of the few asters admitted to the domain of the cottage garden. It was introduced by Amos Perry in 1914 and some authorities say that it was raised in Germany and called 'Kaiser Willhelm' but received a rapid name change due to the imminence of the First World War. An article in the magazine Gardeners' Chronicle, December 21st 1918, states:

> Among the numerous varieties, 'King George', which forms the subject of our coloured supplementary illustration, occupies a very high position … Both in garden and flower markets this handsome perennial aster has already become very popular, and American growers have also recognised its great value.

In the matter of high-volume plant sales, which are all- important in the current garden centre-orientated horticultural environment, 'King George' has been displaced by 'Veilchenkönigin' ('Violet Queen'). In no way are the smaller flowerheads of the latter a match for the broad dimensions of an individual head of 'King George'. But, importantly, 'Veilchenkönigin' produces an abundance of its deep violet heads on erect, bushy sprays with neat green leaves and is a compact plant, highly suitable for sale in the flowering season whereas most of the older cultivars of A. amellus tend to make rather straggly specimens in containers.

CULTIVATION AND PROPAGATION

If their few simple requirements are met, A. amellus cultivars will be long lasting in bloom and long lived in your garden. All cultivars can put on a good display of unabashed daisy-like flowers in the most simple, unrefined form.

Spring is the time to plant them, whether as young plants, larger container-grown stock or divisions from the garden. To do so at any other season will result in the sadness that accompanies the sight of dead, woody stems lacking any sign of nice young shoots springing up around them to herald the promise of a colourful autumn.

PREPARATION

Although native plants of A. amellus appear to be extremely tough and long lived, their cultivated offspring have lost this desirable set of attributes and must be divided every three or four years and planted into a fresh area of soil. If a new site is not feasible it is advisable to replace the old soil with some obtained from a stack of turf. Failing this, buy some bags of sterilized loam or even loam-based potting compost. Replace the soil to a depth of about 30cm (12in). Below this, the original earth must be well broken with a fork, and in clay soils it will do no harm to add some sharp grit. All this excessive gardening activity is designed to combat the threat posed by aster wilt (Verticillium albo-atrium), which is ever ready to shrivel and kill off the flowering sprays of A. amellus, probably not in sufficient quantities to kill the clump but usually enough to look unsightly. Take consolation from the knowledge that you will never need to spray your plants to prevent mildew fungus because A. amellus is reliably resistant to this scourge.

Unless you garden on naturally gritty (or stony) limestone soil, add some limestone grit to the new soil as well as some spent mushroom compost or well-made garden compost. Avoid anything that will make the ground too wet in the winter months. Hoof and horn fertilizer, or something organic with similar properties, can be used lightly as ground preparation and again as a summer feed. The ideal is to have an alkaline, well-drained, medium-loam soil; the plants also need a sunny position.

When I was a boy, our stock of A. amellus cultivars was grown in the sunniest area of the nursery in specially lightened soil. I was fascinated by the method in which the natural Herefordshire clay had been transformed into a great depth of medium to light loam. It appears that, many years previously, tons of the clay topsoil had been baked over dozens of charcoal fires for a long period, producing a light, friable material. Now, due to essential changes in layout, our only patch of decent soil is underneath the glasshouses and polytunnels, although I did manage to rescue a little.

WATERING

A considerable degree of resistance to drought comes naturally with A. amellus cultivars but a hot summer with several weeks without recordable rain brings them to their limit. The first plants to suffer are those planted in spring of the same year, and even established clumps will become so stressed as to need some irrigation. I once made the mistake of assuming that the warmer-climate origins of the species would save me the trouble of watering the plants in a severe drought, and lost a lot of large clumps as a result of my neglect.

DIVISION

If you are lifting and dividing established clumps, by all means use a stout fork to get them out of the ground, then put the fork on one side while you study your clump of woody stem bases with new shoots popping up around them and, hopefully, a good mass of roots. Working from underneath, the aim is to pull your clump apart into sections with three or four flowering stem bases and as many new shoots as possible, plus a good supply of new roots. The actual size of the divisions will depend upon the vigour of the cultivar concerned. Do not attempt to remove sections with just one old stem because these will be too slow to clump again. A short hand-fork, perhaps a strong knife or cleaver and a pair of secateurs will achieve this without wasting many precious shoots. Ancient, woody bits of root and stems, without any new shoots, can be cut away.

A word of caution: nearly all old flowering stems of asters are extremely woody and very sharp at the point where they have been cut down in the autumn. I strongly advise wearing gardening gloves when working with the clumps as there have been some quite nasty accidents, including one in which a farmer's wife in Herefordshire contracted tetanus, which sadly proved fatal, after falling onto a clump of asters with cut-off stems.

Divided sections of a compact cultivar, such as 'Veilchenkönigin', can be planted at about 30cm (12in) apart, spreaders like 'King George' can be spaced at 45cm (18in) and strong growers in the 'Grunder' and 'Lac de Genève' category might be as wide apart as 60cm (24in). A. amellus cultivars are not really happy plants in pots and containers and it is better to use the shorter forms of A. × frikartii or A. thomsonii 'Nanus' if you need large, starry flowerheads for this purpose.

CUTTINGS

Nurserymen will have grown their stocks of A. amellus cultivars from softwood cuttings taken in mid-spring. This method of production will virtually guarantee a plant free from any trace of verticillium wilt. By mid-spring of the following year, the small, pot-grown plants are ready for setting in the garden and will grow with amazing rapidity. Larger, older plants can also be obtained if a better show in the first year is required but all will look at their best in the second and third years after planting.

Young plants from small pots can be planted at the same spacing as divisions and will fill out in their second year. It is also possible to put three or five small plants close together so that they make a better show in the first year and grow together as one clump. More mature plants from larger pots ought to be given their proper spacing.

Plants can nearly always be purchased in the summer and autumn months; they must be placed in an unheated greenhouse or polytunnel in late autumn for planting out in the spring.

SEED

Apart from 'Veilchenköningin' and a few of the more desirable sorts, A. amellus cultivars are generous setters of fertile seed. If sown straight away into pots of loam-based seed compost and placed in a coldframe, there should be a good spring germination. The seedlings can be transplanted into small pots or trays and grown on for planting in a trial bed the following spring. They will flower the same autumn and any showing improvements over existing cultivars can be selected for further trial for qualities such as vigour. The prospect of raising

PLATE IX

A. × *frikartii* 'Eiger'

A. × *frikartii* 'Mönch'

All flowers are shown at approximately ⅔ size

A. *thomsonii* 'Nanus'

A. × *frikartii* 'Flora's Delight'

A. × *frikartii* 'Jungfrau'

A. *pyrenaeus* 'Lutetia'

Beautifully coloured large flowerheads have made A. *amellus* 'King George' (p.114) a popular cultivar of long standing.

a stunner is probably rather less than winning the National Lottery but you never know! In any case, if you have time to spare and space available, the process is entertaining and, unlike many other types of aster, most of the seedlings will be attractive.

SUPPORT

If they are properly sited, there is no need to use supports for any cultivars of A. *amellus*, even the taller ones, because their flowering sprays have such strong stems. On the other hand, if something with lax stems like 'King George' is planted near the edge of a lawn, the person responsible for mowing the grass is likely to become very upset if a few small, twiggy sticks are not used to guide the flowering sprays into appropriate positions. The same goes for pathways, unless you do not object to your flowers being trampled on. Small shrubs, of a nonetheless substantial nature, such as

cultivars of *Potentilla fruticosa* and *Spiraea japonica* are unlikely to object if the flowering sprays of the asters use them for support. The same goes for many herbaceous perennials because the stems of A. *amellus* are not as leafy and heavy as most other asters and are unlikely to cause any damage to their neighbours. If you intend to plant up a whole bed of nothing but A. *amellus* and A. × *frikartii*, they will support each other. But, if an extra degree of tidiness and order is called for, push in some twiggy sticks early in the spring, and allow the asters to grow through them.

IN THE GARDEN

When I planted the first groups of A. *amellus* in the garden I wondered what to associate with them. My first choice was the perhaps obvious one of *Coreopsis verticillata* and *Rudbeckia fulgida* 'Goldsturm'. Of course, the very first dry summer quickly showed me that the rudbeckia was much less drought-resistant than the asters. Sedums then came to mind and I found the softer purple-pink heads of flowers and purple-tinted foliage of

'Joyce Henderson' to be a pleasing change from the universally-planted 'Herbstfreude' ('Autumn Joy').

Although the blue shades of A. amellus mix well with most cultivars in the fleshy sedum genus, the harsher colours found in cultivars with purple-pink rays, such as 'Brilliant' and 'Rosa Erfüllung', always pose more of a problem. A background planting that works well is Eryngium tripartitum, whose generous crop of small, deep blue heads neatly encompass the same flowering season. The use of this plant became even better as the result of one of those happy accidents most plant lovers wish to encounter at least once in their lifetime. Root cuttings are a normal method of producing stock of most eryngiums and these end up in individual pots standing out on a nursery bed in the spring. Looking at such a batch of E. tripartitum some twenty years ago, I noticed one pot where the broad, glossy rounded leaves were brightly variegated with cream and gold, and what green there was had been overlaid to become grey-green. My first reaction was to look for further signs of weedkiller being carelessly dripped onto plants! But this was not the case: something had set off reactions in that one piece of root that eventually produced the plant called Eryngium tripartitum 'Fool's Gold'. The wonderful variegation is retained right through the seasons on the basal leaves and way up the flowering sprays, with the heads being a soft blue. This is where we arrive at the objective of my tale: I had my very own perfect planting partner for A. amellus.

The floriferous cultivars of Chrysanthemum rubellum are hardy in many areas and A. amellus cultivars look well with them. The strong growing 'Mary Stoker' with soft apricot blooms is especially good. I have largely given them up because they encouraged a leaf mining pest that made inroads throughout the entire stock of A. amellus, A. × frikartii and A. thomsonii when they were in their vulnerable rooted cutting stage of growth. I have not heard of this problem occurring in the open garden but I cannot test it for myself because the chrysanthemums hate Colwall winters.

My small rose garden is in a sheltered south-facing corner with a northern backdrop of large shrubs. About 30cm (12in) of imported sandy loam lies on top of a mixture of modelling clay and stones, an inhospitable planting medium resulting from infilling following the removal of a tree stump. I thought A. amellus would look wonderful here with the late flowers on the shrub roses bred by David Austin, and I was right when 'King George' and the rich ochre-yellow of Rosa 'Graham Thomas' got together. 'Framfieldii' has made a massive group between the roses 'Windrush' and 'Gertrude Jekyll', and 'Sonora' stands high by Rosa 'Prospero'.

'Magenta' is a much older rose than the Austin range and I cannot grow it well, always ending up with a small bush and lax branches. This low, droopy habit turned out to be a bonus when combined with a sprawling A. amellus cultivar like 'Moerheim Gem'. The sumptuous rose blooms hang in the aster sprays and the aster sprays attempt to climb into the rose. 'Brilliant' looks quite effective in front of the hybrid musk rose 'Buff Beauty', otherwise the harder pink shades of the A. amellus cultivars are best used among roses that have finished their season of flower. 'Sonia' and 'Peach Blossom' are of sufficiently soft tones to combine happily with yellow, deep pink or red roses. Due to the site being over-hot and much too dry in many summers, the A. amellus cultivars have done best where they have gained a little shade from the taller roses, and a good deal of care and judicious pruning is essential to prevent them being overhung or even swamped by any exuberant variety of rose as they are not good at pushing their growth through covering plants and need their own patch of clear space.

CULTIVARS OF ASTER AMELLUS

The cultivar name is followed by the name of the raiser/introducer (I) and date of introduction if known.

Flowerheads 5cm (2in) across are classed as small; medium flowerheads are 5-6.3cm (2-2½in) across; and large flowerheads are in excess of 6.3cm (2½in) across. The flowering season runs through early autumn into mid-autumn with a few cultivars starting to bloom in late summer. Those described as 'early' will be flowering in the early part of autumn; 'late' indicates a cultivar that flowers well into mid-autumn.

H = height. Heights are based on established specimens; first year plants are often shorter.

'Bessie Chapman' (T. Bones c1928)
Flowerheads deep lavender-blue, large, numerous rays. Sprays strong. H60cm (24in).

'Blaustern' Flowerheads lavender-blue, medium. Sprays compact. H50cm (20in).

'Blue King' (T. Carlile c1954)
Flowerheads bright violet-blue, large, early. Sprays

erect and compact. Clumps small. Leaves grey green. H60cm (24in).

'Blütendecke' (K. Foerster 1950)
Flowerheads purple-blue, medium. H50cm (20in).

'Breslau' (Kock 1959)
Flowerheads violet-blue, small. Sprays erect, well-branched and compact. Clumps small. Leaves small, grey-green. H40cm (16in).

'Brilliant' (T. Carlile c1953)
Flowerheads bright purple-pink. Sprays erect with short branches. Clumps strong. Leaves green. H60cm (24in).

'Butzemann' (Baltin 1957)
Flowerheads violet, small. Sprays erect and compact. H25cm (10in).

'Cassubicus Major' (before 1920)
Flowerheads violet, large. Sprays strong. Clumps strong. Leaves grey-green. H70cm (28in).

'Charlie' (Jones before 1910)
Flowerheads lavender-blue, shaded pink. Sprays compact and bushy. H45cm (18in).

'Doktor Otto Petschek' (Van de Schoot before 1937)
Flowerheads lavender, medium. H60cm (24in).

'Emma Bedeau'
Flowerheads deep lilac. H50cm (20in).

'Festgeschenk' (K. Foerster 1966)
Flowerheads deep lilac, large. H70cm (28in).

'Forncett Flourish' (Metcalf 1996)
Flowerheads violet-blue. H60cm (24in).

'Framfieldii' (before 1907) ♔
Flowerheads lavender, small, late. Sprays erect and well-branched. Clumps compact. Leaves small. H50cm (20in).

'Glucksfund' (K. Foerster 1966)
Flowerheads lilac. H50cm (20in).

'Goliath'
Flowerheads deep lavender, large. H60cm (24in).

'Gründer' (photograph p.2)
Flowerheads lilac-blue, large, late. Sprays erect, strong and well-branched. Clumps strong. Leaves large, grey-green. H80cm (32in).

'Heinrich Seibert'
Flowerheads purple-pink. H50cm (20in).

'Hermann Löns'
Flowerheads lilac-blue. H50cm (20in).

'Jacqueline Genebrier' ♔
Flowerheads rich purple-pink, small, late. Sprays erect

with short branches. Clumps compact. Leaves small, deep green. H75cm (30in).

'Joseph Lakin'
Flowerheads violet, small. Sprays, erect, compact and short-branched. Clumps small. Leaves small, pointed. H45cm (18in).

'King George' (A. Perry 1914; photograph p.112) ♔
Flowerheads rich purple-blue, large, early. Sprays lax, well-branched. Clumps strong. Leaves large, grey-green. H60cm (24in).

'Kobold' (Junge 1920)
Flowerheads violet, small. Sprays erect, compact. Clumps small, rather weak. Leaves small, rounded, deep green. H40cm (16in).

'Lac de Genève' (c1949)
Flowerheads pale lavender-blue, small. Sprays lax with numerous short branches. Clumps strong. Leaves long, pale green. H60cm (24in).

'Lady Hindlip' (T. Carlile 1954)
Flowerheads bright violet, large. H60cm (24in).

'Little Gem' (A. Perry 1904)
Flowerheads rich violet, full-rayed, late. An unusually compact cultivar, but no longer available. H30cm (12in).

A. amellus 'Rosa Erfüllung' produces abundant flowerheads on compact plants.

'Mignon' (Linder 1926)
Flowerheads purple-blue. H50cm (20in).
'Mira' (K. Foerster 1956)
Flowerheads deep lilac. H40cm (16in).
'Moerheim Gem' (H. Ruys 1933)
Flowerheads purple-blue, medium, rays twisted. Sprays very lax with short branches. Clumps compact. Leaves long, mid-green. H50cm (20in).
'Mrs Ralph Woods'
Flowerheads bright purple-pink, medium. Sprays erect and well-branched. Clumps strong. Leaves deep green. H60cm (24in).
'Nocturne' (A. Bloom c1955)
Flowerheads lilac, large, late. Sprays very strong, erect and well-branched. Clumps compact. Leaves broad, stiff, mid-green. H80cm (32in).
'Oktoberkind'
Flowerheads deep violet. H60cm (24in).
'Peach Blossom'
Flowerheads pale purple-pink, medium. Sprays weak with few branches. Clumps small. Leaves small, narrow, pale green. H40cm (16in).
'Praecox Junifreude' (Nonne and Hopker 1928)
Flowerheads pale blue, early. H40cm (16in).
'Praecox Sommergrüss' (Nonne and Hopker)
Flowerheads violet. H50cm (20in).
'Praecox Sonnenwende' (Nonne and Hopker)
Flowerheads bright purple-pink. Sprays are compact. H30cm (12in).
'Profusion' (A. Perry 1915)
Flowerheads lavender-blue, small. A very compact grower with crowded heads, but probably no longer available. H38cm (15in).
'Rosa Erfüllung' ('Pink Zenith') (K. Foerster)
Flowerheads bright purple-pink, late. Sprays erect, bushy. Clumps strong. Leaves small, deep green. H50cm (20in).
'Rosa von Ronsdorf' (G. Arends)
Flowerheads pale purple-pink. H70cm (28in).
'Rotfeuer'
Flowerheads deep purple-pink. Often rather optimistically described in catalogues and books as having 'red' flowerheads. I look forward to the day when a cultivar of A. amellus achieves this distinction. H50cm (20in).
'Rubellus' (before 1920)
Flowerheads purple-pink, large. Sprays strong. Leaves green. H60cm (24in).

The strong flowering sprays of A. amellus 'Sternkugel' are topped by large flowerheads.

'Rudolf Goethe' (G. Arends 1914)
Flowerheads lavender, medium. Sprays well-branched. Clumps strong. Leaves broad and pale green. H75cm (30in).
'Schöne von Ronsdorf' (G. Arends 1911)
Flowerheads pale purple-pink. H50cm (20in).
'Sonia' (T. Bones c1927)
Flowerheads pale purple-pink, large, late. Sprays erect with few branches. Clumps small. Leaves small, grey-green. Generally accepted as being one of the best pale shades. H45cm (18in).
'Sonora' (K. Foerster 1966)
Flowerheads purple-blue, large, mid-season. Sprays erect with short branches. Clumps small. Leaves narrow, deep green. H60cm (24in).

A. amellus 'Veilchenkönigin' has deep violet flowerheads, freely carried on compact plants late in the season.

'Sternkugel' (Lindner 1943)
Flowerheads light violet-blue, large, late. Sprays erect, well-branched. Clumps compact. H50cm (20in).
'Ultramarine' (before 1914)
Flowerheads violet-blue, late. H50cm (20in).
'Vanity'
Flowerheads purple-blue, large. Sprays erect and well-branched. Clumps strong. Leaves broad, grey-green. H45cm (18in).
'Veilchenkönigin' ('Violet Queen') (K. Foerster 1956) ♆
Flowerheads deep violet, small, late. Sprays erect with short, bushy branches. Clumps small. Leaves small, narrow, deep green. Smaller than average flowerheads do not detract from a good display of rich colour. H40cm (16in).
'Weltfriede' (Goos and Konnemann 1950)
Flowerheads violet, small. Sprays erect and well-branched. Leaves grey-green. H50cm (20in).

ASTER × FRIKARTII

Aster amellus is reputed to be tough and long-lived in its native European habitats but usually manages not to achieve the same standards in gardens. I wonder if this is why someone had the notion of creating a hybrid with the Himalayan species, *A. thomsonii*. Perhaps it was the attributes of an extremely long flowering season combined with a graceful appearance that made *A. thomsonii* seem such an attractive partner. I suppose it might just have been another of those happy accidents so frequently upped to the status of a major achievement, but the success rate of obtaining viable seed from a deliberate crossing of these two parents is so minimal that even the most experienced of plant breeders might be more inclined to take up sheep farming than to try.

Let us then look back to the twilight years of Victorian England and assume that the Reverend Wolley-Dod knew what he was doing when he crossed the newly-introduced *A. thomsonii* with *A. amellus*, which had been cultivated in England since at least 1596. The reverend gentleman was a distinguished amateur horticulturist, best remembered today by the hybrid of *Rosa villosa* that bears his name. Indeed, it is fortunate that the rose is still being grown and can commemorate its raiser as although he exhibited flowers from the progeny of his successful aster cross in 1892, no more was heard or seen of this great achievement. Did he consider his hybrid to be of no value as a garden plant and consign it to the rubbish heap, or did he have a gardener of the 'flashing hoe and spade' variety who did away with it? There is no record.

The passion for breeding new varieties of ornamental plants was just as alive in gardeners of the new century as it was with their Victorian predecessors. Promising, recently-introduced plants were always high on the list for pollen transfer and it is a reasonable assumption that numerous efforts would have been made to cross *A. thomsonii* with other aster species. However, it was not until about 1918 that the Swiss nurseryman Frikart managed to produce some seedlings from a cross with *A. amellus*. He gave them the names of alpine peaks – 'Eiger', 'Jungfrau' and 'Mönch' – and followed them in about 1924 with 'Wunder von Stäfa'. A summary description of their distinctive features is that 'Eiger' and 'Jungfrau' look closer in habit to *A. amellus*, whereas 'Mönch' and 'Wunder von Stäfa' might be described as stronger-growing versions of

A. × *frikartii* 'Eiger' (p.120) has the same good qualities as the better-known 'Mönch' and Wünder von Stäfa'.

A. *thomsonii*. The only other recorded hybrid between A. *amellus* and A. *thomsonii* is the cultivar called 'Flora's Delight', which was raised in 1964 by the renowned British plantsman and nurseryman, Alan Bloom. This most modern version of A. × *frikartii* has assumed the habit of a very neat-growing A. *amellus*.

In past years some of the less reliable members of the nursery trade sold plants labelled as 'A. × *frikartii*', without a cultivar name. Many of these offerings turned out to be strong-growing forms of A. *amellus* with inferior flowers. The increased awareness of the gardening public as to the correct naming of plants has, thankfully, largely eradicated this sort of practice.

All of the named cultivars are exceptionally good garden plants and exhibit qualities that are sought after in many other herbaceous perennials. In varying degrees, they all have hybrid vigour, being stronger growing and much longer lived than either parent. The flowering season is legendary, stretching from midsummer well into mid-autumn. My own record is held by 'Flora's Delight', which bore flowers from early summer until late autumn one year. (Of course, much depends upon the weather conditions in any year and the way in which the plant is growing.) Unless the taller-growing 'Mönch' and 'Wunder von Stäfa' are sited where they must look tidy, stakes are not needed. Complete resistance to attack by mildew has been inherited from both parents. Whereas shoots of A. *amellus* cultivars seem rather vunerable to wilting caused by verticillium, this problem is so far unknown to affect A. × *frikartii*. Plants are supposed to be hardy to Z4 in the USA but I suspect that some form of protective covering will be needed in areas where prolonged periods of frost are the norm. Colwall certainly gets frost when it's around. Although a week without any respite would be exceptional, when we have experienced long sessions of frost penetration to root level and below, A. × *frikartii* cultivars have suffered much less damage than those of A. *amellus* growing next door to them. A simple explanation for this would be afforded by the presence in their breeding of A. *thomsonii*, which is virtually an alpine plant.

CULTIVATION AND PROPAGATION

A. × *frikartii* cultivars prefer alkaline soil and a pH of 7 seems very suitable. Good to sharp winter drainage is a must, even if it can only be obtained by the use of grit or sharp sand. A light loam or sandy soil will give the best results: I have found that heavy clay inhibits the production of a satisfactory root system. Since heavy clay is what nature has provided in my own garden, I have resorted to raising the bed levels where groups of this hybrid are to be planted and working in quantities of sharp, gritty sand. A very rich soil is not needed but the texture must be such that moisture and plant food are retained through the summer months. A little well-made garden compost or some spent mushroom com-

A. thomsonii 'Nanus' (p.141) is a free-flowering and graceful aster for rock gardens and raised beds.

post will do the job if added before planting new stock; peat is not as good. I have not tried coir but suspect it would be satisfactory. A spring feed with hoof and horn, or something very similar, will keep the plants happy for a year. Of course, my virtual obsession with making sure of good winter drainage does present the possibility of problems when we run into a long spell of summer drought. Luckily, drought-resistance is a feature of these cultivars and if any show signs of distress, the application of some water will make them respond almost before your eyes.

The safe recommendation is always to plant in an open, sunny position; sites overhung by trees and shrubs or crowded by larger perennials are definitely to be avoided. Having said this, I have had excellent results from all cultivars of A. × *frikartii* when they have been shaded until midday by distant deciduous trees

and shrubs. The main effect of this must be to keep the plants a little cooler in hot weather while the deciduous nature of the woody plantings means that the area is not shaded and damp over the winter.

DIVISION

A. *thomsonii* has passed on the wonderful attribute of making nice, tight clumps packed with luscious-looking new shoots in all cultivars except 'Flora's Delight'. It is impossible to mistake their distinctive shoots for any other aster.

The clumps should be divided every three years or so. It is unwise, not to say foolhardy, to move them at any time other than the early spring, just as the shoots are beginning to hit ground level. Sections of 7.5-10cm (3-4in) in diameter are ideal for the original Frikart cultivars. Do the best you can with 'Flora's Delight': you might only be able to get sections of about 5cm (2in). Replanting on the same site seems to be acceptable, provided the ground is thoroughly prepared. I usually like to include some good turf loam or (pre-packed) sterilized loam when putting any type of plant back into its original spot. As a general rule moving by even a foot or two will avoid the possibility of nematode problems. When planting groups leave 30-45cm (12-18in) between the plants of 'Mönch' and 'Wunder von Stäfa' and about 30cm (12in) between the other varieties, except A. *thomsonii* 'Nanus' which might go down to 20cm (8in). Allow singleton plants enough room to expand over several years without being swamped by their neighbours.

It appears that none of the cultivars are able to produce fertile seed, thus ruling out this method of increasing stocks.

CUTTINGS

In commercial horticulture A. × *frikartii* cultivars are propagated by softwood cuttings taken in spring. They are an absolute joy because the shoots are freely produced and easy to handle and prepare. In a mist unit virtually 100 per cent will root in a sand and peat or a coir compost. The latter, in cells, has proved especially good because it drains well and saves root disturbance when potting on. Rockwool plugs have recently been used successfully for the same reason. If you are using a closed frame with bottom heat, the cuttings should be taken earlier in the season and removed from the par-

ent plants a little below ground level where the stems are still white. A peat and sand mixture seems to suit these cuttings best.

Once rooted, the young plants can be potted into 7.5cm (3in) pots (some growers use 9cm/3½in) and grown on in frames or polytunnels until the following spring. The plants must not become too wet through the winter and it pays to have some horticultural fleece at the ready for very cold weather. In an exceptionally severe winter a little heating for frost protection is advisable. They can then be moved into larger containers for sale, or planted out.

CULTIVARS OF ASTER × FRIKARTII

As available today, 'Mönch' and 'Wunder von Stäfa' look the same to me. They both grow up to a good 90cm (36in) high and have flowerheads reaching 8cm (3in) across with up to 50 rays, each of which is 4mm (⅙in) wide and pale lavender. The rays are arranged in two rows and are often slightly curled and twisting. Opinion varies as to how the colour must be described: for those who have the latest copy of the Royal Horticultural Society's colour chart, it matches at 'violet-blue 90C'. The flowering sprays are freely produced and have thin but strong, green stems and lots of branches with solitary heads at the ends. The leaves are oblong, deepish green and somewhat rough to touch.

Much variation in height, diameter of flowerheads and intensity of ray colour can be observed in plants growing under different conditions. For example, I grow a clump of 'Mönch' in poor, stony soil, in full sun, near the garden entrance. It is given a hint of fertilizer each spring and only gets watered in a drought if I suddenly remember about it. The height of this specimen is down to 60cm (24in) and the heads are reduced to 5-6cm (2-2½in) across, while the ray colour is noticeably deeper and more dull. First-year growth from divided clumps also often results in a height reduction and sturdy flowering sprays that do not fall. In their second year they will adopt the typical, rather graceful, arching effect normally associated with these cultivars.

Both 'Mönch' and 'Wunder von Stäfa' have received Awards of Garden Merit from the Royal Horticultural Society. I would vote for similar accolades to be awarded to 'Jungfrau' and 'Flora's Delight' because they are of distinctly different appearance and are superb garden plants.

'Jungfrau' has a compact stature, at 60-70cm (24-28in), and its flowerheads are 5cm (2in) across with up to 50 violet rays; even to the casual observer quite obviously a different colour to that of the taller cultivars. (The reference in the RHS colour chart is 'violet 87B'.) Also, the rays are formally set around a small disc creating a much tidier flowerhead than the other cultivars. Leaves are deep green and the sturdy flowering sprays have short, upright branches on their upper reaches. Whereas 'Mönch' and 'Wunder von Stäfa' require consideration as to whether or not to shove in some twiggy supports, this dilemma does not arise with 'Jungfrau' because the sprays are truly self-supporting.

This sturdy habit is further exemplified by **'Flora's Delight'**, which is a cross between A. *amellus* 'Sonia' and A. *thomsonii* 'Nanus' and grows to only 45cm (18in) high. The flowerheads are borne on sturdy, well-branched sprays with flat tops. They are 4cm (1½in) across and have lilac-coloured rays that pale with age. (The RHS official colour is 'violet 84A'.)

The leaves are smaller than those of the other cultivars and grey-green. The hybrid vigour of 'Flora's Delight' has been channelled into the production of flowering sprays, which seem to appear in endless succession. Clumps are small and rather weak when compared to the other cultivars, although they might well be stronger than the A. *amellus* parent. This is a plant to be treasured in raised beds or large rock gardens and will need careful chaperoning in the rough and tumble of a mixed border.

Very similar to 'Jungfrau', **'Eiger'** (photograph p.117) has identical flowerheads, produced less freely. But the flowering sprays are a little taller at 80cm (32in) and they are lax, having the same arching effect as the tall cultivars. The thin branches, bearing solitary heads, are often purple tinted. Although lacking the touch of quality apparent in the other cultivars, its flowering season is just as long.

IN THE GARDEN

'Mönch' and 'Wunder von Stäfa' head the list of asters that were deemed 'acceptable' by the main corps of gardening writers and broadcasters until the more recent awakening of interest in the genus as a whole. There is little doubt that plants such as these deserve every bit of praise they receive: they are of fairly easy culture with a season of flowering extending to four months

and do not have any disease problems. The whole group can generally be relied upon as excellent mixers in beds and borders.

Like A. *amellus* (see p.105), they are suitable for grouping with roses where their soft tones of lavender-blue will give a beautiful foiling haze of colour, and are happy with their arching wands supported by low bushes of *Spiraea japonica* and *Potentilla fruticosa*. Another idea is to grow pink and red pyramids of fragrant sweet peas behind them. A favourite combination of mine is to combine them with *Coreopsis verticillata* 'Moonbeam' whose flower colour and overall daintiness make for a perfect blend. In herbaceous borders they complement the late summer show, then put the other plants to shame by continuing to bloom into the autumn months.

Among shrubs with silver or golden leaves, their broad flowerheads do not look out of place. Try them grouped around the sunny side of *Eucryphia* × *intermedia* 'Rostrevor', whose luxuriant white cups and white fluffs of stamens will tower and shine above them as early autumn arrives. I have grown A. × *frikartii* cultivars in all these situations and more; you might as well ask where I have not grown them. However, the one place where they will stand out like Cinderella before she had the aid of her fairy Godmother is in a bed of A. *novi-belgii* cultivars. Whether the A. *novi-belgii* cultivars' brilliant colours and formality make the A. × *frikartii* cultivars appear dismal, or whether the refinement of the latter make the former look too brazen is purely a matter of opinion.

All of the cultivars of A. × *frikartii* look at home in a bed of A. *amellus* where the practical side of gardening is made easier because they all need similar conditions of cultivation. 'Jungfrau' and 'Flora's Delight' are very successful and long flowering in containers, but the pots ought to be placed in an unheated greenhouse or polytunnel in late autumn to prevent damage from excessive wet or frost, and the plants should be taken up and replanted in new potting compost every spring, after being carefully divided (if they are large enough). If you need shorter specimens in containers try planting them up each spring with young stock that has been raised from cuttings taken in the previous year. Whether in containers or in the garden, such plants rarely seem to make their full height until their second season of growth.

8

OTHER ASTER SPECIES

Asters inhabit the edges of arctic regions, the plains and mountains of Europe, Asia and Northern America. They are natives of woodlands, field edges, riverbanks and swamps, roadside verges and waste land. Given a genus of plants so diverse, generalization on cultivation is not possible and one must be sensibly guided by the soil and climatic conditions of each species' native habitats.

The robust plants with spreading clumps can invariably be propagated from divisions, offset shoots or soft tip cuttings as an alternative to raising stock from seed. Species with compact root systems and tufted clumps are often easier to seed-raise than to divide but the majority will provide suitable material for springtime cuttings from the tips of new growth. Propagation is not usually a great problem with asters. Guidelines for seed sowing are given on p.122, growing new plants from cuttings is discussed on p.83, and divisions, offsets and potting composts are covered on pp.47-48. Some of the Asiatic and quite a few of the more obscure North American species will provide enthusiastic growers with a suitable challenge for their skills. Many of the lesser-known aster species have been sadly neglected while their more prolific cousins have spawned huge numbers of cultivars. Adding new plants to the garden is always a special joy for plant lovers and the discovery that an untried or unknown species has many desirable qualities justifies their enthusiasm.

The diversity in such a large genus as *Aster* makes it almost certain that a little bit of thought will come up with a suitable site for a species or cultivar in virtually any garden in the temperate zones of the world. I have also seen asters being cultivated in gardens of equatorial regions and, on the whole, it is an experience not to be repeated, but had the grower been aware of the existence of a species such as *Aster carolinianus*, the results might have proved to be worth the effort.

Certain groups of asters, such as *A. novi-belgii*, have become dominant in gardens and commercial production due to their readiness to produce large numbers of desirable cultivars. Other species have their own special attributes and could easily be more suitable for the prevailing growing conditions than the more traditional range of asters. Indeed, growing conditions play an important role in defining the usefulness of many plants as additions to our gardens. A species that has every appearance of a spindly weed in its native habitat can readily change from Cinderella into a princess when given the benefits of good soil and thoughtful cultivation; the reverse is also true in that neat-growing, free-flowering plants that look beautiful in the wild state are quite prone to becoming robust, leafy weeds when given too rich a diet. If you wish to adopt a safe and fairly trouble-free approach to your gardening it is probably best to stick to the tried and tested cultivars, specially developed to give the best results in gardening situations. But I somehow suspect that the vast majority of gardeners have an inbuilt urge to grow at least some plants that are a little unusual. The range of aster species hardly grown in gardens is enormous and there are many excellent plants waiting to repay any efforts put into a little experimentation.

SPRING- AND SUMMER-FLOWERING SPECIES

In contrast to the vast array of autumn-flowering asters, which have an easy time selling themselves because there is little competition in the garden at that time of the year, the smaller numbers of cultivated asters that flower in the spring and early summer months have to work that bit harder to convince us they are valuable additions to the garden or alpine house. Some of the finest look marvellous in their often mountainous native habitats, only to prove impossible to cultivate to similar standards. Many of the more interesting of these early-flowering species only feel at home when planted in a rock garden or raised bed, and some of them will need the additional comfort of protection from wetness during the winter.

On the whole, spring- and summer-flowering asters share common growth characteristics that are unlike the majority of the later-flowering members of the genus. Those that are typically small-growing herbaceous perennials mainly form a low, compact mound of leaves with usually erect flowering stems, either having few branches or often unbranched. The flowerheads can be expected to be comparatively large and to be carried singly on the stems. Again, unlike many autumn-flowering asters, the stems are likely to have very few leaves. The more precisely alpine members of the genus may have low rosettes or mats of small leaves, supported by woody branches. This type of species will not retract below ground each autumn and produce new shoots from underground in spring: it rests on the surface and, without a good covering of winter snow, is vunerable to both weather and physical damage.

CULTIVATION

Although it is difficult to generalize, it is pretty certain that the majority of these asters will need to grow in a raised bed, rock garden pocket or pot containing a loam-rich compost mix with plenty of sharp grit in it. Give them a situation that is sunny without being overhot, where plenty of moisture can be added during the spring and summer, and where nature's supply of winter moisture will drain quickly and completely away.

A surprising number of aster species will germinate easily from spring-sown seed, where the temperature is between 10-20°C (50-70°F) and details of this procedure can be found on p.47. *Aster alpinus* and its colourful varieties fall into this trouble-free category.

The seed of the more idiosyncratic alpine species will benefit from conditioning treatment before being sown. Such seed is sown in early to midwinter, in the usual way, and the containers must then be placed in an unheated frame outdoors, where they will be exposed to cold but protected from excessive wet and predation from mice and birds and so on. I frequently sow the seeds straight off the plant, not waiting for winter. As with so many horticultural procedures, watering is critical as the seeds must have taken up some moisture before going into freezing conditions, for the conditioning to be fully effective. Seedlings ought to appear in the spring and will be encouraged by being removed to a greenhouse where night temperatures are maintained at about 10°C (50°F). Normally, one would not dream of getting alpines into heat but it is a good idea to speed the development of the seedlings beyond the stage where they are so very vulnerable to numerous pests. They will then probably need pricking out into small pots or trays before being returned to 'outdoor' temperatures.

This simple procedure can work well. But there will be years when the winter temperatures are not low enough for a sufficient period to condition the seeds properly – recent winters in the British Isles, for example. The process of artificially conditioning seeds can only be considered when gardeners are fortunate enough to have equable household arangements, ie consent to take up a little space in the domestic refrigerator! Mix the seeds with a small handful of grit or vermiculite, which is just moist and not soggy, place the mixture into strong polythene bags and tie the tops securely. Remember to label each bag. Pack the bags into a plastic food container and store them in the refrigerator for about six to eight weeks. After this period prepare some pots of seed compost and carefully sprinkle the contents of the bags on to the surface of the seed compost and water it well so that it settles firmly. I would usually transfer these seeds to a frost-free greenhouse to germinate but, if your timing coincides with mid-spring, an outdoor frame would do just as well.

Having obtained your established plants, by whatever means, it is necessary to propagate the stock on a regular basis to keep your plants young, vigorous and, consequently, floriferous. Those species with tufted growth can be lifted and divided into smaller sections and directly replanted into a refreshed soil mix. The mat-forming species can be grown from cuttings but seed is the recommended method, unless a particular form or cultivar is to be increased.

Although it is asking for trouble to make an attempt at recommending just one type of potting compost for growing the members of such a varied genus, particularly as every keen gardener will have their own favourite mixture, what I will say is that I have grown a wider range of asters than most people, in the compost mentioned on p.48, making suitable variations in the grit content to accommodate particular species. I also think that asters, more than most plants, hate anything approaching stale soil or 'tired' potting compost, making frequent repotting and replanting an essential element in successful cultivation.

A SELECTION OF SPRING-AND EARLY SUMMER-FLOWERING SPECIES

The following is a personal selection. There are many others. My best advice is to read what I have to say then ignore it if you wish. You have little to lose and might have much to gain.

Aster albescens (DC.) Hand.- Mazz. (c1840)
(syn. *Microglossa albescens*)
This is so unlike most other members of the genus that one might be inclined to opt for the synonym. On the other hand, many modern botanists have adopted the above classification and the plants are worthy of a place in suitable gardens. This species grows in the form of a broadly bushy shrub. The tiny flowerheads have white or pale blue rays and are carried in very large numbers on broad corymbs from mid- to late summer. The leaves are elliptic, lanceolate or ovate, 2.5-10cm (1-4in) long, entire or crenate-toothed, often white-tomentose beneath. The smaller versions are decorative in containers and this makes them easier to protect in winter in colder areas. Cut them back severely so that they make new growth for each season. Himalaya and W. China. Hardy to Z6. H60-180cm (24-72in), F10-13mm (½in).

Aster × alpellus hort. (*A. alpinus × A. amellus*)
This compact plant is more soundly perennial than *A. alpinus*. In summer the branched flowering sprays bear prominent heads with lavender-blue rays and orange disc florets. **'Triumph'** has white rays and orange discs. An interesting hybrid but not widely available. Garden origin. Hardy to Z3. H20-30cm (8-12in), F to 5cm (2in).

Aster alpigenus (Torr. & A. Gray) A. Gray
A deep taproot supports a tuft of linear-spathulate or oblanceolate leaves, up to 15cm (6in) long. Each wiry stem carries one glorious deep violet or purple-rayed flowerhead in summer. Mountains of W. USA. Hardy to Z7. H20cm (8in), F to 4cm (1½in).
subsp. andersonii (A. Gray) Onno This subspecies is usually found further to the south-west. It is a low, mat-forming plant with linear to linear-elliptic leaves and purple-rayed flowerheads. F not usually exceeding 3.5cm (1½in).
subsp. haydenii (T.C. Porter) also compact, is sometimes available.

Aster alpinus L. Alpine aster ♔ (photograph p.124)
This species forms comparatively large, spreading mats of pubescent, oblong-spathulate to lanceolate leaves, mostly in basal rosettes, with a few on the stems. The large flowerheads have violet to purple-blue rays, sometimes white or purple-pink, and yellow disc florets. They are carried singly on each stem in spring and early summer. European mountains, W. and central Asia, Iran, Siberia, W. North America: Alaska to Colorado. Hardy to Z3. H20-30cm (8-12in), F to 5cm (2in).

This is the most widely cultivated and easiest to grow of all the alpine asters. Plants tend to be short-lived – the more so if planted in rich soil – making frequent propagation essential. Seed sowing is the best method and many strains will reproduce faithfully, although double-flowering cultivars may not be so successful. These can be divided just after flowering; some care will be needed to establish them in dry weather. Among the cultivars are: **'Abendschein'**, a very choice variety with bright pink rays, H to 25cm (10in); **'Albus'**, with white rays, H also to 25cm (10in); **'Beechwood'**, pale violet-blue flowerheads, H20cm (8in); **'Dunkel Schöne'**, with deep purple-blue flowerheads a little later than some others, H30cm (12in); **'Happy End'**, a pink cultivar, H25cm (10in); **'Nancy Perry'** (Perry 1915), which freely produces its double, lavender-blue flowerheads, H25cm (10in); **'Roseus'**, pale purple-pink, H15cm (6in); **'Trimix'**, an excellent seed strain with single flowers of various colours that can be purchased separately, H20cm (8in); **'Wargrave Variety'**, with large, pale mauve-pink rays, H20cm (8in); and **'White Beauty'**, a white-rayed cultivar, H25cm (10in).

The varied cultivars of the easily grown A. *alpinus* (p.123) are invaluable for spring colour in a rock garden.

Aster asteroides (DC.) Kuntze (1912)
This plant was previously known as A. *lichiangensis* and a good form is an undoubted jewel. The tuberous roots support stems rising from a neat basal rosette of bright green, ovate to lanceolate leaves, each up to 4cm (1½in) long. The flowerheads, with rich purple-blue rays, are borne singly on wiry stems in early summer. Lesser forms may have pale violet rays. The species is not very easy to grow but a worthwhile challenge. Tibet, Bhutan, W. China. Hardy to Z6. H to 15cm (6in), F to 5cm (2in).

Aster bellidiastrum (L.) Scop. (1769) Daisy-star aster
The most desirable forms of this species are only about 15cm (6in) high; taller ones can be rather coarse. The solitary flowerheads have white or sometimes purple-pink rays and yellow discs, in mid-spring. Spathulate to elliptic leaves are in a basal rosette. A variable plant reminiscent of a lawn daisy (*Bellis*), it needs a cool, humus-rich soil with summer moisture in a partially

shaded rock-garden site. Mountains of S. Europe. Hardy to Z6. H15-40cm (6-16in), F2.5cm (1in).

Aster brachytrichus Franch.

A compact tuft of obovate-spathulate or obovate, hirsute leaves, 6cm (2½in) long, produces stems bearing solitary flowerheads with narrow, pale violet-blue rays and yellow discs. China. Hardy to Z6. H to 30cm (12in), F5cm (2in).

Aster caucasicus Willd.

This species has rather leafy stems that bear corymbs of 1-6 flowerheads in summer. These have purple-blue rays. The ovate to oblanceolate, scabrid, serrate leaves are up to 15cm (6in) long. Clumps are vigorous enough to be divided. S. Central Europe. Hardy to Z6. H to 60cm (24in), F5cm (2in).

Aster dahuricus (DC.) Benth. ex Bak.

Unlike most of the other species in this section, this a slender perennial with oblong-linear leaves. The white or pale violet flowerheads are borne in summer. Border soil. Siberia. Hardy to Z2. H to 1m (40in). F4cm (1½in).

Aster farreri W.W. Sm. and Jeffrey

An attractive perennial with leafy stems rising from a neat clump of lanceolate, dark green, hirsute leaves, up to 12.5cm (5in) long. The solitary flowerheads with narrow, bright violet rays and orange-gold disc florets are borne from early to midsummer. Tibet and W. China. Hardy to Z4. H to 60cm (24in), F3.2cm (1½in), some forms up to 6cm (2½in).

Do not be misled by the flowering height of A. *farreri*. Take note of its homeland and remember that it is likely to be happy on a rock garden and not in a border. I wish it would be kind enough to live longer in Herefordshire – however, it grows well from seed.

Aster flaccidus Bunge. (A. *purdomii* Hutch.)

On the lines of a hairy version of A. *alpinus*, with a basal cluster of hirsute, oblanceolate, undulate leaves. The solitary flowerheads have up to 40 pale violet-blue rays, and pale yellow discs in midsummer. China, Afghanistan, Mongolia, Siberia. Hardy to Z6. H to 15cm (6in), F4cm (1½in).

Aster glomeratus (Nees) Bernh. (1898) Bernhard's aster

A leafy perennial with flowerheads that have only 6 rays; borne in midsummer, these are are dull white and the disc florets quickly become brown. The basal leaves are cordate; those higher on the plant tend to be ovate.

A plant of moist thickets and swamps, where it makes strong clumps. E. North America. Hardy to Z3. H to 90cm (36in), F2.5cm (1in).

Aster himalaicus C.B. Clarke

A plant closely allied to A. *alpinus*, with solitary flowerheads in summer. The rays are violet and the discs brownish-yellow. Its leaves, up to 7.5cm (3in) long, are obovate-spathulate to narrow elliptic. Nepal to China. Hardy to Z6. H15-25cm (6-10in), F3.5cm (1½in).

Aster lingulatus Franch.

This is said to be a desirable plant with large flowerheads and bright violet or lavender rays, around yellow or orange disc florets. Erect stems usually have several heads clustered at their apex and the stems carry large leaves all the way up. China. Hardy to Z5. H30cm (12in). F4cm (1½in).

Aster lipskii Komar.

A graceful plant, akin to A. *flaccidus*, with slender, hairy stems and lanceolate leaves in a basal clump. Solitary flowerheads, in early summer, have deep violet-blue ray florets with yellow discs. Tibet. Hardy to Z6. H to 45cm (18in), F to 6.5cm (2¾in).

Aster oreophilus Franch. (1916)

Another species where you need the luck of the draw to provide you with a good form. The stems are purple tinted and carry a solitary flowerhead (sometimes two) in early summer. The ray florets in a good form should add up to 40 and will be a pleasant shade of violet-blue. Leaves oblanceolate to spathulate, shallowly dentate. W. China. Hardy to Z6. H of the best 30cm (12in) or less; the best in the wild state to 60cm (24in), F5cm (2in).

Aster peregrinus Pursh.

The nearly leafless stems carry 2 or 3 flowerheads with violet or white rays in summer. Leaves are spathulate or linear-oblanceolate in a tufted mound. Canada. Hardy to Z3. H to 70cm (28in) but better forms are 30cm (12in), F2.5cm (1in).

Aster porteri A. Gray

This species is widely found as a native plant of Colorado and will need light soil that drains really sharply during wet months of the year. The flowerheads are tiny, as with A. *ericoides*, with crisply white ray florets, which are likely to fade to light purple-pink. Arching flowering sprays carry thousands of these heads in broad corymbs in midsummer. The leaves are linear or linear-spathulate. The largest are up to 10cm (4in) long, but most are much smaller, becoming minute high on the sprays. A superb species to bring floral life to a rock garden during the heat of summer, when so many truly alpine plants are sulking. Central USA. Hardy to Z4. H of the best around 30cm (12in), others 60-90cm (24-36in), F to 18mm (¾in).

Aster savatieri Makino (syn. *Gymnaster savatieri* (Makino) Kitam.)
Flowerheads with blue or white rays are borne on erect flowering sprays, branched at the top into loose corymbs, above compact, spreading clumps in summer. The leaves, to 6cm (2½in) long and 3cm (1¼in) wide, are oblong or oblong-ovate, coarsely incised-toothed and short pubescent on both sides. Woods on mountains in Honshu, Shikoku and Kyushu, Japan. Hardy to Z7. H20-50cm (8-20in), F to 4cm (1½in).

This plant has also found itself in the genera *Boltonia* and *Asteromoea* in accordance with various botanical schools of thought and definitely belongs to the grey area of 'when is an aster not an aster'.

Aster scopulorum A. Gray. Wes. Crags aster
This is a compact, tufted plant with a dense mound of hairy leaves that are almost gems in their own right, being only 14mm (½in) long with tiny hairs, elliptic to oblong or linear and pale green with white margins. The solitary flowerheads, in summer, have violet or purple-blue ray florets. Utah, Oregon, Montana, Wyoming, California and Nevada. Hardy to Z7. H to 12.5cm (5in), F2.5cm (1in).

Aster souliei Franch. (1918) (*A. forrestii* Stapf.)
A plant with similarities to *A. farreri* and *A. diplostephioides*, having tufts or rosettes of leaves which are spathulate, oblanceolate or obovate and up to 10cm (4in) long. The stems carry large, solitary heads, with about 50 very thin, spidery rays of pale lavender or violet-blue and richly orange discs, in early summer. A lovely thing for careful cultivation on a rock garden or raised bed. George Forrest, the Scots plant collector, was one of my boyhood heroes and I am always sad to be reminded that his glorious aster proved to have been an earlier discovery. S.W. China, Tibet, Bhutan and Burma. Hardy to Z5. H to 30cm (12in), F7.5cm (3in).

Aster staticefolius Franch.
I can find no modern reference to this species, which can be either a miniature shrub or more of a cushion plant, depending upon its location. *The Present Day Rock Garden*, by Samson Clay (1937), includes a photograph of but one species of aster, among the many described. The honour has gone to a photograph of *A. staticefolius*, taken by no less an authority than George Forrest, growing in scree conditions in Yunnan, China. The plant is yet another of Forrest's rediscoveries, having been first found by the great Abbé Delavay, 20 years previously. Forrest took the trouble to count the flowerheads on just one plant and arrived at a massive total of 400. The flowerheads, borne in summer, have about 17 purple-blue, lavender or purple-red rays and small, yellow discs. There are many fine, woody branches, each bearing a rosette of small, oblanceolate to spathulate leaves. S.W. China. Hardy to Z6. H as a shrubby plant 60cm (24in), but in exposed scree conditions it will be a low cushion, F to 5cm (2in).

Aster stenomeres A. Gray
A woody rootstock supports dense, leafy tufts. The pale green leaves are only up to 3cm (1¼in) long and are spathulate to linear, entire, rigid and with tiny hairs. The stems bear solitary flowerheads with violet ray florets in summer. N.W. North America: British Columbia, Washington, Idaho, Montana. Hardy to Z4. H to 30cm (12in), F5cm (2in)

Aster stracheyi Hook. f.
A mountain aster, from an altitude of up to 5,000m (16,000ft), behaving like a strawberry plant in sending forth runners to maintain its creeping habit of growth – about 20cm (8in) across. Its leaves are up to 5cm (2in) long, obovate-spathulate, slightly dentate and noticeably pubescent or villous, as often befits a plant from great heights. The solitary flowerheads have narrow, recurved ray florets of pale violet or purple-blue with small yellow discs, and are borne in summer. In cultivation a rock garden scree that is cool, and probably therefore partially shaded, ought to provide a suitable home if an alpine house is not available. W. Himalaya. Hardy to Z6. H5cm (2in), F1.3-3.8cm (½-1½in).

Aster thomsonii see p.141.

Aster tongolensis Franch. (*A. subcaeruleus* S. Moore)
Hardly ever grown in the form of its typical species, this is a great provider of cultivars. In its wild state, *A. tongolensis* is a spreading plant with oblong or oblong-lanceolate leaves, to 9cm (3½in) long and slightly pubescent. The solitary flowerheads have lavender-blue ray florets and orange discs and are borne in late spring and early summer. W. China to India. Hardy to Z8. H30-40cm (12-16in), F3.8-5cm (1½-2in).

The many cultivars are extremely free flowering and are suitable as cut flowers. **'Berggarten'** has large heads of lavender-blue rays and bright orange discs, H40cm (16in). **'Berggartenzwerg'** has bright violet-blue rays, H20cm (8in). **'Leuchtenburg'** has violet rays and orange discs, H40-50cm (8-20in). The rich orange disc of **'Napsbury'** is surrounded by deep violet ray florets, H to 30cm (12in). The rays of **'Sternschnuppe'** are lilac-blue, H40cm (16in). **'Wartburgstern'** has violet-blue rays, H to 40cm (16in).

Aster tricephalus C.B. Clarke
This species has very narrow blue or white rays on erect flowering sprays that carry 1-3 heads in summer. The leaves are ovate-spathulate at the base of the plant, oblong on the stems. Sikkim and Nepal. Hardy to Z7. H to 40cm (16in), F5cm (2in).

Aster vahlii (Gaudich.) Hook. and Arn.
This cannot lay claim to being one of my favourite plants. It resembles, but is vastly inferior to A. *alpinus* and only merits mention because of its location far down in the southern hemisphere – Falkland Is. and Tierra del Fuego. Hardy to Z6.

Aster yunnanensis Franch. (1912) (A. *vilmorinii* Franch.)
Flowering in early summer, this species has lanceolate or oblanceolate, dark green leaves at its basal clump, with those higher on the plant being ovate. They are 5-16cm (2-6in) long. Each stem carries 2-6 flower-heads with numerous, broad ray florets of a good shade of deep lavender-blue with deep brown disc florets. W. China. Hardy to Z5. H to 60cm (24in), F6.5cm (2¾in).

LATE SUMMER- AND AUTUMN- FLOWERING SPECIES

The species featured in this chapter are those from which few if any cultivars have been developed; for those that also flower during this period but have many cultivars see chapters 3, 5, and 6. Unless otherwise stated they flower from late summer and into autumn. H = height, F = diameter of flowerhead.

Aster acuminatus Michx. (1803) Whorled aster, Mountain aster
Wiry sprays with short, erect branches bear flower-heads, said to be fragrant, with 12-18 twisted and recurved, white rays, sometimes tinged purple; the disc

A. *tongolensis* 'Berggarten' is the best known of several cultivars of this species and is good for late-spring displays.

florets are purple tinted. The leaves, to 15cm (6in) long, are elliptic to obovate, acuminate, dentate, glabrous. They are scattered on the stem so as to appear whorled. The clumps creep. Moist woodland in S. Canada and N.E. USA. Hardy to Z4. H30-90cm (12-36in), F3cm (1¼in).

Aster adnatus Nutt.
This is said to be a fairly tall plant with wand-like stems bearing small leaves and few, erect branches.

Aster adscendens Lindl. (1834) Western aster
In late summer, slender, stiff sprays, with short branches at the top, bear heads with violet rays. The leaves are linear-lanceolate or linear-oblong and 2.5-7.5cm (1-3in) long. Prairies and moist banks in W. Nebraska to Wyoming, Montana, Colorado, New Mexico and Nevada. Hardy to Z4. H15-60cm (6-24in), F2.5cm (1in).

Aster amellus see p.105.

Aster amethystinus Nutt. (1841) Amethyst aster
Strong, compact clumps produce long, lanceolate leaves, rough to the touch, and strong sprays with erect branches towards the top. The heads, opening in mid- to late autumn, have 20-30 violet-blue rays and deep yellow to brownish disc florets. Moist soil in Vermont and Massachusetts to New York, Pennsylvania, Illinois, Iowa and Nebraska. Highly likely to have hybridized with A. novae-angliae, A. oblongifolius and A. ericoides. Some authorities now list this plant as A. × amethystinus. Hardy to Z3. H to 1.6m (5½ft), F19mm (¾in).

Aster anomalus Engelm. (1843) Many-rayed aster
In early autumn this species produces heads, with 30-45 bright violet rays, on strong sprays with short branches towards the top. The leaves are thin, the lower ones cordate, ovate or ovate-lanceolate, pubescent, the upper one smaller, lanceolate, oblong or linear. Recommended for partial shade; drought-resistant. Limestone cliffs in Illinois, Missouri and Arkansas. Hardy to Z5. H to 90cm (36in), F2.5cm (1in).

Aster azureus Lindl. (1835) Sky-blue aster
This species bears slender, erect flowering sprays that are branched at the top, with small leafy bracts. In early to mid-autumn it has flowerheads with 10-20 bright blue rays. The leaves are cordate, ovate or lanceolate and 5-15cm (2-6in) long. Prairies and woodland edges. Ontario, W. New York, Georgia, Minnesota, Kansas, Alabama and Texas. Hardy to Z3. H30-120cm (12-48in), F2.5cm (1in).

Aster bakerianus Burtt, Davy ex C.A. Smith
The solitary flowerheads have pale to deeper blue or white rays and pale yellow disc florets. They are borne on sturdy sprays, with a few short branches. The clumps are tuberous and spreading with ovate-oblong to oblong-lanceolate leaves, 5-12.5cm (2-5in) long. South Africa. Hardy to Z6. H to 30cm (12in), F to 5cm (2in).

Aster bigelovii A. Gray (1878)
This biennial species has oblong-spathulate, hispid leaves; those on the stem are ovate-oblong. The rays are lilac; the disc florets yellow. Colorado. Hardy to Z5. H75cm (30in), F5.5cm (2¼in).

Aster carolinianus Walter (1788)
A lax shrub with straggling sprays with thin branches bearing flowerheads with pale purple rays and yellow disc florets from mid- to late autumn. The leaves are oblong-lanceolate to elliptic, grey-green, 5-10cm (2-4in) long and slightly downy. Florida to North Carolina. Hardy to Z8. H to 4m (12ft), F2.5cm (1in).

I have managed to grow large, straggly plants but have so far been unable to persuade them to flower – even when taken under cover for the winter. Colleagues in favoured states of the USA obtain staggering results!

Aster chapmanii Torr. & A. Gray
Slender, unbranched sprays bear solitary heads with violet rays. Leaves are linear-spathulate to filiform and up to 18cm (7in) long. Florida. Hardy to Z8. H to 1m (40in), F13mm (½in).

Aster chilensis Nees.
Small flowerheads, carried in large panicles from late summer to early autumn, have violet to pale purple rays and yellow discs. The leaves are oblanceolate, serrulate and to 10cm (4in) long. Dry soils in California. Hardy to Z8. H30-120cm (12-48in).

Aster ciliolatus Lindl. (as A. lindleyanus Torr. & A. Gray 1841)
From early to mid-autumn the few strong sprays, with upright branches, produce heads with pale violet to lavender rays. Ovate to cordate leaves, up to 10cm (4in) long, and vigorous clumps. In open places from Labrador to Mackenzie, Alberta, Maine, New York, Michigan and Montana. Hardy to Z2. H45-90cm (18-36in), F2.5cm (1in).

A leafy plant which makes a reasonably handsome clump in a border. A compact form with deep-coloured rays was in existence in 1892 but seems to have been lost.

Aster claytoni Burgess. (1898) Clayton's aster
Flowerheads usually have 6 white rays and are borne in early autumn on lax sprays with short, open branches. The stems are reddish; the leaves ovate-lanceolate. Sunny or slightly shaded, rocky places in Maine, New York, mountains in Virginia. Hardy to Z4. H to 45cm (18in), F to 2.5cm (1in).

Aster coloradensis A. Gray (syn. Machaeranthera coloradensis (A. Gray) Osterh., Xylorrhiza coloradensis (A. Gray) Rydb.)
This has a woody base, greyish foliage and rosy purple flowerheads. It should be a rock garden-plant and is likely to need deep, well-drained, stony soil. Colorado. Hardy to Z5. H15cm (6in).

Aster × commixtus (Nees.) Kunth. (*A. herveyi* A. Gray 1867)
Erect, open-branched sprays bear heads with violet-blue rays and yellow discs. The leaves are ovate and 5-15cm (2-6in) long in vigorous, spreading clumps. Dry soil in E. Massachusetts, Rhode Island, Connecticut and Long Island. Hardy to Z6. H to 90cm (36in), F3cm (1¼in).

Cultivated for many years in the UK, **A. 'Twilight'** seems to be identical to this recently-renamed hybrid. Ours is an excellent, easy-going aster which quickly makes a colony and gives plenty of colour in late summer and early autumn. I have never seen a hint of mildew on the plants and they do not need any supports. Simply divide the wide mats of shoots when you wish to tidy them up or, perhaps, prevent them from swamping a neighbouring plant.

Aster concinnus Willd. (1809) Narrow-leaved smooth aster
Erect sprays, branched into panicles, bear heads with violet or purple rays in mid-autumn. The leaves are light green, lanceolate to linear and 2.5-7.5cm (1-3in) long. Woodland in Connecticut to Pennsylvania, Virginia, North Carolina, Missouri and Arkansas. Hardy to Z4. H30-90cm (12-36in), F2cm (¾in).

Aster concolor L. (1763) Eastern silvery aster
Elliptic-oblong to lanceolate leaves, to 6cm (2½in) long, are silky, grey-green. The flowerheads, borne late in the season, have lavender, violet or pinkish rays and yellow discs, and are held in narrow racemes on slender sprays with few, erect branches. The clumps are small and woody. Dry, sandy soil in E. Massachusetts and Rhode Island to Florida, Tennessee and Louisiana, mostly near the coast. Hardy to Z4. H to 80cm (32in), F2.5cm (1in).

Aster conspicuus Lindl.
Erect-branched sprays form a corymb bearing heads with violet rays. The leaves are ovate to obovate, dentate, scabrid above, hirsute beneath. British Columbia, Washington, Oregon, South Dakota. Hardy to Z4. H to 1m (40in), F4cm (1½in).

Aster cordifolius see p.93.

Aster curtisii Torr. & A. Gray
Strong flowering sprays, branching into a panicle, bear heads with bright lilac rays. Ovate-lanceolate leaves to 10cm (4in) long. N. America. Hardy to Z5. H60-90cm (24-36in), F3.5cm (1½in).

Aster curvescens Burgess. (1898) Dome-topped aster
Flowerheads have about 8 creamy white rays and discs that turn purple-brown, on erect sprays, with short, ascending branches, in late summer. The leaves are ovate to lanceolate. Moist soil and shade in New England, New York, Virginia. Hardy to Z4. H45-105cm (18-42in), F2.5cm (1in).

Aster depauperatus (Porter) Fernald. (1908) Serpentine aster
Widely-branched, slender sprays bear heads with white rays from early to mid-autumn. Leaves are spathulate to oblanceolate and 1.3-3cm (½-1¼in) long; those on the stem are linear and 2.5cm (1in) or less. Serpentine barrens, S. Pennsylvania and W. Virginia. Hardy to Z5. H10-38cm (4-15in), F18mm (¾in).

Aster diplostephioides (DC.) C.B. Clarke
In spite of a burdensome name, this is among the most beautiful of alpine asters to give late colour for rock garden enthusiasts. It produces small clumps with oblanceolate to linear-lanceolate leaves, up to 8cm (3in) long, in basal tufts. Produced from late summer to early autumn, the flowerheads have numerous, very narrow, pale violet-blue rays and orange-brown discs; the flowering sprays are wiry and leafless with solitary heads. High altitudes in Kashmir and China. Hardy to Z5. H to 45cm (18in), F to 7.5cm (3in).

Aster divaricatus L. (1753) White wood-aster
Opening late summer to early autumn, the flowerheads have 6-9 narrow and unevenly spaced, white rays and yellow discs, turning brown. The wiry sprays droop to the ground and are much-branched and brown. Leaves broadly oval to triangular, deep green, 6cm (2½in) wide; clumps vigorous. Open woodlands and thickets in dry soil in Quebec to Manitoba, Georgia and Tennessee. Hardy to Z4. H to 45cm (18in), F2.5cm (1in).

This species is not only tolerant of a shaded site but actually grows best there, and also seems to thrive on lack of attention. Insignificant as one small plant, it comes into its own when used as large drifts of groundcover. Gertrude Jekyll had the brilliant idea of allowing its sprawling stems to hang over the leaves of bergenias and the combination of clouds of little white stars and heavy, bronze-red autumn leaves is worth aiming for. The cultivar **'Perseus'** was said to have darker, firmer and more wrinkled foliage. **'Raiche Form'** is currently said to be an improvement on the type species.

Aster drummondii Lindl. (1835) Drummond's aster

A. *divaricatus* (p.129) is one of the comparatively few asters that are truly happy in a shaded site.

Flowering in mid-season, this species has wiry sprays with stout, greyish stems and short horizontal branches. The heads have 8-15 lavender-blue rays and yellow disc florets. Leaves, up to 15cm (6in) long, are cordate at the plant's base; the upper ones are broadly lanceolate and rough. Clumps dense. Dry soil, wood edges and on prairies in Ohio to Minnesota, Kentucky, Arkansas and Texas. Hardy to Z5. H1.3m (4½ft), F13mm (½in).

Aster dumosus L. (1753) Bushy aster, Rice-button aster

Heads with 15-30 lavender, violet or white rays and yellow discs are borne on sturdy sprays, branching into mounds or with short, finely divided branches, from late summer to mid-autumn. The leaves are up to 12.5cm (5in) long and linear-lanceolate or narrow-elliptic. Clumps are mostly strong; some spread, others are compact. Extremely variable. Usually in sandy soil

in Massachusetts to W. New York, Ontario, Florida, Louisiana and Missouri. Hardy to Z3. H20-100cm (8-40in) – mostly about 40cm (16in), F13mm (½in).

This is a parent of many compact and dwarf cultivars. These are sometimes still catalogued under A. *dumosus*, but most authorities have now accepted their inclusion under cultivars of A. *novi-belgii* (the other parent). The retention of A. *dumosus* as a group name for the cultivars has the obvious benefit of readily indicating that these are compact in stature.

Aster elliottii
Available in the USA, this is a tall-growing species from moist areas of Florida.

Aster ericoides see p.97.

Aster falcatus Lindl. White prairie aster
Widely branched, erect sprays bear heads with 20-30 white rays. The leaves are linear or oblong-linear and up to 4cm (1½in) long. New Mexico. Utah and Arizona. Hardy to Z4. H to 80cm (32in), F2.5cm (1in).

Aster falconeri (C.B. Clarke) Hutch. (1906)
The late-summer flowerheads of this species have very narrow, violet-blue rays, white at the base, and bright yellow discs. The flowering sprays are sturdy and erect with solitary heads. Oblanceolate leaves, to 15cm (6in) long, are in basal tufts forming small clumps; shorter leaves on stems of the sprays. Another late flowering treat for the rock garden, where careful cultivation in scree conditions will give the best chance of success. Himalaya in Pakistan and Nepal. Hardy to Z6. H to 40cm (16in), F to 8cm (3in).

Aster fastigiatus Fisch.
From late summer to early autumn, erect sprays, branched at the top into dense corymbs, bear many very small flowerheads with white or purple rays. Leaves thick, linear-lanceolate or lanceolate, 5-12.5cm (2-5in) long and up to 15mm (½in) wide; numerous smaller leaves on stems. On waste ground and near rivers in lowland areas of Honshu, Shikoku, Kyushu in Japan, also Korea, Manchuria and China. Hardy to Z4. H30-100cm (12-40in), F9mm (⅜in).

Aster faxonii Porter. (1894) Faxon's aster
Strong sprays have branches forming a corymb of flowerheads with clear white, sometimes purple rays, in late summer. Firm, lanceolate or linear-lanceolate leaves are 5-12.5cm (2-5in) long. Moist cliffs in Maine and Vermont to Pennsylvania, Wisconsin and North Carolina. Hardy to Z4. H to 1.5m (5ft), F2.5cm (1in).

Aster fendleri A. Gray (1849) Fendler's aster
In late summer produces solitary or a few sprays, with a few short branches at the top forming a small raceme. These bear heads with 10-15 pale violet rays and yellow disc florets. The few, rigid leaves are linear, up to 4.5cm (1¾in) long, with ciliate margins. One of the finest asters for a rock garden. Dry soil on plains in Nebraska and Kansas to Colorado and New Mexico. Hardy to Z5. H15-30cm (6-12in), F to 3.8cm (1½in).

Aster foliaceus Lindl. (1853) Leafy-bracted aster
Flowerheads with about 30 lavender, violet or purple-pink rays, and yellow disc florets are borne on stout sprays with erect branches towards the top in late summer. Up to 12.5cm (5in) long, the leaves are oblong-lanceolate to obovate and deep rich green. Small clumps. Mountains of Quebec, Oregon to Alaska. Hardy to Z2. H to 90cm (36in) – frequently around 40cm (16in), F to 5.5cm (2¼in).

This is not likely to be one of the easiest plants to grow but it is rather magnificent and well worth the challenge for alpine-plant enthusiasts. Most of the lush-looking foliage grows in a basal clump and several strong flowering sprays will stand above these mounds. The grower's skill is tested in striking a balance so that the quantity of foliage does not appear to overwhelm the display of flowerheads. The most sought-after form has rich violet flowerheads. A humus-rich, moist soil is essential through the growing and flowering season and, in lowland regions at least, good winter drainage. If soil conditions are damp enough, a sunny situation is acceptable, although the plants are probably easier to manage where they are shaded from the sun through the hottest hours of the day. They should be divided each spring to avoid the formation of mats of leaves that do not throw up any flowering sprays.

Aster fragilis Willd. (1803)
Erect sprays branch into an open panicle bearing heads with violet, purple-tinted or white ray florets. Leaves, up to 10cm (4in) long, are linear-lanceolate, mucronate, minutely serrulate or entire. E. USA. Hardy to Z5. H to 1.2m (4ft), F18mm (¾in).

Aster × frikartii see p.116.

Aster fuscescens Bur. & Franch. (1914)
Rounded corymbs, about 15cm (6in) across, bear heads with about 15 violet rays and yellow to orange discs. The sprays are erect and the stems purplish with fine white hairs. Ovate, cordate, hirsute leaves are up to 12.5cm (5in) long. A tough border plant. China, Tibet and Burma. Hardy to Z6. H60cm (24in), F3cm (1¼in).

Aster glaucodes S.F. Blake
Erect sprays, branched into dense corymbs, bear flowerheads with rays that are purple or pinkish-tinted white. Leaves, up to 3cm (1¼in) long, are linear-oblong, acute, glaucous. Utah, Michigan, Idaho, Wyoming, Arizona and Colorado. Hardy to Z4. H to 60cm (24in), F to 2.5cm (1in).

Aster glehnii F. Schmidt
White flowerheads are borne on strong sprays, branched into a dense corymb, from early to mid-autumn. The leaves are oblong to linear and crowded in strong clumps. Grassy places in Hokkaido to Sakhalin and S. Kuriles, Japan. Hardy to Z7. H to 1.5m (5ft), F13mm (½in).

Aster gracilis Nutt. (1818) Slender aster, Tuber aster
In late summer, slender sprays, branched into a corymb, bear violet to purple flowerheads with 9-15 rays. The basal leaves, to 6.5cm (2½in) long, are elliptic, entire; those on the stem are linear, to 9cm (3½in). The clumps are woody. Dry, sandy soil in New Jersey to Kentucky, Tennessee and South Carolina. Hardy to Z5. H30-45cm (12-18in), F2cm (¾in).

Aster grandiflorus L. (1753) Large-flowered aster
Flowerheads with numerous, deep violet or purple-blue rays and deep yellow discs are borne from early to mid-autumn in the wild, late autumn to early winter in cultivation in the British Isles. The sprays are strong with short, stiff branches; the stems brown and hairy. Oblong or lanceolate-oblong leaves are rough, and the clumps are small. Dry soils in Virginia and east of the mountains to Florida. Hardy to Z7. H30-75cm (12-30in), F5cm (2in).

A truly beautiful aster for areas where late autumn sunshine and moderately low rainfall at that season can be assured. Could be a worthwhile cool conservatory or greenhouse pot plant for those of us in less favoured climates. The species first flowered in England in 1720, from seed collected in Virginia by Mark Catesby. Through the late eighteenth and nineteenth century *A. grandiflorus* gained popularity as the 'Christmas Aster' because its richly coloured flowerheads appeared so late in the year and some good results were achieved in years when the autumn frosts did not spoil their show. Growers frequently cut the sprays before the buds opened and allowed them to develop fully indoors.

Aster greatae Parish
Sprays are branched in an open panicle and bear heads with pale purple rays and yellow discs. The leaves, mostly at the base of the plant, are oblanceolate to lanceolate-elliptic, up to 15cm (6in) long. California. Hardy to Z8. H to 1.2m (4ft), F2.5cm (1in).

Aster hauptii Ledeb.
Heads with numerous purple rays are borne on erect sprays with few branches. Leaves are linear-oblong or linear. Siberia. Hardy to Z2. H60cm (24in), F5cm (2in).

Aster hemisphaericus Alexander. Southern aster
Rigid, few-branched sprays bear flowerheads on short stalks in the leaf axils; rays violet-blue, disc florets pale yellow. The leaves are smooth, thick, hard and linear with the midrib prominent beneath. The clumps are small. Sandy soil, open woods and prairies in the USA, N. to Missouri and North Carolina. Hardy to Z7. H60-90cm (24-36in), F3.5cm (1½in).

So far with me, this species has produced a rather leafy clump and not enough flowering sprays to make it really showy; other growers who have the benefit of warmer gardens have been more successful and find it a worthwhile addition.

Aster hirsuticaulis Lindl. (1836) Hairy-stemmed aster
Slender, erect sprays, with short, ascending branches and pubescent stems, bear heads with white rays from early to mid-autumn. Leaves are linear-lanceolate to lanceolate, up to 15cm (6in) long. Woods and thickets in New Brunswick to Pennsylvania, Kentucky and Michigan. Hardy to Z4. H45-90cm (18-36in), F about 2cm (¾in).

Aster ianthinus Burgess. (1898) Violet wood-aster
Flowerheads with 10-13 deep violet rays are borne on erect sprays with short branches near the top from late summer to mid-autumn. Leaves orbicular to oblong, 12.5cm (5in) long. Shaded banks and woodlands; Maine to Lake Erie and West Virginia. Hardy to Z4. H60-90cm (24-36in), F2.5cm (1in).

Aster indamellus Grierson (1886)
Flowering from late summer to early autumn, this is an attractive little plant, reminiscent of A. *amellus*. It has sprays, loosely branched towards the top, with heads of 20-30 violet rays. The leaves, up to 5cm (2in) long, are oblong, entire or dentate, finely pubescent. Kashmir and Nepal. Hardy to Z6. H20-25cm (8-10in), F to 3.8cm (1½in).

Aster integrifolius Nutt.
The species has purple or violet rays and yellow discs. The erect flowering sprays are branched at the top. Thick, glabrous to white-pilose leaves, to 20cm (8in) long, are oblanceolate to elliptic. California, Montana and Colorado. Hardy to Z7. H70cm (28in), F3cm (1¼in).

Aster junceus Ait. (1789) Rush aster
In late summer, few-branched, slender sprays, forming small panicles, bear violet or white heads. The leaves are firm, glabrous, narrowly linear and 7.5-15cm (3-6in) long. Swamps and bogs from Nova Scotia to British Columbia, New Jersey, Ohio, Wisconsin and Colorado. Hardy to Z3. H30-90cm (12-36in), F2.5cm (1in).

Aster junciformis Rydb.
Slender sprays, with branches in an open panicle, carry white, pale blue or lavender heads. The leaves, to 8cm (3in) long, are linear to lanceolate or oblong-linear. New Jersey, Quebec, Colorado, Idaho, Alaska. Hardy to Z2. H to 90cm (36in), F2cm (¾in).

Aster kumleinii Fries ex A. Gray (syn. A. *oblongifolius* var. *rigidulus*)
Sprays branch into bushy mounds and bear heads with bright violet-blue rays. Hardy to Z9. H to 60cm (24in), F2.5cm (1in). **'Dream of Beauty'** has pink rays.

Aster laevis see p.74.

Aster lanceolatus Willd.
Flowerheads, with white or pale violet-blue rays and pale yellow disc florets, are produced, late in the season, on strong sprays with purple-tinged stems and upright branches forming a graceful spire. Making vigorous, spreading clumps, with pale green lanceolate leaves, this species is sometimes invasive. Moist soil in New Brunswick to W. Ontario and Montana, S. to New Jersey, Virginia, Kentucky, Louisiana and Missouri. Hardy to Z4. H to 1.8m (6ft), F2cm (¾in).

'Edwin Beckett' (before 1902) has flowerheads of 2.5cm (1in) and very pale violet-blue rays. The flowering sprays branch into elegant pyramids, Although the clumps are vigorous they tend to be less invasive than the typical species. Both are good in wild garden plantings and useful for cutting.

Aster lateriflorus see p.102.

Aster ledophyllus A. Gray
Erect sprays, with few branches, bear flowerheads with purple-blue ray florets. The leaves, to 6cm (2½in) long,

are narrow-lanceolate to elliptic-oblanceolate, sessile, tomentose beneath. California and Washington. Hardy to Z6. H60cm (24in), F2.5cm (1in).

Aster linariifolius L. (1753) Stiff-leaf aster
With lavender-blue rays and pale yellow disc florets, the flowerheads of this species are borne on stiff and erect sprays, with few short, upright branches, in early autumn. Very narrow linear, rigid, deep green leaves, to 3.8cm (1½in) long, are tightly packed on the stems; clumps small. Quebec to Florida and Texas, Wisconsin and Montana. Hardy to Z4. H30-45cm (12-18in), F2cm (¾in).

Forms **'Albus'**, **'Purpureus'** and **'Roseus'** are recorded, with white, purple and pink rays respectively. I have only grown the form with blue rays and can strongly recommend it as a rock garden plant where its neat habit and glorious flowerheads can be fully appreciated. Good winter drainage is essential.

Aster lindleyanus Torr. & A. Gray (1841) Lindley's aster
The few-branched, strong sprays produce heads with 10-20 blue or violet rays in early to mid-autumn. The thick leaves are cordate to ovate or lanceolate; longest 10cm (4in). Open places from Labrador to Mackenzie, Alberta, Maine, New York, Michigan and Montana. Hardy to Z4. H to 1.8m (6ft), F2cm (¾in).

Aster linosyris (L.) Bernh. Goldilocks
Flowerheads consisting only of deep yellow disc florets (no ray florets) are borne on wiry sprays with short, upright branches, numerous at the top, in early autumn. Leaves very narrow-lanceolate, pale green, flax-like. Small woody clumps. Somewhat of a curiosity but quite a decorative garden plant for sandy or otherwise well-drained soil. Sunny, dry slopes and heathland in S. and S.E. Europe, including British Isles. Hardy to Z4. H to 60cm (24in), F2cm (¾in).

'Gold Dust' is slightly earlier-flowering, more compact and with deeper-coloured flowerheads. A form with white rays is recorded but is said to be inferior. A cross with *A. sedifolius* was raised in Miss Ellen Willmott's famous garden at Great Warley. It was soon discarded as being merely an oddity.

Aster longifolius Lam. (1783) Long-leaved aster
In late summer, strong, open-branched sprays bear flowerheads with violet to pale purple rays, often more than 30 per head, and small, yellow disc florets. Stems often purple-tinged; numerous leaves are lanceolate,

deep green and up to 20cm (8in) long; clumps strong. This has been cultivated in gardens for about 200 years and so must be among the numerous parents of the present race of *A. novi-belgii* cultivars. Labrador, Saskatchewan, New England, Ontario and Montana. Hardy to Z3. H90cm (36in), F2.5cm (1in).

Aster lowrieanus Porter. (1894) Lowrie's aster, Fall aster
Branched into a loose panicle, the erect sprays bear flowerheads with light blue rays, in mid-autumn. Firm, ovate to ovate-lanceolate leaves. Woods in Connecticut and S. New York to Pennsylvania, Ontario, North Carolina and Kentucky. Hardy to Z4. H to 1.2m (4ft), F18mm (¾in).

Aster maackii Regel
Flowerheads with pale lavender rays and yellow disc florets are borne on sturdy sprays with short, upright branches towards the top. Leaves up to 10cm (4in) long, lanceolate, hairy. The clumps are rhizomatous and spreading. Japan, Korea and Manchuria. Hardy to Z7. H1m (40in), F to 3.8cm (1½in).

Aster macrophyllus L. (1763) Large-leaved aster
In late summer, strong, open-branched sprays hold up to 80 flowerheads, each with 10-16 pale lavender, violet or white rays and yellow discs. The stems are often purple-red tinted and hairy. Leaves ovate-cordate, broad and coarse, up to 15cm (6in) long; clumps woody and spreading. Dry soil in shade; Canada to Minnesota and North Carolina. Hardy to Z3. H90cm (36in), F2.5cm (1in).

Quite handsome clumps of foliage but the flowerheads lack impact. However, all is redeemed when the heads set seed. From then on the sprays are decorative for as long as they can last through the autumn and winter months. The following, written by Thoreau on August 26th 1856, appears in *The History and Folklore of North American Wildflowers* by Timothy Coffey:

> Sailed across to Bee Tree Hill. This hillside, laid bare two years ago and partly last winter, is almost covered with *Aster macrophyllus*, now in its prime. It grows large and rank, two feet high. On one count, seventeen central flowers withered, one hundred and thirty in bloom and half as many in bud. As I looked down from the hilltop over the sprout land, its rounded grayish tops amid the bushes I mistook for gray, lichen clad rocks, such was

its profusion and harmony with the scenery,
like hoary rocky hilltops amid bushes.

Aster miqueliana Hara. (syn. *Kalimeris miqueliana*)
Violet ray florets on slender sprays. Leaves to 9cm
(3½in) long, ovate-cordate, acute to acuminate,
incised-serrate, pilose. Japan. Hardy to Z7. H90cm
(36in), F2.5cm (1in).

Aster missouriensis Britton. (1898) Missouri aster
Much-branched sprays bear heads with white rays in
early to mid-autumn. The stems are pubescent and the
leaves are oblong-lanceolate, up to 10cm (4in) long.
Moist soil in Kansas, Missouri and Iowa. Hardy to Z3.
H60cm (24in), F2cm (¾in).

Aster modestus Lindl. (1834) Great northern aster
In late summer, erect sprays bear heads with 35-45 purple or violet rays. The stems are pilose and leafy with a
few short branches; the leaves lanceolate, serrulate or
entire, up to 13cm (5in) long. Moist soils in W.
Ontario to Minnesota, Oregon and British Columbia.
Hardy to Z3. H about 1m (40in), F3cm (1¼in).

Aster multiflorus Aiton. (1789) Dense-flowered aster,
White wreath aster
Flowerheads with 10-20 white rays and large yellow
discs are borne on erect sprays with bushy branches
forming a pyramid at the end of late summer to mid-
autumn. The crowded, rigid leaves are deep green,
linear or linear-oblong and rough. A variable plant
included by some authorities in *A. ericoides*. Dry open
places; Maine and Ontario to Alberta, Georgia, Texas
and Arizona. Hardy to Z3. H1.2m (4ft) or more, F10-
15mm (½in).

Aster multiformis Burgess. (1898) Various-leaved
aster
Sprays are erect with a few upright branches and, in
late summer, bear heads with about 13 white rays.
Large leaves are cordate at base of plant; higher ones
are ovate to lanceolate. Moist shade in Maine to W
New York, Pennsylvania and Maryland. Hardy to Z4.
H30-60cm (12-24in), F2cm (¾in).

Aster nemoralis Ait. (1789) Bog aster
Flowerheads consist of 15-25 pale purple-blue to pale
purple-pink rays and yellow disc florets. In late summer
and early autumn, erect, unbranched sprays carry a
solitary head or have several heads on short stalks. The
leaves are very numerous, linear to oblong, tapering at
both ends, sessile and toothless. The clumps are thin
and spreading. Acid bogs; New Jersey to N. New York,

Ontario, Newfoundland and Hudson Bay. Hardy to Z2.
H15-60cm (6-24in), F to 3.2cm (1½in).

Aster nobilis Burgess. (1898) Stately aster
In late summer, strong sprays, branched into an open
panicle, bear heads with 13-15 violet or blue rays.
Thin, firm leaves are deep green and orbicular to
oblong; basal and lower leaves up to 23cm (9in) long
by 15cm (6in) wide. Leaf mould-rich soils from Lake
Champlain to Lake Erie. Hardy to Z4. H1.2-1.5m
(4-5ft), F2.5cm (1in).

Aster novae-angliae see p.76.

Aster novi-belgii see p.24.

Aster oblongifolius Nutt. (1818) Aromatic aster
Strong sprays with open branches and woody, hairy
stems flower through early and mid-autumn. The flowerheads have 20-30 violet, rarely lavender or pink, rays
and yellow disc florets. Pale green leaves are oblong or
lanceolate-oblong, to 8cm (3in) long, and rough on
compact clumps. On prairies and bluffs, especially on
limestone, central Pennsylvania to Minnesota, North
Dakota, Nebraska, Colorado, Virginia, Tennessee and
Texas. Hardy to Z9. H to 1m (40in), F to 2cm (¾in).

If freedom of flower production over a long season
counts for anything *A. oblongifolius* and its offspring
deserve to be much more widely planted by gardeners.
The most aromatic parts of the plant are said to be the
green-tipped bracts below the rays. The variable
species has already provided gardeners with the selection known as **'Fanny's Aster'**, which is similar but
smaller. Rays violet; flowerheads are freely carried over
a long period on bushy sprays, with many branches
which spread horizontally. H about 50cm (20in),
F18mm (½in).

'October Skies' has purple-blue flowers and is said to
be highly tolerant of drought and poor soil. H45cm
(18in). **'Raydon's Favourite'** is taller than the typical
species with larger flowerheads.

Aster occidentalis (Nutt.) Torr. & A. Gray
Lavender or violet rays and yellow disc florets are borne
on slender sprays with few short branches. The stems
are red tinted, the leaves are linear-oblanceolate and
entire, and the clumps are creeping. Alaska to California. Hardy to Z3. H50cm (20in), F2.5cm (1in).

Aster oolentangiensis Riddell
Heads with lavender or pink rays are borne in late summer to mid-autumn on erect sprays, branched into
open panicles. Leaves thick and firm, lanceolate or

ovate, cordate or sub-cordate, hispid above, pubescent beneath, to 13cm (5in) long. Prairies in mid- and N. Louisiana. Hardy to Z5. H to 1.5m (5ft), F2.5cm (1in).

Aster paludosus Ait. (1789) Southern swamp aster
In early to mid-autumn, slender sprays with few branches produce heads with 20-30 deep violet rays. The leaves are linear, rigid, glabrous and 5-15cm (2-6in) long. Swamps in Kansas, Missouri to Texas, E. to North Carolina and Florida. Hardy to Z5. H30-75cm (12-30in), F to 5cm (2in).

Aster parviceps (Burgess) Mackenzie & Bush (1902) Small-headed aster
Wiry, well-branched sprays bear heads with white rays and brownish discs in late autumn. At the base, the leaves are spathulate; those on the stem are linear to linear-lanceolate; 3-7cm (1¼-3in) long Small clumps. Dry, open woodlands and prairies, Illinois, Iowa and Missouri. Hardy to Z3. H30-80cm (12-32in), F15mm (½in).

Also known as A. ericoides var. parviceps, this is not an exciting garden plant but is cultivated in the form of **'Edi Niedermeier'** (Reuther 1982), which is used for the production of flowers for drying for winter flower arrangements. H70cm (28in).

Aster patens Ait. (1789) Late purple aster, Spreading aster
In early autumn this species produces mostly solitary heads, with 20-30 purple-blue or violet (rarely pink) rays and yellow disc florets, at the ends of thin branchlets. The sprays are wiry and weak with few, widely spreading branches. The broadly ovate to oblong leaves, rough and up to 15cm (6in) long, are lobed at the base where they clasp the hairy stems. Variable. Dry, open places, including open woods, Maine to N. New York, Minnesota, Florida, Louisiana and Texas. Hardy to Z4. H30-100cm (12-40in), F2.5cm (1in).

Aster patulus Lamarck
Sturdy sprays with bushy, spreading branches bear flowerheads with violet or white rays. The leaves are bright green, to 15cm (6in) and oval or oblong-lanceolate. Clumps are vigorous and spreading. S.E. USA. Hardy to Z4. H to 1.2m (4ft), F2.5cm (1in).

Aster paucicapitatus Robinson
In late summer, erect sprays each hold 1-4 heads with white rays, aging pink. Entire, elliptic or elliptic-oblong leaves. N.W. USA. Hardy to Z6. H40cm (16in), F to 4cm (1½in).

Aster phlogifolius Muhl. (1804) Thin-leaved purple aster
Flowerheads with numerous, purple-blue rays are carried singly or in small groups on slender sprays, with short branches, in early autumn. Leaves are lanceolate to oblong-lanceolate. Woods and thickets from New York to Ohio, North Carolina and Tennessee. Hardy to Z4. H to 90cm (36in), F to 5cm (2in).

Aster phyllodes Ryd. (1910) Large-bracted aster
Slender, erect-branched, leafy sprays bear flowerheads with purple ray florets in late summer. Leaves are oblong-lanceolate and up to 10cm (4in) long. Wet ground in W. Nebraska and E. Colorado. Hardy to Z3. H60-90cm (24-36in), F about 2.5cm (1in).

Aster piccolii Hook. (1899)
Lax sprays, branched into open corymbs, produce heads, each with about 30 lilac ray florets and yellow discs. Oblong, dentate leaves to 10cm (4in) long. China. Hardy to Z6. H to 90cm (36in), F to 5cm (2in).

Aster pilosus Willd. (1803) Frost-weed aster
Each flowerhead has 15-20 white rays, aging purple-pink and deep yellow disc florets. These are produced on strong sprays, with numerous upright branches forming a wide spire through early autumn. Narrow, lanceolate leaves are slightly hairy. Strong clumps. Dry thickets, clearings, fields and roadsides, N.E. USA. Hardy to Z5. H to 1m (40in), F15mm (½in).

var. demotus (Blake) ♛ is slightly taller at 1.5m (5ft) and is the most commonly cultivated form. It is certainly free with its flowerheads, and showy when planted *en masse*. The heads are densely packed on the sprays and little of the small green leaves is visible at flowering time. In its native land this aster turns wide acres of many states white and is the dominant species along with the tall goldenrod, *Solidago altissima*.

Aster praealtus Poir. (A. salicifolius Ait.)
In mid-autumn, strong, short-branched sprays produce flowerheads with purple-blue or white rays. Clumps are woody and spreading. Leaves are thick and hairy and to 13cm (5in) long. Michigan to Georgia, W. to Nebraska and S. into Arizona and N. Mexico. Hardy to Z4. H to 1.6m (5½ft), F2.5cm (1in). A. praealtus should not be confused with A. salicifolius Lam. (1783).

var. nebraskensis (Britt.) Wieg. (A. *nebraskensis* Britt. 1898) is probably a better garden plant, with purple-blue rays, wiry, very erect sprays with few, short, upright branches, and thick, upward-pointing, lanceolate to oblong-lanceolate leaves. A distinctive feature is the way in which the flowerheads are supported by short, leafy branchlets. Lake shores in central Nebraska. H to 90cm (36in), F2.5cm (1in).

Aster prenanthoides Muhl. (1804) Crooked-stem aster

Sturdy sprays, with stems that often zigzag, have upright, open branches. In late summer and early autumn they produce heads with 20-30 pale violet or white rays and yellow disc florets, turning purple. The leaves are thin, ovate to lanceolate, serrated, light green and the clumps strong and creeping. One of the more attractive and compact-growing species when cultivated in gardens. Moist soil in Massachusetts to Minnesota, Virginia, Kentucky and Iowa. Hardy to Z4. H to 90cm (36in), F2.5cm (1in).

Aster pricei Britton. (1901) Miss Price's aster

Widely branched sprays with pubescent stems, bright purple or pink rays, and oblanceolate to linear-lanceolate leaves, up to 5cm (2in) long. Flowers in mid-autumn. Dry soil in Kentucky and North Carolina. Hardy to Z3. H30-75cm (12-30in), F2.5cm (1in).

Aster pringlei p.99.

Aster ptarmicoides (Nees.) Torr. & A. Gray (1841)

In late summer and early autumn, bears flowerheads with 10-20 white or creamy white rays and creamy white or very pale yellow discs. Sprays are thin and rigid with short, stiff branches towards the top. The leaves, up to 20cm (8in) long, are linear-oblanceolate, firm and bright green, and the clumps are small. Dry or rocky soil in Massachusetts, Vermont and Ontario to Saskatchewan, Illinois, Missouri and Colorado. Hardy to Z3. H40-70cm (16-28in), F2cm (¾in).

A thoroughly desirable and compact plant for rock gardens, well-drained small borders and containers. The form **'Major'** has slightly larger flowerheads and only grows to 20cm (8in) but is somewhat less graceful than the taller forms. **'Rosea'**, with pink-flushed rays, H about 20cm (8in), was introduced by Amos Perry in 1936 but seems to have been lost. The cultivar **'Summer Snow'**, flowering from midsummer and H45cm (18in), is recorded as being raised by T. Huber as recently as 1987. There is no trace of it being offered commercially.

Aster puniceus L. (1753) Red-stalk aster, Purple-stem aster

In late summer and early autumn, this species produces flowerheads with 20-40 violet, purple-blue, rarely purple-pink or white, rays and small yellow disc florets. The sprays are strong with open branches and noticeably hairy, purple-red stems. Rich green leaves, up to 16cm (6in) long, are oblong-lanceolate, broad and rather coarse. Clumps are vigorous. A variable species. Swamps in Newfoundland to Ontario, Manitoba, Minnesota, Georgia, Tennessee, Ohio and Michigan. Hardy to Z3. H1.2-1.5m (4-5ft), F3-4cm (1¼-1½in).

When cultivated in moderately wet or even boggy summer conditions, A. puniceus is a handsome plant with an abundance of lush, brightly coloured foliage and stems, standing robustly upright and needing minimal support. The flowerheads are freely produced, towards the tips of the branches on large sprays. Although large, they are something of a disappointment in that the rays invariably curl up, giving the appearance of 'going over' for several weeks.

The nineteenth century variety **'Lucidulus'** had very pale rays and neater foliage but grew to 1.65m (5½ft). Also from that era was **'Pulcherrimus'** with flowerheads of 4cm (1½in) and white rays, lightly flushed violet and attractively twisted. This bloomed later – from mid-autumn. **'Sulphurea'** raised by Amos Perry in 1922 was said to have soft-yellow rays.

Aster purpuratus Nees. (1832) Southern smooth aster

Slender sprays, branched into loose panicles bearing flowerheads with 5-10 blue or violet rays in early autumn, and linear-lanceolate leaves, 5-15cm (2-6in) long. Virginia and West Virginia to Georgia and Texas. Hardy to Z4. H to 90cm (36in), F2cm (¾in).

Aster pyrenaeus Desfontaines ex DC. (1805)

From late summer to mid-autumn, sturdy sprays with spreading branches produce flowerheads with 20-30 lilac-blue rays and pale yellow disc florets. Leaves oblong-lanceolate and clumps strong and compact. Well-drained soil in Europe – E. and W. Pyrenees. Hardy to Z6. H60-90cm (24-36in), F4cm (1½in).

'Lutetia' (Cayeaux 1912), the cultivar available commercially, has been variously catalogued as A. amellus and A. × frikartii. It certainly displays the desirable trait of hybrid vigour and might well be associated with the former species. There is also a reference to a hybrid with A. thomsonii, which might account for the A. × frikartii listing. The flowerheads, with palest lilac-blue rays, are extremely freely borne on well-branched, arching sprays. These rise from vigorous yet tight, woody clumps, enabling one plant to cover more than a metre (yd) of ground. The flowering season is early and mid-autumn. Given good weather during the latter period, my specimens have even provided some colour in late autumn. A sunny position seems to be essential and good winter drainage is another prime ingredient for success. Alkaline soils give better results than those with a low pH value.

Maintenance could not be much easier, since it is only necessary to split the clumps every third or fourth year and staking positively spoils its looks. It is also completely resistant to mildew. So why is this marvellous plant not in every garden worthy of the name? True, many gardeners regard the colour as little more than 'washy', but this is not really important when plantings are associated with other flowers. For instance, I have had great success with growing *Nerine bowdenii* through it. Another colourful factor is the amount of late butterflies attracted to the generous supply of flowerheads.

Aster radula Aiton (1789) Low rough aster, File-blade aster
Sturdy sprays with upright branches towards the top bear heads with 20-30 bright violet rays and yellow disc florets, in late summer. Mid-green, oblong-lanceolate leaves are 5-8cm (2-3in) long, the upper surface rough. Clumps are vigorous. Swamps and moist soil in Newfoundland to Delaware, Pennsylvania, Maryland and West Virginia. Hardy to Z5. H to 60cm (24in), F2-4cm (¾-1½in).

Differs from *A. × commixtus* in starting to flower some weeks earlier and being much more compact and bushy. Also the clumps are more densely packed with shoots and less woody. This most desirable species, which is resistant to mildew and requires no support, brings a cheerful mound of blue to perennial borders at a time when yellow flowers begin to dominate the scene. It associates well in mixed plantings with coreopsis and rudbeckia.

Aster reevesii (A. Gray) Bergmans. Reeves aster
In early autumn, flowerheads with white rays and yellow disc florets are carried on sturdy sprays with slender, leafy branches forming a small pyramid above small clumps. Small linear-lanceolate leaves are up to 6cm (2½in) long. Probably a form of *A. ericoides*, the plant is described in Ranson's *Michaelmas Daisies and other Garden Asters*, and mentioned here because of

The delicately coloured flowerheads of *A. pyrenaeus* 'Lutetia' last for many weeks through the autumn.

its apparent compactness. Said to need well-drained soil and a sunny position. Hardy to Z3. H20-30cm (8-12in), F15mm (½in).

Aster retroflexus Lindl. (*A. curtisii* Torr. & A. Gray 1892)
Flowerheads with purple-blue rays and pale yellow disc florets are borne on strong sprays, with branches forming an open spire, in late summer and early autumn. Leaves linear-lanceolate and clumps compact. Mountains in North Carolina, Georgia and Tennessee. Hardy to Z5. H1m (40in), F2cm (¾in).

Aster roscidus Burgess. ex Britton & A. Brown (1898) Dew-leaf aster
Heads of 14-16 broad, clear violet rays and yellow discs, soon turning red, are borne on sprays that are branched at the top, in late summer. Leaves are cordate to orbicular, up to 13cm (5in) long, glandular, scented when young. The clumps are very leafy. Slight shade in good

soil; Maine to Pennsylvania and Michigan. Hardy to Z4. H to 90cm (36in), F about 2.5cm (1in).

Aster sagittifolius Willd. (1804) (*A. cordifolius* subsp. *sagittifolius*) Arrow-leaved aster
From early to mid-autumn, strong, wiry sprays with upright branches forming a long, open spire, bear heads of small pale yellow disc florets and 10-15 pale violet, pale purple-blue or white rays. The stems are noticeably purple tinted. Thin leaves; lower ones heart- or arrow-shaped, ovate-lanceolate, upper ones lanceolate. Strong clumps. Dry soil in New Brunswick to Ontario, North Dakota, New Jersey, Georgia and Missouri. Hardy to Z3. H to 1.5m (5ft), F2cm (¾in).

Aster salicifolius Lam. (1783) Willow aster
This species flowers in mid- to late autumn, producing heads with violet, purple-blue or white rays and yellow discs on bushy-branched, strong, slender sprays. The firm, bright green leaves are lanceolate or linear-lanceolate in vigorous, spreading clumps. Moist soil from Maine to Massachusetts, Florida, Ontario, Texas and Colorado. Hardy to Z4. H60-150cm (24-60in), F2cm (¾in).

Closely allied to *A. lanceolatus* and equally well suited for late colour in the more untamed areas of the garden. It is sad that the cultivar 'Tresserve' is no longer available. This was said to have heads of more than 3cm (1¼in) diameter with pale purple-pink rays and bushy growth only 45cm (18in) high. In addition, the flowering season extended well into late autumn.

Aster × salignus Willd. (*A. lanceolatus* × *A. novi-belgii*)
Spreading clumps, with ovate-lanceolate to linear-lanceolate leaves, produce strong sprays of short, upright, open branches. Flowerheads have very pale violet-blue rays and pale yellow disc florets. An escapee of garden origin and now widely naturalized, especially in N. and central Europe. Hardy to Z3. H to 1.2m (4ft), F2.5cm (1in).

Drifts enliven many a railway journey made in mid- and late autumn in Britain. Quite variable; some forms might be worth returning to wilder areas of the garden.

Aster scaber Thunb.
White ray florets, strong sprays, branched at the top into a loose corymb and deep green cordate to ovate-deltoid leaves in strong clumps. Woodland and thickets in hills; Hokkaido, Honshu and Kyushu in Japan, Korea, Manchuria and China. Hardy to Z7. H to 1.5m (5ft), F to 2.5cm (1in).

Aster schreberi Nees. (1818) Schreber's aster
In late summer and early autumn, sturdy, arching flowering sprays, with short branches towards the top, produce widely spaced flowerheads with about 10 white rays and yellow disc florets, quickly turning brown. Pale green leaves, somewhat rough, are thin, broad and cordate at the base; upper ones are ovate-oblong to lanceolate. Clumps strong, spreading. Edges of woods and other partially shaded areas in New York to Michigan and Virginia. Hardy to Z3. H60-90cm (24-36in), F3.2cm (1⅛in).

Close in habit to *A. macrophyllus* but the flowering sprays are more lax and the leaves paler green. Although not a show-stopper, this species is useful among shrubs or in shaded areas where the quiet overall effect is welcome.

Aster sedifolius L. (*A. acris*)
Flowerheads with about 8-12 lavender-blue, pale purple-pink or white rays and small, pale yellow discs are borne on sturdy sprays, with much-divided, wiry, upright branches, from the beginning of late summer well into early autumn. Narrow, linear to broadly lanceolate or elliptic leaves are blue-green and up to 8cm (3in) long. Clumps strong. Well-drained soil; S. and E. central Europe, E. Europe and N. Asia. Hardy to Z6. H to 1.2m (4ft) – usually 60-80cm (24-32in), F to 3.5cm (1⅜in).

Cultivated in the British Isles for 250 years and still not seen in every garden! True, the individual flowerheads have thinly spaced rays and are nothing to write home about, but when gathered together in their hundreds in a broad, flat-topped spray, the effect is nothing short of spectacular. There is also the bonus of an easily discernible, melliferous fragrance – a benefit neglected by most other asters. Other bonus points are earned by not succumbing to mildew and happily growing into a larger clump year by year without the need for constant division. On the down side, the flowering sprays do become much too heavy for their supporting stems, especially in wet weather, and some discreet form of staking is called for. However, this task can be avoided in two ways – either set your group of *A. sedifolius* in the border so that its sprays can lean against such stalwart plants as *Sedum* 'Herbstfreude' ('Autumn Joy'), or, in suitable parts of the garden, simply let nature take its own course and allow the flowering sprays to sprawl. I did this once and pushed the stems around to allow clumps of *Sedum spectabile* and *Inula ensifolia* to poke through them. The leafy centres of the aster clumps were partially screened by some arching, un-staked sprays of *A. × frikartii* 'Mönch'. Looking at this small list of companion plants you can deduce that *A. sedifolius* enjoys a sunny, well-drained spot. However, plants will flourish in partial shade if the area does not become too soggy in the winter months.

'Nanus' (photograph p.140) is a compact form with lavender-blue rays. H about 45cm (18in) – an early description put the height at no more than 30cm (12in). 'Roseus' with pale purple-pink rays is a plant I have yet to see although a French nursery are listing a cultivar called 'Rosenkissen'. 'Mrs Berkeley' was being grown in Britain in 1920 and had larger than average heads, bearing crisp white rays. 'Golden Star', raised before 1910, was said to have very small, white rays and prominent golden disc florets. H to 90cm (36in) tall. A number of other cultivars, including 'Antiope', 'Cassiope', 'Elfin', 'Fairy' and 'Lovely', have been recorded. It seems a pity that some enterprising plant breeder has not yet sought to create a new range of cultivars of this reliable species that would appeal to modern plant buyers.

subsp. *canus* ((Waldst. & Kit.) Merxm.) is sometimes dignified as a distinct species with pale lavender rays and yellow disc florets in late summer. The flowering sprays are wiry with a few short branches towards the top. Leaves are grey-green with cobwebby, white hairs. Moors and heathlands in Hungary and Austria. H75cm (30in), F to 2cm (¾in).

Aster sericeus Vent. (1800) Western silvery aster
Slender sprays, with short branches towards the top, carry flowerheads in a flat-topped panicle in late summer to early autumn. The heads have 15-25 purple-blue to rosy-purple or white rays. The silvery, silky leaves are oblong-lanceolate, lanceolate to oblong or elliptic and upward-facing; the clumps are small and woody. Dry open places; Illinois to Minnesota, Manitoba, South Dakota, Tennessee, Missouri and Texas. Hardy to Z4. H30-60cm (12-24in), F2.5cm (1in).

Aster shortii Lindl. (Hook.) (1834) Short's aster
In early to mid-autumn, flowerheads with 10-15 purple-blue, sometimes pinkish or white rays and pale yellow discs are carried on wiry sprays with slender branches forming a panicle. Thick leaves are narrowly ovate to lanceolate and the compact clumps are woody.

Edges of woods and banks; Pennsylvania to Virginia, Georgia, Illinois, Wisconsin and Tennessee. Hardy to Z4. H60-120cm (24-48in), F2.5cm (1in).

This is a species that is capable of making a good display when cultivated and deserves to be more often seen in gardens.

Aster sibiricus L. Arctic aster
Numerous sprays, branched into a low mound, bear heads, with 15-30 pale violet-blue rays, singly or in loose corymbs in late summer. Leaves ovate-lanceolate to oblong, firm, mid-green; clumps spreading. Banks of streams and rivers in mountains in N. Russia, parts of Norway, Siberia and E. Asia and far N.W. North America. This is a quiet little plant that will bring some interest to rock gardens at the end of the summer and is one of the few species to inhabit both the Old and the New World. Hardy to Z3. H15-40cm (6-16in), F2.5cm (1in).

A. sedifolius, shown here with *Sedum* 'Herbstfreude', is well-suited for a summer display in mixed borders.

A. *sedifolius* 'Nanus' (p.139) produces huge numbers of lavender-blue stars on compact plants.

Aster sikkimensis Hook.

Numerous heads with blue rays are borne on erect sprays, branching into large corymbs. The stems are purple-brown and the leaves lanceolate, entire or sub-serrate. An attractive plant which deserves to be more widely planted in gardens. Himalaya. Hardy to Z6. H1.2m (4ft), F2cm (¾in).

Aster spathulifolius Maxim.

Blue-purple rays and pale yellow discs are carried in solitary heads on long branchlets on sturdy sprays, branched from the base; late summer to mid-autumn. Leaves at base are 3-9cm (1¼-3½in) long and 1.5-5.5cm (½-2¼in) wide, thick, obovate or orbicular and densely hairy; upper leaves spathulate, up to 1.5cm (½in) long. Clumps small and woody. Listed by a few growers and worth trying on rock gardens. Rocky places near seashores, Japan – Honshu, Kyushu and Korea. Hardy to Z4. H25cm (10in), F3.5-4cm (1½in).

Aster spectabilis Ait. (1789). Low showy aster, Seaside purple aster

In late summer to early autumn, stiff sprays, with few short branches, bear heads with 15-30 bright purple-blue rays and pale yellow discs. Thin, spreading clumps have firm, dull green leaves up to 15cm (6in) long and 3cm (1¼in) wide; lower leaves are oval, upper ones are linear-oblong. Dry, sand soil, pine barrens near coast; Massachusetts to Delaware. Hardy to Z3. H15-60cm (6-24in), F3.2cm (1½in).

The individual flowerheads are very reminiscent of A. *amellus* but they are not carried in such large numbers on the leafy sprays, which rise rather sparsely from a weak clump. I have achieved some success when growing this species in the same bed as A. *amellus* cultivars and in light soil among roses. It is not susceptible to mildew. Plants must be divided every second year and replanted into 'freshened' soil. Quite effective on a rock garden.

Aster subspicatus Nees. (A. *douglasii* Lindl.)

Heads with violet rays and yellow discs open on slender

sprays with upright branches in late summer and early autumn. The lanceolate leaves are up to 12.5cm (5in) long; the clumps are compact. California to Alaska and E. Montana. Hardy to Z2. H1m (40in), F3.2cm (1½in).

Aster surculosus Michx. (1803) Creeping aster
Slender sprays, with few if any branches, bear heads with 15-30 violet rays in early autumn. Firm, lanceolate or linear leaves, 5-7.5cm (2-3in) long. Sandy or gravel soils in Kentucky, North Carolina and Georgia. Hardy to Z3. H25-45cm (10-18in), F2cm (¾in).

Aster tanacetifolius H.B. & K. (1851) Tansy-leaf aster
An annual species, sometimes included in the genus *Machaeranthera*. It has much-branched sprays with heads of 15-25 violet-purple rays and pinnate to entire leaves. S.W. USA. Hardy to Z8. H30-60cm (12-24in), F2.5-5cm (1-2in).

Aster tardiflorus L. (1763) Northeastern aster
Branched into corymbs near the top, the sprays carry heads with 20-30 violet rays, from early to mid-autumn. The leaves are lanceolate, oblong-lanceolate or ovate-lanceolate, serrate, 7.5-15cm (3-6in) long. Beside streams in New Brunswick to Pennsylvania. Hardy to Z4. H to 90cm (36in), F2.5cm (1in).

Aster tataricus L. f.
Hairy-stemmed sprays have short branches at the top forming a corymb that carries heads with 15-20 violet or purple rays and yellow disc florets in mid- to late autumn. Coarse, pale green leaves, up to 50cm (20in) long, are elliptic, dentate in vigorous clumps. Wet places in N., N.E. and N.W. China, Korea, Japan and E. Siberia. Hardy to Z3. H to 2m (6½ft), F3.5cm (1½in).

The leaves are some of the largest to found in the genus and can be decorative in wild areas of the garden. The flowering season tends to be so late that bad weather can damage the heads; however, sprays will open and last well in water if cut and taken inside. A selection called **'Jindai'**, H to 1.5m (5ft), is offered.

Aster tenebrosus Burgess. Long-leaved wood-aster
In late summer, few sprays, branched into a broad corymb, bear heads with white rays and pale yellow discs, becoming purple-brown. Very thin and smooth leaves are broadly oblong and coarsely toothed, up to 10cm (4in) long. Moist, shaded woods in New York to Virginia. Hardy to Z4. H90cm (36in), F3cm (1¼in).

Aster tenuifolius L. (1753) Perennial salt-marsh aster
Pale purple or white ray florets are borne in solitary heads on sparsely branched sprays in early to mid-

autumn. The stems are glabrous and fleshy with linear to lanceolate leaves 5-15cm (2-6in) long; branches have tiny leaves. Salt marshes on the coast of Massachusetts to Florida. Hardy to Z3. H30-60cm (12-24in), F2.5cm (1in).

Aster thomsonii C.B. Clarke ♔
Around 20 lavender-blue rays and yellow discs are borne in heads on wiry sprays with slender branches from midsummer to mid-autumn. Hairy stems and ovate to elliptic, pale green leaves, rough to touch and up to 10cm (4in) long, are produced in small clumps. Well-drained soil, edges of woods in W. Himalaya, Pakistan and Uttar Pradesh. Hardy to Z7. H90cm (36in), F to 5cm (2in).

The first aster to gain an AGM and now, it seems, only available in its compact form **'Nanus'**. This charming plant has similar characteristics but is only 30cm (12in) high, making it eminently suitable for growing in small borders, raised beds, rock gardens and, also, in containers. A sunny position is usually recommended however, I have had great success with a group planted in a raised bed where they get a little shade for two or three hours in the middle of the day. Whatever the site, good winter drainage is a must. I once used generous quantities of gritty sand to make up a bed surrounding a shrub rose ('Barrone Prevost') and had glorious displays of 'Nanus' for about five years until an exceptionally severe and prolonged frosty spell was followed by lots of wet weather towards the end of the winter.

Another danger to be guarded against, with this aster more than most, is slugs and snails. A good quantity of small, succulent shoots are produced in tight, little clumps and, in much the same way as campanulas, seem to attract these slimy pests from other areas of the garden. I am careful to keep some stock plants potted and tucked safely into a frame for the winter months. It is one insurance policy well worth the cost to preserve such a lovely plant with a flowering season to outstrip most other herbaceous perennials. There are no problems with mildew and stakes are quite unnecessary. Clumps should be divided every two or three years to keep them vigorous. This must only be done in spring, just as the shoots are starting to move. It can be a tricky job which needs to be carried out on a bench with the aid of a good knife. The best method of increasing one's stock is by taking softwood cuttings later in the spring and rooting them in a mist unit. Virtually a hundred per cent will root, but they will need some care to bring them through their first winter, under cover.

Two cultivars have been recorded: **'Robinsonii'** was said to have pale blue flowers, larger than the typical plant. H to 60cm (24in); and **'Winchmore Hill'** is described as 'forming an erect, spreading bush, 75cm (30in) in height and 90cm (36in) and more across, blooming July to late autumn, a lovely shade of soft blue'. A hybrid between *A. thomsonii* and *A. amellus* produced the well-loved *A. × frikartii* cultivars (see p.119).

Aster tradescantii L. (1753) Tradescant's aster, Michaelmas daisy

Flowering from late mid-autumn into late autumn, this species has strong sprays, with upright, slender branches from the leaf axils, forming a graceful panicle of heads with white rays and yellow discs. Leaves bright green, linear-lanceolate or lanceolate, 7.5-15cm (3-6in) to 15cm (6in) long; clumps vigorous, spreading. Fields and swamps, shores in Quebec, Michigan, New York, Maine to Virginia, Ontario, Illinois and Missouri. Hardy to Z4. H60-150cm (24-60in), F to 15mm (½in).

So many species have been mistakenly sold for *A. tradescantii* over the years that it is not surprising to find considerable doubt as to the true identity of the first aster to reach England from the New World. Some authorities consign the 1753 version to *A. lateriflorus* but the above description is not recognizable as *A. lateriflorus*. There is a distinct possibility that what we are talking about here is a garden form belonging to *A. lanceolatus*. This latter is certainly more in keeping with a love of moist soil. Whatever the botanical truth, I grow two versions of Tradescant's aster and neither of them closely resembles any other asters in the collection. My original plant grows to 1.5m (5ft) and, although in no way striking, can always be relied upon for some late autumn flowers. The more recent addition is only about 80cm (32in) high and has much narrower leaves, up to 10cm (4in) long, of a rather more intense green. Both will survive in ordinary, moderately dry soil conditions, but give them summer moisture and their display will be lifted above the indifferent.

Aster trinervius Roxb. ex. D. Don.

White rays and yellow disc florets are produced in heads on wiry, slender- and open-branched sprays in mid-autumn. Leaves lanceolate to elliptic, dentate in vigorous, spreading clumps. W. Nepal to S.W. China and Japan. Hardy to Z7. H to 1m (40in), F to 2cm (¾in).

subsp. *ageratoides* var. *microcephalus* ((Miq.) Mac.) has heads with pale violet-blue rays on sturdy sprays with open branches towards the top; mid- to late autumn. Leaves linear, dentate, 3.5-6cm (1½-2½in) long, deep green. Japan. H to 40cm (16in), F2cm (¾in).

var. *harae* (Makino) has purple-blue rays, strong, slender sprays with short, open branches, purple-tinted stems and linear-lanceolate or lanceolate leaves and flowers mid- to late autumn. Japan. H70cm (28in), F2.5cm (1in).

Much botanical confusion surrounds these oriental asters. They are variously included in *A. ageratoides* and *A. trinervius*, and *The Flora of Japan* lists over 40 varieties, subspecies and forms. It would take an ardent enthusiast to claim that the individual heads have any great attraction and a lot of gardeners have difficulty in appreciating the beauty in a clump of sprays. For my part, I am prepared to see beauty in any plant that has the courage to produce blooms at the end of late autumn in Herefordshire. They certainly last well as cut flowers and probably deserve to be developed for this specific use. I have grown plants from spring cuttings which bloomed beautifully at Christmas in a greenhouse kept just frost free. There should be no problems with mildew and virtually no stakes are needed. A number of cultivars, usually listed under *A. ageratoides*, are coming onto the market and look promising for wild areas of the garden. **'Asran'** bears narrow, open-spaced rays of pale violet-blue through mid-autumn. H to 70cm (28in), F3.8cm (1½in).

Aster tripolium L. Sea aster

A short-lived or annual species, producing sturdy sprays, with erect branches towards the top, bearing heads with lavender to violet rays and yellow disc florets from late summer to mid-autumn. Leaves rather fleshy, linear-lanceolate to linear in small clumps. Salt marshes, estuaries and coasts, Japan, Korea, N. China, Manchuria, E. Siberia, Europe (including British Isles) and N. Africa. Hardy to Z6. H to 60cm (24in), F to 3.2cm (1½in).

Unless you have a muddy, salty, coastal garden, this

may not be the plant for you. This short-lived or annual species further exemplifies the extensive range of conditions in which native asters can be found.

Aster turbinellus Lindl. (1835) Prairie aster
Flowering in mid-autumn, this species produces sturdy sprays with wiry, open branches bearing heads with 10-20 pale violet-blue rays and yellow disc florets. Stems are smooth and purple-tinted and the oblong-lanceolate to lanceolate leaves, 5-8cm (2-3in) long, are pale blue-green, smooth and firm. Clumps compact. In dry soil, especially on prairies, in Illinois to Missouri, Nebraska, Kansas, Louisiana and Arkansas. Hardy to Z5. H60-100cm (24-40in), F2.5cm (1in).

Much confusion reigns as to the true identity of this species. I am quite satisfied that the description above, as given in Britton and Brown (see Reading About Asters, p.155), fits the plant that has been cultivated since the nineteenth century (along with a white and a pink-tinted form, neither of which seems to be available now). However, there is another plant, which received an AGM; it came to me as a hybrid of A. turbinellus and its characteristics, including vigour, seem appropriate to that status. One school of thought believes that the true species is not being cultivated and both plants are usurpers to the title. From the gardeners' point of view, we have two totally different plants, both of considerable merit, whatever the nomenclature experts decide.

The plant described above is useful in mixed borders and for cutting. It grows 1-1.2m (40-48in) in cultivation with very distinctive foliage, and its flowering sprays are formed into graceful, open-branched panicles, bearing 1-2 heads at the ends of short branchlets, notable for having many small bractlets. Mildew is rarely a problem and the clumps can be left for three or more years before being divided. It grows well under a variety of soil conditions and is certainly tolerant of drought. However, like many such plants, the best results come from fertile soil, good cultivation and good winter drainage. Staking is usually not required.

The plant that received the AGM is of unknown origin; I have no better name for it than **A. turbinellus Hybrid**. This grows to 1.2-1.5m (48-60in) with flowerheads up to 3.2cm (1½in); each has 20-30 bright violet-blue rays. They are borne singly at the tips of thin branchlets on strong sprays with many wiry branches. Deep rich glossy green leaves are linear-lanceolate and

stems are tinted purple-brown. Clumps are strong and tightly packed with shoots. There can be no doubt that this is the more colourful plant and it still retains a graceful habit of growth, although its additional vigour results in the production of more flowering sprays in a denser grouping, so some support is advisable. I have noticed a considerable amount of foliage discoloration if plants are subjected to very dry conditions in summer conditions. It is also possible for mildew to attack the leaves. The best results will be obtained from plants grown in the same way as the cultivars of A. novi-belgii (see p.32).

Aster umbellatus Mill. (1768) Flat-topped white aster
White rays, up to 15 in a head are slightly reflexed; the disc florets are yellow. They are borne from late summer on strong sprays with short, upright branches forming a broad, flat-topped umbel. Leaves, up to 16cm (6½in) long, are broadly lanceolate, mid-green and rough. Clumps vigorous with strong, spreading shoots. Moist soil on woodland edges and thickets in Newfoundland to Minnesota and S. to Georgia and Kentucky. Hardy to Z3. H to 2m (6½ft), usually less in cultivation, F2cm (¾in).

A wonderfully stately plant that looks so unlike most other asters that botanists once assigned it to the genus *Doellingeria*. The earliness of the flowering period means that it is not an ideal companion for the later-flowering asters and makes a happier association with the many other herbaceous perennials still at their best through late summer. The umbels make a decorative feature after the ray florets have faded and the discs have expanded into fluffy seedheads with a slightly silvery sheen. Gertrude Jekyll was the first garden designer to make use of generous groups of this species.

I have never seen a hint of mildew on it and consider preventive spraying to be quite unnecessary. The height of most cultivated plants seems to be around 1.2-1.5m (4-5ft) but the sprays are so strong that support is not needed on any but the most exposed sites. It is best not to divide the woody-centred clumps too frequently. The strong shoots which spread widely are not as numerous as with many other asters and are inclined to break off, without any roots attached, when disturbed. The tips of these shoots root reasonably well if the cuttings are taken early and the knife is used below ground level through a white-coloured section of the shoot.

Aster undulatus L. (1753) Wavy-leaf aster
Sturdy sprays, with upright branches forming stiff pyramids, bear flowerheads with 15 pale lavender to violet rays, reflexed as they mature, and deep yellow disc florets, through early autumn. Strong clumps have hairy stems and thick and rough, lanceolate-ovate to ovate leaves with wavy edges. This species can flourish in partial shade when growing in a light, humus-rich soil. Found in dry woods and clearings; New Brunswick and Ontario to Minnesota, Florida, Alabama, Louisiana and Arkansas. Hardy to Z5. H30-120cm (12-48in), F2.5cm (1in).

Aster × versicolor see p.75.

Aster vimineus Lam. (1783) Small white aster
Flowering in early to mid-autumn, this species has narrow sprays with many short branches. The 15-30 rays are white and the discs are golden-yellow discs. Linear-lanceolate leaves, up to 10cm (4in) long, mostly much smaller, are green to grey-green. Clumps strong, compact. Moist soil; Ontario to Florida, W. to Minnesota and Arkansas. Hardy to Z5. H60-120cm (24-48in), F10-15mm (½in).

This species is often included with *A. lateriflorus* or said to be synonymous with *A. fragilis* (Willd.); another indication of just how difficult it is positively to identify many of the aster species. I grow three distinct forms which differ mostly in height and leaf colour and share common features such as rather crowded, little flowerheads, massed on graceful sprays, with feathery foliage.

A. Perry's catalogue of 1910 lists no less than eight cultivars, including such delights as 'Cassiope', 'Orphir' and 'Prince Charming'. A footnote to the catalogue page states: 'the vimineus group contains the most fairy-like blossoms imaginable, small flowers densely set on waving stems and, either for decoration or cutting, invaluable.' Also around 1910, Mr. H.J. Jones raised and introduced, through his Lewisham nursery, a cultivar called 'Golden Rain' with creamy-white ray florets and deep yellow discs. H only 45cm (18in). Cultivars with pinkish or pale violet rays have also been recorded.

There should be no problems with mildew, and clumps of *A. vimineus* can be divided into smaller sections about every third year. The taller forms need some support to prevent rain damage. Good for borders, cutting and large containers.

Aster violaris Burgess. ex Britton & A. Brown (1898) Violet-leaf aster
Slender, erect sprays, with slender branches virtually forming an umbel, bear heads with 12-15 narrow, pale violet ray florets in early to mid-autumn. Leaves broadly oval, thin, firm and bluish-green. Shaded, moist areas, sometimes among rocks in New York, from the Hudson to Lake Erie. Hardy to Z4. H to 60cm (24in), F2cm (¾in).

× Solidaster luteus Wehrh. (*Aster × Solidago*)
In late summer, sturdy sprays, with short, upright branches forming a dense, flat-topped panicle, bear flowerheads with lemon-yellow rays and golden-yellow disc florets. Leaves up to 15cm (6in) long, are narrow, lanceolate to linear-elliptic and the clumps are small and inclined to be weak. Garden origin. Hardy to Z5. H to 75cm (30in), F10mm (½in).

This attractive plant was discovered around 1910 in the nurseries of Leonard Lille near Lyon in France. It is assumed to be a natural, bi-generic hybrid between *A. ptarmicoides* and an unknown *Solidago* species. A form of *A. ptarmicoides*, which produces flowerheads with soft yellow rays, was discovered in Saskatchewan towards the end of the nineteenth century and named 'Lutescens'. This might also be a hybrid with a *Solidago* species.

The pleasing yellow and greenish colour of the heads of × *Solidaster luteus* makes it easy to mix with most other late-summer flowers, and the compact stature of the plant is also invaluable. Cut-flower production is a major commercial use for the various × *Solidaster* cultivars and forms.

Good, fertile soil, which drains well in the winter months, is essential if the modest clumps of shoots are still going to be there in the spring. Slugs and snails must also be guarded against. In spite of their slow rate of increase, the clumps must be divided each spring to encourage new growth. Tip-cuttings, rooted in spring, give virtually a hundred per cent success and grow on into much better stock for planting up the following spring than could be obtained by division.

× *Solidaster* 'Lemore' ♆ is still often catalogued as a *Solidago*. It is somewhat more vigorous than the earlier hybrid and tends to flower later, into early autumn. One of the most recent cultivars of × *Solidaster* is called 'Super' and is of great value as a commercial cut flower. H to 90cm (36in).

9

ASTERS IN NORTH AMERICA

by Pamela J. Harper

In a poll to determine the bestselling genera in the USA, which was carried out by the Perennial Plant Association in 1994, asters did not rank in the top twenty. In 1997, nearly a hundred different species could be obtained from mail-order nurseries, but this is only a fraction of the total number of species in what is a predominantly American genus. However, these figures probably understate the popularity of asters – few gardens lack a plant or two – and the present fervour for native plants and naturalistic gardens can only increase their status. Dan Hinkley at Heronswood near Seattle perhaps summed up the attitude towards asters when he said: 'The plants sell well in a steady sort of way but not overwhelming. By the time they are blossoming in the nursery, many pople have stopped thinking about gardening.'

Plant popularity polls can be misleading: not many nurseries sell more than a handful of different species or cultivars of asters, and what that handful consists of differs markedly from one region to another. There are few, if any, asters that could earn high marks in every region, but there are numerous garden-worthy species for each State. Were the figures aggregated, asters would undoubtedly score higher.

HARDINESS

One of the reasons that different asters are popular in different areas is, of course, climate. American gardeners have not only cold-hardiness to consider but also heat-hardiness. Gardeners everywhere must occasionally contend with summer drought but in some regions of America, summers are always dry, and in many regions they are always unpleasantly hot. This affects flowering time, which differs considerably from one region to another, as also does the length of the bloom period. Late-blooming asters are best where autumns are long and sunny; where cold weather sets in early, they are less successful, though many are somewhat frost-resistant.

It is not, then, remarkable, that no single aster makes the top twenty in every region, rather it is to be marvelled at that any plant is rugged enough to survive a climate where winter lows may drop below –34.5°C (–30°F), protracted highs top 38°C (100°F), and months go by without measurable rain. And many asters do more than survive – they flourish, some with weed-like profligacy by means of seed, running roots, or both. (A word of caution on this point: an aster that is not native to the area in which you wish to grow it is sometimes a better choice than the one that you see locally, flourishing in the rough and tumble of roadside or woodland fringe. When transplanted into the comparative luxury of the garden this will certainly grow taller and may become invasive.)

COLD-HARDY ASTERS

Cold-hardiness has long been evaluated in America, with plants keyed to hardiness zone maps, but with so many variables these serve only as a rough guide. Local input – from horticulutral societies, botanic gardens or enthusiastic gardening friends and neighbours – is best. Some of the most effective asters for cultivation were passed around by generations of gardeners before attracting the attention of nurserymen.

Having carried out its own tests of hardiness, Gardens North, a mail-order nursery in Ontario, Canada, sells seed of three species with a zone 3 rating (winter lows of –40°C (–40°F): *A. alpinus*, *A. amellus*, and *A.*

A. *novi-belgii* 'Professor Anton Kippenberg' (see also p.66) is a reliable dwarf cultivar with a tough constitution.

sibiricus. Other ultra-hardy species include A. *ericoides*, A. *lateriflorus* and A. *macrophyllus*.

As one might expect from a species with a native range that includes Newfoundland, the New York aster, A. *novi-belgii*, is well adapted to cold winters. Where summer heat or drought prevail these shallow-rooting asters are usually short-lived and scarcely justify the effort of applying fungicides, watering and staking (the taller kinds). The need for frequent division is another count against them, and where autumns are long and sunny, nurseries find that asters cannot compete with the chrysanthemums on sale at the same time. An extensive range of A. *novi-belgii* hybrids is offered by nurseries in cool-summer regions, especially the Northeast and the Pacific Northwest. No figures are available but what is seen in gardens, but catalogues suggest that 'Professor Anton Kippenberg' leads the pack with 'Jenny' a close runner-up.

COLD- AND HEAT-HARDY ASTERS

Some asters are very adaptable, coping alike with cold winters and hot summers. Apart from the basic New England aster (A. *novae-angliae*), these include A. *cordifolius*, A. *ericoides*, A. *lateriflorus* and A. *laevis*.

The New England aster does quite well in the south, where other 'yankees' may wilt in the heat, advises one catalogue. New England asters are also less prone to mildew and need less frequent division than New York asters, but they usually need staking, have undistinguished foliage, and flower for a shorter time than such aster-like perennials as *Kalimeris pinnatifida* (syn. *Astermoea mongolica*) and white- or pink-flowered *Boltonia asteroides*, so these are understandably more popular where summer temperatures stay high. Where the growing season starts early and summers are hot, New England asters may flower as early as July. It is customary to shear them, which delays flowering and keeps them more compact. If left to flower and then sheared, they often flower again.

'Andenken an Alma Pötschke' is probably the most widely grown New England aster, admired for its glowing cerise-with-a-hint-of-scarlet colouring and its relatively compact habit. In my coastal garden in Virginia it is matched by a crape myrtle (*Lagerstroemia indica*) called 'Prairie Lace', which flowers at the same time. Violet-blue 'Hella Lacy', introduced by journalist Allen Lacy and named after his wife, has almost ousted the older, similar 'Treasure'. In my garden 'Hella Lacy' attracts more bees and butterflies than any other aster – also, alas, the praying mantis, which sometimes leaves the ground beneath the plants littered with the wings of the butterflies it has devoured. 'Harrington's Pink', found growing wild in Quebec more than 50 years ago, remains in demand but is getting some competition from a recent American introduction, the 90-120cm (36-48in) 'Honeysong Pink', which has brilliant rich pink blooms with lemon-yellow centres.

Though introduced as a selection of New England aster, 'Purple Dome' is more prone to foliar diseases than most of this group. Spotted alongside a road in Pennsylvania by Robert Seip and introduced by the Mount Cuba Center for the Study of Piedmont Flora, its low, dense habit – unusual in New England asters – brought it instant acclaim. In my garden, however, it became diseased in its second year and so was discarded.

The 1.2m (4ft) stems of the popular A. *cordifolius* hybrid 'Little Carlow' need staking if they are to stay upright, but where there is room for it to sprawl, it looks pretty with its billowing mass of blue flowers spread over the ground. Heavy rain at flowering time leaves it looking bedraggled so it isn't at its best where summer storms are frequent.

The self-supporting A. *ericoides* grows wider than high, and looks cloud-like with its tiny leaves and host of flowers in late summer or autumn. Many selections are available, in white, pink, lilac, blue or violet. In the wild, it is found in dry, sunny wasteland. The untamed look of this species makes it well suited to the natural-istic gardens at present in vogue. Those preferring manicured gardens tend to think it weedy.

The longer one gardens, the more one recognizes the importance of good foliage. Good can mean glossy and healthy, delicately fern-like, bold and handsome, coloured grey, chartreuse, purple (brownish), or varie-gated, or simply inconspicuous. A. *lateriflorus* 'Horizon-talis' scores on two counts: its small, neat leaves and their dark coppery-purple colouring, darkest in the form 'Prince'. Dubbed the calico aster, its wide-angled branches are smothered in later summer or early autumn with small pink-eyed, white daisies.

A. *laevis* first came to my attention in the catalogue of Nancy Goodwin's Montrose Nursery. She wrote: 'This plant was found in an old garden near here … It is lovely at all seasons with smooth, blue-green rosettes of leaves with reddish tints throughout the winter and marvellous violet-blue flowers on 5ft stalks in the fall. The leaves appear almost succulent.' Demand for this species rocketed when, in 1995, the Mount Cuba Cen-ter for the Study of the Piedmont Flora introduced A. *laevis* 'Bluebird', which had appeared as a seedling in a Connecticut garden. Tall, dark-stemmed A. *laevis* 'Calliope', which has recently arrived here from Eng-land, is already being acclaimed.

HEAT-HARDY ASTERS

Heat-hardiness evaluations will probably always be tentative. A zone number does not suffice: zone 9 embraces parts of both Florida and Southern Califor-nia but growing conditions in these regions are very different. Plants that thrive in dry heat may rot in humid heat, some cannot endure summer drought, and some need a winter resting period. The Italian

Creating large clumps of colour year in year out, A. 'Little Carlow' (see also p.95) is a first-class, 'no fuss' hybrid.

aster, A. *amellus*, is one of the most drought enduring. Though cold-hardy, it is easier to establish in regions with dry summers and mild winters. 'Rudolph Goethe' is the selection most often grown. In the same regions, the evergreen shrub aster, *Felicia fruticosa* (formerly A. *fruticosus*), can also be seen. This puts on a fine spring to early summer show of lavender daisies in dry, sunny sites, but does not survive winter freezes.

In the Southeast, summers are hot and humid and winters relatively mild. Southern Perennials and Herbs, a nursery in Mississippi, has found that the following species enjoy, or at least put up with, these conditions: A. *adnatus*, A. *azureus*, A. *carolinianus*, A. *concolor*, A. *ericoides*, A. *hemisphaericus*, A. *laevis*, A. *lateriflorus*, A. *linariifolius*, A. *novae-angliae*, A. *oblongifolius*, A. *praealtus*.

'Climax' and 'White Climax', believed to be derived from a native species, possibly A. *laevis*, also put up

Compact, bushy growth and a long flowering season distinguish the sun-loving A. 'Fanny's Aster'.

with these conditions. They make 2m (6ft) pyramids of flower, blue or white respectively, in late summer, and have healthy, mildew-free foliage. Another plus point is that they do not have to be staked, a task the average home owner is unwilling to carry out.

The finest asters for the Southeast's long, sunny autumn days were introduced by the keen-eyed owners of two North Carolina nurseries, both, sadly, now closed. From Nancy Goodwin at Montrose came 'Our Latest One', followed by 'Fanny's Aster' (named by Ruth Knopf after her maid), described as follows in her 1992 catalogue: 'No longer is 'Our Latest One' our latest aster to bloom. We were given this plant from an old garden in South Carolina and simultaneously the same one from Pennsylvania and now we have asters all through November. It is violet-blue, just one shade darker than 'Our Latest One', but in every other way similar.'

Left unsheared, 'Fanny's Aster' reaches about 90cm (36in). I shear mine, sometimes twice, which prevents it sprawling, without destroying its grace. It flourishes in the same sunny corner – in sandy soil with some competition from tree roots – as the button chrysanthemums 'Mei Kyo' (pink), 'Bronze Elegance' and yellow 'Nantyderry Sunshine', for any of which it makes a fine companion. Many other asters with vigorous habits, especially the taller A. novi-belgii cultivars, respond well to shearing in early summer. This can sometimes diminish their susceptibility to powdery mildew and makes them sturdier plants when they come into flower.

To what species 'Our Latest One' and 'Fanny's Aster' belong is still uncertain, but they are very similar to one that flowers a week or two earlier and which was introduced by Allen Bush of Holbrook Farm & Nursery as A. oblongifolius var. angustatus 'Raydon's Favourite'. Raydon was Raydon Alexander of San Antonio, Texas, who had known it for thirty years and called it his favourite aster.

Another introduction by Allen Bush was 'Miss Bessie', spotted by Edith Eddleman in a Louisiana garden, shared by its owner and named after her. Slightly taller than 'Fanny's Aster' and 'Raydon's Favourite', with smaller flowers of a similar violet-blue, this is the very last to flower, often still in bloom at the end of November. Plant it in poor soil to limit its rapid spread.

In 1997 Charles and Martha Oliver of The Primrose Path Nursery in Pennsylvania introduced A. *oblongifolius* 'October Skies', a compact 45cm (18in) form found growing on their land.

No Southeastern garden should be without the climbing aster, Aster *carolinianus*. In the wild it usually inhabits wet ground but this is not essential. Pale violet flowers about 2.5cm (1in) across are of rather ragged form, but what they lack in quality they make up for in quantity, with thousands upon thousands packed into far flung shawls of foliage-obliterating bloom in late October and November. What makes this species unique is its ability to climb. In the wild it clambers over bushes and into trees to heights as much as 4m (12ft). At about 5cm (2in) intervals, stiff 30cm (12in) side branches grow out horizontally, each in a different direction. Once a few of these have lodged themselves across a twig or branch the aster has its scaffolding in place. If the searching stems find no means of support they loll and interlace, piling up branch over branch, much as one might stack sticks when starting a fire, becoming an intricately interwoven, self-supporting structure. It can be trained on a sunny trellis, outhouse, arbour or fence. Stems root where they touch the ground, by which means it steadily extends its terrain.

HEAT AND SHADE

That hostas head the perennials popularity polls is not surprising, given that so many American homes are built on heavily wooded sites. 'What can I grow in the shade?' is a very common question, usually asked in a despairing tone of voice. Where summers are comparatively cool, asters do best in open, sunny sites, but in regions scarcely habitable without air conditioning (would that one could extend this from homes and cars to gardens), a bit of shade in the hottest hours of the day is acceptable to many asters, and preferred by some. Unfortunately, respite from hot sun often comes at the cost of ground moisture lost to the thirsty roots of the trees that cast the shade. Provided the light is good, or can be made so by thinning the trees, the white wood-aster, A. *divaricatus*, tolerates root competition. Indeed, this may be the best place for it, for in conditions that are moister and richer conditions, its self-sown seedings are so abundant, and so widely dispersed, that weeding them out is very time-consuming. Found in dry thin woodland and clearings frm Maine to Alabama, A. *divaricatus* opens its white starry flowers in late summer or autumn, on slender, sometimes zigzag, usually sprawling (not unattractively) wiry stems that in nursery-sold plants are usually dark, though not always so in the wild. Selected forms with larger flowers are occasionally available.

What kinds of trees comprise the woodland in part determines what will grow among them. The dense roots of maples and sweetgums (*Liquidambar*) absorb all available moisture and make it hard for other plants to get a toehold. Oaks and pines are more benign and A. *grandiflorus* can be found growing among them, especially along cleared trails, from Virginia south to Florida. This is a showy species, with 5cm (2in) violet flowers on leafy 60-90cm (24-36in) stems in autumn.

ASTERS IN A RANGE OF SIZES

Asters range in height from dwarfs to giants. The Tatarian or Siberian aster, A. *tataricus*, is the tallest I have seen, quite capable of exceeding 2.5m (8ft) in some American gardens. Shrugging off heat and cold alike, it has long been grown in America but until recently few could identify what it was they were growing. Not an American native, it is often thought to be, having become naturalized in some regions. Butterfly-attracting flowers of pale violet-purple are borne in late summer or autumn atop stout stems that seldom need staking. This is a healthy, easy and desirable aster for the back of the border or in sunny bays among shrubs, with one caveat: dense, weed-suppressing clumps of basal leaves as much as 60cm (24in) long spring from rhizomatous roots that spread quite rapidly in good, moist soil. A. *tataricus* 'Jindai', dubbed the dwarf Tatarian aster (all things being relative) is a 1.2m (4ft) selection with flowers of a slightly brighter purple-blue. It was found in Tokyo's Jindai Park.

At the other extreme come asters suitable for rock gardens, raised beds, or the front of small borders. The annual seed list of the North American Rock Garden

A. × *frikartii* 'Mönch' (see also p.119), America's favourite aster, is highly regarded as an excellent, trouble-free planr.

Society contains a dozen or more dwarf species. Each is keyed by number to the donor of the seed, which is helpful in deducing whether a species not tried before is likely to thrive in one's own locale. Seed of A. *alpinus*, for example, comes from several sources but all in regions with fairly cool summers. Curiously, the two sources for A. *subspicatus*, a West Coast native, are France and Germany.

From his base in South Dakota the late Claude Barr spent much of his life exploring the 'beauties of the plains', and that is the title of his book, published in 1982. One of the Great Plains natives he introduced, *Aster kumleinii* 'Dream of Beauty', is well suited to rock gardens in regions where summers are hot and dry. Flowering in late summer or early autumn, it makes a pretty little mound of pink for a week or two.

Among the best dwarf asters for East Coast gardens is A. *linariifolius*, native over a wide range from Quebec to Florida, usually in dry sandy or rocky sites, and variously known as stiff aster, savoury-leafed aster or pine-starwort. A compact, dainty plant that never engulfs its neighbours, it varies in height from 15-45cm (6-18in). Upright stems clad in mere slivers of leaf, which are bractlike on the upper part of the plant, divide into several stiffly ascending branches, each crowned with a single violet-blue daisy about 2.5cm (1in) across. A. *vimineus* 'Lovely' is suitable for large rock gardens. At about 60cm (24in) it cannot be called a dwarf, but it has an appropriate compact daintiness, with fine-textured foliage and small blue flowers in early autumn.

AMERICA'S FAVOURITE ASTER

It is ironic that, with such a wealth of native species from which to choose, America's favourite aster is the non-native A. × *frikartii*. Poorly adapted to weather extremes, it is seldom long-lived, but it flowers for longer than any other aster and many gardeners are willing to treat it as an annual and replant it every spring. For many years 'Wunder von Stäfa' was the only selection available. 'Mönch' is now more common. Canyon Creek Nursery in California also offers 'Jungfrau', commending it for its compact, more upright habit and deeper-coloured flowers. Though generally considered a tender perennial, A. × *frikartii* has a better chance of winter survival if the temptation to tidy it away in autumn is resisted and it is not cut back until early spring.

As an alternative to A. × *frikartii* I suggest the showy aster, A. *spectabilis*. This is a rhizomatous species found in sandy, acid coastal pinelands from Massachusetts to South Carolina. It makes a more or less evergreen carpet of dark green feathery leaves from which rise 30-45cm (12-18in) branching stems bearing 4cm (1½in) violet-blue flowers for about a month in late August and September. –10°C (15°F) is its probable hardiness limit but it has not been widely tested. It has the same grace and charm as A. × *frikartii* and is much longer-lived.

Great strides have recently been made in studying the riches of America's native flora. This has resulted in many fine asters being brought into our gardens. More are sure to follow.

APPENDICES

Although I have tried to avoid complex terminology in this book, there are some places where, in the interests of accuracy and brevity, it was necessary to use the standard terms applied to plant parts. These are defined here.

Achene A small, dry, hard, non-splitting fruit with one seed.

Alternate Of leaves, arranged singly at different heights on the stem.

Anther The enlarged part of the **stamen**, holding the pollen.

Axil The upper angle where the leaf joins the stem.

Bracts Modified leaves associated with the flower.

Calyx The outer circle of floral leaves (sepals), usually green, sometimes like petals. They may be separate or joined. In asters they are reduced to pappus hairs.

Capitulum see **Head**.

Ciliate Bearing a marginal fringe of fine hairs.

Compound Divided into two or more lesser parts.

Cordate Heart-shaped.

Corolla The coloured inner floral envelope.

Corymb A flat-topped or dome-shaped cluster of flowerheads (flowers).

Cultivar A 'cultivated variety'; a distinct assemblage of plants arising and/or maintained in cultivation which, when reproduced sexually or asexually, retains its distinguishing character. The term is sometimes seen shortened to cv.

Deltoid (**deltate**) Of leaves, shaped like an equilateral triangle and attached to the stem by the broad end.

Dentate Toothed.

Disc The round centre of a flowerhead comprising lots of very small tubular disc **florets** (disc flowers), surrounded by a circle of **ray florets** (ray flowers).

Divaricate Spreading far apart.

Elliptic Widest at or near the middle.

Elongate Lengthened as if stretched or extended.

Entire Describing a leaf without lobes or teeth.

Fertile Able to reproduce sexually: stamens producing viable pollen, fruit bearing seed, and so on.

Floret A very small flower, usually part of a dense **inflorescence**.

Glabrous Without hairs.

Head A crowded cluster of stalkless (or nearly stalkless) flowers.

Hirsute With long coarse or stiff hairs.

Hispid With stiff, bristly hairs.

Hybrid A plant resulting from a cross between different **species**.

Inflorescence The arrangement of the flowers and their associated parts.

Involucre A circle of **bracts** supporting a flower or **inflorescence** (as in Asteraceae).

Lanceolate Lance-shaped: long, widest at the base and tapering to the apex.

Lateral On or to the side.

Ligule In Asteraceae, the strap-shaped limb of a **ray floret**.

Linear Of leaves, long and narrow with parallel veins.

Oblanceolate Inversely **lanceolate**.

Oblong Of leaves, longer than broad, with nearly parallel sides.

Obovate Inversely **ovate**.

Ovate Broadest below the middle.
Panicle An elongated, branched **inflorescence**.
Paniculate Having flowers in **panicles**.
Pappus In Asteraceae, the hairs, bristles or scales at the tip of the **achene**.
Petal One of the segments of the **corolla**, usually coloured.
Pilose With long, soft, straight hairs.
Pistil The central female organ of a flower.
Pubescent With short, soft, downy hairs.
Raceme A simple, elongated **inflorescence**, each flower having its own small stalk.
Ray The flat, strap-shaped blade that encircles the disc florets (as in Asteraceae). Also referred to as ray **floret** or ray flower.
Receptacle The enlarged or elongated end of the stem to which the floral parts are attached.
Recurved Curved downward or backward.
Sagittate Shaped like an arrowhead.
Scabrid/Scabrous Rough to touch.
Serrate Saw toothed (teeth pointing forward).
Sessile Without a stalk.
Simple Of a leaf, not compound.
Spathulate Spatula-shaped. Oblong, tapering narrowly at the base and rounded at the apex.
Stamen The male organ of a flower, comprising filament and **anther**.
Stigma The uppermost part of the **pistil**, which receives the pollen.
Stolon A shoot, at or below the surface of the ground, that produces a new plant at its tip.
Style The slender stalk on the ovary, bearing the **stigma**.
Subulate Awl-shaped, tapering from a narrow base to a fine, sharp point.
Suckering Producing underground stems.
Turbinate Turban- or top-shaped.
Type Of a **species**, the original or 'type' specimen; often indicates the typical form in cultivation.
Umbel An umbrella-like **inflorescence** with all flowerstalks radiating from the same point.
Undulate Of a margin, with a wavy surface.
Verticillate Arranged in a **whorl** or ring.
Villous Shaggily **pubescent**.
Viscid With a sticky or gelatinous covering.
Whorl Three or more leaves (or flowers) radiating from a single point.

APPENDIX 2
ASTERS FOR SPECIAL PURPOSES

These lists of asters for special uses are not intended to be fully comprehensive and are quite simply my suggestions for some of the most suitable plants for particular purposes and a purely esoteric choice in most cases.

Cut flowers
Nearly all cultivars in the A. *novi-belgii*, A. *ericoides*, A. *cordifolius* and allied hybrid groups can be used, but some are more attractive for this purpose than others.

A. *novi-belgii*
white
 'Albanian'
 'Blandie'
pale pink
 'Fellowship'
 'Priory Blush'
 'Timsbury'
deeper pink
 'Autumn Rose'
 'Mary Deane'
 'Sheena'
deep purple-pink
 'Lawrence Chiswell'
 'Margery Bennett'
 'Sophia'
red
 'Coombe Radiance'
 'Guardsman'
 'Helen Ballard'
purple
 'Coombe Rosemary'
 'Pride of Colwall'
 'Thundercloud'
lilac
 'Fair Lady'
 'Sarah Ballard'
 'Schöne von Dietlikon'
blue-purple to violet
 'Davey's True Blue'
 'Gurney Slade'
 'Harrison's Blue'
 'Mary Ann Weil'

blue
 'Anita Ballard'
 'Blue Radiance'
 'Climax'
 'Dauerblau'
 'Madge Cato'
 'Marie Ballard'

A. *amellus*
 'Brilliant'
 'Grunder'
 'Nocturne'
 'Veilchenkönigin'
A. *cordifolius*
 'Chieftain'
 'Elegans'
 'Sweet Lavender'
A. *ericoides*
 'Esther'
 'Pink Cloud'
 'White Heather'
 'Yvette Richardson'
A. × *frikartii*
 'Jungfrau'
A. 'Hon. Vicary Gibbs'
A. *lateriflorus*
 'Lady in Black'
A. 'Little Carlow'
A. 'Ochtendgloren'
A. 'Photograph'
A. *pringlei*
 'Monte Cassino'
A. 'Ringdove'

Asters suitable for moist soils

A. acuminatus
A. curvescens
A. foliaceus
A. junceus
A. lanceolatus
A. modestus
A. multiformis
A. novi-belgii cultivars
A. paludosus
A. phyllodes
A. prenanthoides
A. puniceus
A. radula
A. salicifolius
A. tataricus
A. tenuifolius

Asters suitable for dry soils

A. amellus cultivars
A. commixtus
A. concolor
A. drummondii
A. dumosus
A. ericoides
A. fendleri
A. × frikartii cultivars
A. gracilis
A. grandiflorus
A. hemisphericus
A. laevis
A. lateriflorus
A. linosyris
A. macrophyllus
A. multiflorus
A. oblongifolius
A. patens
A. pilosus
A. pricei
A. pringlei
A. ptarmicoides
A. pyrenaeus
A. sagittifolius
A. × salignus
A. sedifolius
A. sericeus
A. 'Snow Flurry'
A. spectabilis
A. surculosus
A. tradescantii
A. trinervius
A. turbinellus
A. versicolor

Asters suitable for containers

A. alpinus and
  cultivars
A. ericoides 'Cinderella',
  'Esther', 'Golden
  Spray', 'Lovely'
A. × frikartii 'Flora's
  Delight', 'Jungfrau'
A. lateriflorus
  'Horizontalis', 'Prince'
A. 'Little Carlow'
A. novi-belgii cultivars
  including 'Chatterbox',
  'Christine Soanes',
  'Chequers', 'Dietgard',
'Dolly', 'Guardsman',
  'Jenny', 'Lady in Blue',
  'Lawrence Chiswell',
  'Lisa Dawn', 'Little
  Pink Lady',
  'Remembrance',
  'Rosebud', 'Trudi Ann'
A. 'Ochtendgloren'
A. 'Photograph'
A. pringlei 'Monte
  Cassino'
A. 'Snow Star'
A. thomsonii 'Nanus'
A. tongolensis cultivars

Asters suitable for rock gardens

A. × alpellus
A. alpinus and cultivars
A. asteroides
A. diplostephioides
A. falconeri
A. foliaceus
A. linariifolius
A. ptarmicoides
A. scopulorum
A. sibiricus
A. 'Snow Flurry'
A. soulei
A. staticefolius
A. stracheyi
A. tongolensis cultivars

Companion plants for asters

Some of the many plants suitable for growing with autumn-flowering asters, particularly cultivars of A. novi-belgii.

Aconitum carmichaelii
Anemone × hybrida
  cultivars
Chrysanthemum rubellum
  cultivars
Coreopsis verticillata
  cultivars
Chrysopsis mariana
Eupatorium maculatum
Eupatorium purpureum
Euphorbia dulcis
  'Chameleon'
Helianthus 'Gullicks
  Variety'
Helianthus 'Lemon
  Queen'
Helianthus 'Monarch'
Helianthus decapetalus
  'Triomphe de Gand'
Heterotheca villosa
Kalimeris 'Shogun'
Leucanthemella serotina
Physalis alkekengi
Physostegia virginiana
  'Variegata'
Rudbeckia fulgida
  cultivars
Rudbeckia subtomentosa
Salvia uliginosa
Sanguisorba canadensis
Schizostylis coccinea
  cultivars
Sedum 'Herbstfreude'
Sedum 'Joyce Henderson'
Sedum 'Morchen'
Solidago caesia
Solidago canadensis
Solidago 'Cloth of
  Gold'
Solidago 'Goldenmosa'
Solidago 'Le Raft'
Solidago rugosa
  'Fireworks'
× Solidaster luteus

APPENDIX 3
A. NOVI-BELGII CULTIVARS WITH CERTAIN ADVANTAGES

Those that can be left undivided for several years

'Autumn Rose'	'Mary Deane'
'Baby Climax'	'Professor Anton
'Bewunderung'	Kippenberg'
'Blue Eyes'	'Queen Mary'
'Blue Danube'	'Richness'
'Bridesmaid'	'St. Egwin'
'Cecily'	'Snowdrift'
'Climax'	'Starlight'
'Erica'	'Sunset'
'Little Boy Blue'	

Those that appear to be less subject to mildew

This mildew-resistance relies on the asters being well-cultivated and not under stress. This is not a list of recommended cultivars, merely those that might be worthwhile trying if mildew cannot be readily prevented by spraying.

'Algar's Pride'	'Lassie'
'Baby Climax'	'Little Boy Blue'
'Blue Eyes'	'Mary Deane'
'Carlingcott'	'Orlando'
'Climax'	'Priory Blush'
'Destiny'	'Remembrance'
'Dietgard'	'Richness'
'Fair Lady'	'Royal Velvet'
'Fellowship'	'Sarah Ballard'
'Gayborder Royal'	'Tapestry'

APPENDIX 4
THE AWARD OF GARDEN MERIT

The Award of Garden Merit (♀) is given by the Royal Horticultural Society to recognize plants of outstanding excellence for garden use, whether grown in the open or under glass. The AGM is of practical value to gardeners in that it highlights exceptional plants among the tens of thousands currently offered in the international horticultural trade.

APPENDIX 5
HARDINESS ZONES

The references to hardiness in this book are based on the following table giving the range of average annual minimum temperature for each climatic zone.

Zone	degrees F	degrees C
1	< -50	< -45.5
2	-50 to -40	-45.5 to -40.1
3	-40 to -30	-40.0 to -34.5
4	-30 to -20	-34.4 to -28.9
5	-20 to -10	-28.8 to -23.4
6	-10 to 0	-23.3 to -17.8
7	0 to + 10	-17.7 to -12.3
8	+10 to +20	-12.2 to -6.7
9	+20 to +30	-6.6 to -1.2
10	+30 to +40	-1.1 to +4.4.
11	< +40	< +4.4.

APPENDIX 6
WHERE TO SEE ASTERS IN THE BRITISH ISLES

The Picton Garden, Walwyn Road, Colwall, Near Malvern, Worcestershire WR13 6QE (NCCPG National Collection of Autumn-flowering Asters)

The National Trust, Upton House, Near Banbury, Oxfordshire OX15 6HT (NCCPG National Collection of *Aster amellus*, *A. cordifolius*, *A. ericoides*)

Temple Newsam Estate (Rose Garden), Leeds LS13 0AD. Correspondence to M. Walker, The Farmhouse, Redhall Lane, Leeds LS17 8NB (NCCPG National Collection of *A. novi-belgii*)

Waterperry Gardens Limited, Waterperry, Near Wheatley, Oxfordshire OX33 1JZ

APPENDIX 7
ASTERS READILY OBTAINABLE IN NORTH AMERICA

A. *acuminatus*

A. *adnatus*

A. 'Alert'

A. *alpigenus* subsp. *haydenii*

A. *alpinus* and 'Albus', 'Happy End', 'Dunkle Schöne'

A. *amellus* and 'Rudolph Goethe'

A. *anomalus*

A. *azureus*

A. *bellidiastrum*

A. *bigelovii*

A. 'Bill's Big Blue'

A. 'Climax'

A. *carolinianus*

A. *chilensis*

A. *coloradensis*

A. *concolor*

A. *cordifolius* and 'Aldebaran', 'Elegans', 'Sweet Lavender'

A. *curtisii*

A. *diplostephioides*

A. *divaricatus* and 'Raiche Form'

A. *drummondii*

A. *elliottii*

A. *ericoides* and 'Blue Star', 'Brimstone', 'Cinderella', 'Erlkönig', 'Enchantress', 'Esther','Lovely', 'Pink Cloud', 'White Heather'

A. *farreri*

A. *fendleri*

A. *flaccidus*

A. *foliaceus*

A. × *frikartii* 'Flora's Delight', 'Mönch', 'Wunder von Stäffa'

A. *grandiflorus*

A. *hemisphericus*

A. *himalaicus*

A. 'Honeysong Pink'

A. 'Hon. Vicary Gibbs'

A. *kumleinii* 'Dream of Beauty'

A. *laevis* and var. *geyeri*, 'Bluebird', 'Calliope'

A. *lateriflorus* and 'Coombe Fishacre', 'Horizontalis', 'Prince'

A. *linariifolius*

A. 'Little Carlow'

A. 'Lombarda'

A. *macrophyllus* and *macrophyllus* 'Albus'

A. 'Miss Bessie'

A. *novae-angliae* 'Andenken an Alma Pötschke', 'Harrington's Pink', 'Hella Lacy', 'Purple Dome', 'Rudelsburg'

A. *novi-belgii* – numerous cultivars

A. *nepaulensis*

A. *oblongifolius* 'Fanny's Aster', 'October Skies',

'Raydon's Favorite'

A. *oolentangiensis*

A. 'Our Latest One'

A. *patens*

A. *pilosus* var. *demotus*

A. 'Pink Star'

A. *pringlei* 'Monte Cassino'

A. *ptarmicoides*

A. *puniceus*

A. *pyrenaeus*

A. *sedifolius* 'Nanus'

A. *sericeus*

A. *sibiricus*

A. *simplex*

A. *spathulifolius*

A. *spectabilis*

A. *stracheyi*

A. *subspicatus*

A. *tanacetifolius*

A. *tataricus* and 'Jindai'

A. *tortifolius*

A. *umbellatus*

A. *yunnanensis*

APPENDIX 8
READING ABOUT ASTERS

Clay, Samson *The Present Day Rock Garden* (T.C. & E.C. Jack, London, 1937).

Erhardt, Anne und Walter *PPP Index, The European Plant Finder* (Eugen Ulmer GmbH & Co, Stuttgart (Hohenheim), 1995).

Farrer, Reginald *The English Rock Garden* (T.C. & E.C. Jack Ltd, London, 1928).

Gleason, H.A. *The New Britton and Brown Illustrated Flora of Northeastern United States and Adjacent Canada* (Hafner, 3rd edition 1968, New York).

Griffiths, Mark *Index of Garden Plants* (Royal Horticultural Society, The Macmillan Press Limited, London and Basingstoke, 1994; and Timber Press, Portland, Oregon, USA).

Levine, Carol et al. *A Guide to Wildflowers in Winter* (Yale University Press, New Haven & London, 1995).

Lord, T. et al *The RHS Plant Finder* (Dorling Kindersley, London, published annually).

Ohwi, Jisaburo *Flora of Japan* (Smithsonian Institution, Washington, 1965).

Peterson, R.T., and M. McKenny *A Field Guide to the Wildflowers of Northeastern and North-Central North America* (Houghton Mifflin, Boston, 1968).

Ranson, E.R. *Michaelmas Daisies and other Garden Asters* (John Gifford Limited, London, 1946).

Robinson, William *The English Flower Garden* (John Murray, London, 10th ed., 1907; and Sagapress, USA).

Schollkopf, W. *Astern* (Ulmar, Stuttgart (Hohenheim), 1995).

Wharton, Mary E. & Roger W. Barbour *A Guide to the Wildflowers & Ferns of Kentucky* (The University Press of Kentucky, Lexington, 1971).

APPENDIX 9
WHERE TO BUY ASTERS

Europe

In Europe we are fortunate in having two comprehensive directories of commercial sources of garden plants: *The RHS Plant Finder* (published by the Royal Horticultural Society) and *The PPP Index* (published by Anne and Walter Erhardt). Although a great many of the old aster cultivars have been lost over the years, sufficient remain available and new introductions arrive each year. The availability of aster species is quite limited and largely confined to a few of the most showy and easily grown sorts. Growers who wish to try their hand at a species not in the commercial catalogues must turn to suppliers of wild plant seeds, such as hardy plant societies and rock garden or alpine garden societies, or possibly establish contact with a botanical collection.

The list below is a selection of the best nurseries offering asters.

✴ indicates nurseries offering a good range of asters but no mail order.

✿ denotes nurseries with a large range of asters and mail order service.

❁ identifies specialist growers of asters.

✿ Georg Arends, Monschaustrasse 76, 42369 Wuppertal, Germany

Brabant-Colas, Chemin du Renard, St. Didier de Formans, 01600 Trévoux, France

✴ Bridgemere Nurseries, Bridgemere, Near Nantwich, Cheshire, CW5 7QB, England

The Beth Chatto Gardens Limited, Elmstead Market, Colchester, Essex CO7 7DB, England

✿ Les Jardins de Cotelle, 76370 Derchigny-Graincourt, France

Cotswold Garden Flowers, 1 Waterside, Evesham, Worcestershire, WR11 6BS, England

✴ Demmel, Baumschulenstrasse 3, 82402 Seeshaupt, Germany

Eastgrove Cottage Garden Nursery, Sankyns Green, Little Witley, Near Shrawley, Worcestershire, WR6 6LQ, England

✿ Feldweber, A-4974, Ort im Innkreis 139, Germany

Jean Loius Ferraud, Jardins de Montagne, Caramptran, 74420 Habére-Lullin, France

Kaytie Fisher, The Nursery, South End Cottage, Long Reach, Ockham, Surrey, GU23 6PF, England

✿ ❁ Four Seasons, Forncett St. Mary, Norwich, Norfolk, NR16 1JT, England

Gardiner's Hall Plants, Braiseworth, Eye, Suffolk, IP23 7DZ, England

✿ Hans Götz, 77761 Schiltach, Germany

✿ Heinrich Hagemann, Walsroder Strasse 324, 30855 Langenhagen-Krähenwinkel, Germany

Fritz Häusserman, Schützenhausweg 43-47, 70499 Stuttgart, Germany

Hoo House Nursery, Hoo House, Gloucester Road, Tewkesbury, Gloucestershire, GL20 7DA, England

✿ Kayser & Siebert, Wilhelm-Leuschner-Strasse 85, 64380 Ronsdorf, Germany

✿ ❁ Heinz Klose, Rosenstrasse 10, 34253 Lohfelden, Germany

✿ ❁ Uwe Knöpnadel, Friesland Staudengarten, Husumer Weg 16, 26441 Jever-Rahrdrum, Germany

Hans Kramer, Hessenweg 41, 6718 TC Ede, Holland

Langthorn's Plantery, High Cross Lane West, Little Canfield, Dunmow, Essex, CM6 1TD, England

Pépiniéres Michel Lumen, Les Coutets, 24100 Creysse-Bergerac, France

Elizabeth MacGregor, Ellenbank, Tongland Road, Kircudbright, Dumfries and Galloway, DG6 4UU, Scotland

Milton Garden Plants, Milton-on-Stour, Gillingham, Dorset, SP8 5PX, England

✿ Monksilver Nursery, Oakington Road, Cottenham, Cambridgeshire, CB4 4TW, England

✿ Jardin du Mont des Oiseaux, 31220 Mondavezan, France

✴ Gudrun Müller, Nordenstädter Strasse 90, 65239 Hochheim am Main, Germany

✴ Maria und Erich Niederstadt, Riedweg 15, 32107 Bad Salzuflen, Germany

The Nursery Further Afield, Evenley Road, Mixbury, Near Brackley, Northamptonshire, NN13 5YR, England

✿ ❁ Old Court Nurseries, Colwall, Malvern, Worcestershire, WR13 6QE, England

Ernst Pagels, Deichstrasse 4, 26789 Leer, Germany

✿ Rolf Peine, Indistriestrasse 51, 82194 Gröbenzell, Germany

Perhill Nurseries, Worcester Road, Great Witley, Worcestershire, WR6 6JT, England

Perryhill Nurseries, Hartfield, East Sussex, TN17 4JP, England

✽ Th. Ploeger en Zn. B.V., 3731 EB De Bilt, Holland

Jean-Yves Poiroux, le Petit Beauregard, 85340 Olonne sur Mer, France

✽ Reuther, Gärtner Strasse 11, 88107 Baar-Ebenhausen, Germany

R.V. Roger Limited, The Nurseries, Pickering, Yorkshire, YO18 7HG, England

✿ ❀ Rougham Hall Nurseries, Ipswich Road, Rougham, Bury St Edmunds, Suffolk, IP30 9LZ, England

Walter Schmid, Straubenmühle, 73460 Huttlingen, Germany

✿ Staudengartnerei Schöllkopf (inh. Roselinde Frank & Regine Peter), Postfach 7137, 72735 Reutlingen, Germany

✿ Werner Simon, Staudenweg 2, 97828 Marktheidenfeld, Germany

✿ Plantes Vivaces Specker, 168 Rue de Mulhouse, 68300 Saint-Loius, France

Wolfgang Sprich, Papierweg 20, 79400 Kandern, Germany

✿ Helmut Stade, Beckenstrang 24, 46325 Borken-Marbeck, Germany

Paul Theoboldt (ims. Hartmut Theoboldt), Auf de Scheibe 2, 88326 Aulendorf, Germany

Ulverscroft Grange Nursery, Priory Lane, Ulverscroft, Markfield, Leicestershire, LE67 9BP, England

✿ Waterperry Gardens Limited, Waterperry, Near Wheatley, Oxfordshire OX33 1JZ, England

Wauschkuhn, An der B3, 34346 Hann.-Münden, Germany

Willumeit, Heidelberger Landstrasse 179, 64297 Darmstadt-Eberstadt, Germany

✿ Gräfin von Zeppelin (inh. Aglaja von Rumohr), 79295 Sulzburg-Laufen, Germany

✽ Longin Ziegler, Oberzeig, 8627 Grüningen, Switzerland

✿ Pieter Zwijnenburg Jr., Hakve Raak 18, 2771 AD Boskoop, Holland

North America

Andre Viette Nursery, PO Box 1109, Fishersville, Virginia 22939

Arrowhead Alpines, PO Box 857, Fowlerville, Michigan 48836

Busse Gardens, 5873 Oliver Avenue SW, Cokato, Minnesota 55321

Canyon Creek, 3527 Dry Creek Road, Oroville, California 95965

Carroll Gardens, 444 E. Main Street, Westminster, Maryland 21157

Crownsville Nursery, PO Box 797, Crownsville, Maryland 21032

Forest Farm, 990 Tetherow Road, Williams, Oregon 97544

Gardens North, 5984 Third Line Road North, RR3, North Gower, Ontario K0A 2T0, Canada

Goodness Grows, PO Box 311, Lexington, Georgia 30648

Heronswood Nursery, 7530 NE 288th Street, Kingston, Washington 98346

Klehm Nursery, 4210 North Duncan Road, Champaign, Illinois 61821

Kurt Bluemel Inc, 2740 Greene Lane, Baldwin, MD 21013

Native Gardens, 5737 Fisher Lane, Greenback, Tennessee 37742

Plant Delights Nursery, 9241 Sauls Road, Raleigh, North Carolina 27603

Plants of the Southwest, Route 6, Box 11A, Agua Fria, Santa Fe, New Mexico 87501

Primrose Path, RD2, PO Box 110, Scottdale, Pennsylvania 15683

Prairie Nursery, PO Box 306, Westfield, Wisconsin 53964

Siskiyou, 2825 Cummings Road, Medford, Oregon 97501

Southern Perennials and Herbs, 98 Bridges Road, Tylertown, Mississippi 39667

Sunlight Gardens, 174 Golden Lane, Andersonville, Tennessee 37705

Tripple Brook Farm, 37 Middle Road, Southampton, Massachusetts 01073

We-Du, Route 5, Box 724, Marion, North Carolina 28752

Woodlanders, 1128 Colleton Avenue, Aiken, South Carolina 29801

For other US sources see *Gardening by Mail* by Barbara J. Barton (Tusker Press, PO Box 1338, Sebastopol, California 95473)

INDEX

Page numbers in *italics* refer to illustrations

ACKNOWLEDGMENTS

I would like to thank the following people for their help and contributions: Pamela J. Harper who wrote the chapter about asters in the USA; Brian Young whose diligent research over many years has unearthed much useful information about asters and the people who have grown them, and without whose help much of the book would not have been possible; Beth Chatto for kindly supplying the details about Aster 'Snow Flurry'; Ron Watts who has generously helped and encouraged the building of our aster collection; and Meriel Picton, my long suffering wife, who has taken more than her fair share of running the nursery to allow time for me to write this book.